*The Politics of Rich and Poor*

# THE POLITICS
## OF
# RICH AND POOR

*Wealth and the
American Electorate
in the Reagan Aftermath*

## KEVIN PHILLIPS

*Random House*    *New York*

Grateful acknowledgment is made to the following for permission to reprint previously published material:

*The Economist:* Three charts from the following issues of *The Economist*: January 14, 1989, April 15, 1989, and June 17, 1989. Copyright © 1989 by The Economist Newspaper Ltd. All rights reserved. Reprinted by permission.

*Financial Times:* Excerpt from "Weary Bush Seeks to Hammer Home his Message" from the November 8, 1988, issue of the *Financial Times*. Reprinted by permission.

*Financial World Magazine:* Chart from *Financial World Magazine*, 1989. Reprinted by permission of *Financial World* magazine.

*Fortune Magazine:* Adaptation of chart from the article "The Bull Market's Biggest Winners" from the August 8, 1983, issue of *Fortune* magazine. Copyright © 1983 by Time, Inc. Adaptation of *"Fortune* Magazine's 1987 Billionaires List" from the September 12, 1988, issue of *Fortune* magazine. Copyright © 1988 by Time, Inc. All rights reserved. Reprinted by permission.

*GRANT's Interest Rate Observer:* Chart from the June 24, 1988, issue of *GRANT'S Interest Rate Observer*. Reprinted by permission of *GRANT'S Interest Rate Observer*.

*The Gridiron Club of Washington, D.C.:* Excerpt from the Gridiron Club parody of George Bush from March, 1988. Reprinted by permission of The Gridiron Club of Washington, D.C.

*Milton Moskowitz:* Excerpt from "The Selling of America," by Milton Moskowitz, from the January 24, 1988, issue of the *Los Angeles Times*. Copyright © 1988 by Milton Moskowitz. Reprinted by permission.

*Mother Jones:* Excerpt from "You've Got to Spread It Around," by Jim Hightower, from the May 1988 issue of *Mother Jones*. Copyright © 1988 by Foundation for National Progress. Reprinted by permission of *Mother Jones* magazine.

*The New Republic:* Excerpt from "The Executive's New Clothes," by Robert Reich, from the May 13, 1985, issue of *The New Republic*. Copyright © 1985 by The New Republic, Inc. Reprinted by permission of *The New Republic*.

*The Urban Institute:* Chart from *Challenge to Leadership: Economic and Social Issues for the Next Decade*, edited by Isabel V. Sawhill (Washington, D.C.: The Urban Institute Press, 1988). Chart reprinted by permission.

*Washington Post Writer's Group:* Excerpt from "What Dukakis Should Be Saying," by George F. Will, from the September 15, 1988, issue of *The Washington Post*. Copyright © 1988 by The Washington Post Writer's Group. Reprinted by permission.

Library of Congress Cataloging-in-Publication Data
Phillips, Kevin P.
The politics of rich and poor : wealth and the American electorate
in the Reagan aftermath / by Kevin Phillips.
p.  cm.
ISBN 0-394-55954-1 : $19.95
1. Wealth—United States.  2. Poor—United States.  3. United States—Economic policy—1981–  4. Voting—United States.  5. United States—Politics and government—1981–1989.  I. Title.
HC110.W4P48  1990
339.2'2'097309048—dc20      89-43419

Manufactured in the United States of America
6 8 9 7

TO ANDREW AND ALEC

# *Foreword*

From the White House to Capitol Hill, a critical weakness in American politics and governance is becoming woefully apparent—the frightening inability of the nation's leaders to face, much less define and debate, the unprecedented problems and opportunities facing the country.

Politicians from both parties seem unsure whether the economy is strong or weak, whether the United States is globally winning (over Russia) or losing (to Japan). Though there are some important distinctions between the Republican and Democratic disabilities—and the threats they pose to America's future—both parties seem rudderless on a sea of compromise, caution and confusion.

Both are out of step with a world that is profoundly changing, a world in which American politics hasn't kept pace. George Bush has chosen to imitate Eisenhower's low-key style, but imitating Ike in the 1990s makes as little sense as imitating Queen Victoria in the 1930s. From Eastern Europe to world financial markets and rising concern about a U.S. recession, the inescapable turbulence of the 1990s is already closing in on the Bush White House.

The failure of the Bush administration to develop a national strategy was predictable, not just because of Bush's own pref-

erence for compromise, but because of the unavoidable con-
straints on a former vice president following two terms of the
president to whom he was subordinate. In such situations, re-
active politics and caution are inevitable. Bush cannot identify
national problems because to do so would identify many of his
own party's failings. The limitations of such follow-up presi-
dencies deserve attention because the governing party's weak-
nesses become national disabilities, a dilemma that worsens
when the opposition is also second-rate and confused—which
is a kindly characterization of post-Reagan Democrats.

The Republicans at least know they have a problem with the
"vision thing." George Bush and Bob Dole both grumbled about
it during the 1988 campaign. But the Democrats have seemed
even more bewildered, and their inability during the 1980s to
goad and pressure the Republicans has been central to the larger
national failure.

This is hardly the first time that U.S. political leaders have
danced around the edges of a developing national unease. In
the 1850s Democratic and Whig party chieftains waltzed around
slavery and sectionalism, just as the established parties skirted
the growing economic crisis in the decade before William Jennings Bryan forced populism onto center stage in 1896. The
complacent bipartisan dialogues of the late 1920s—congressional Democrats were joining the Chamber of Commerce in
pushing tax cuts right up through 1927–28—bore no relation
to what would develop after the crash in 1929. Even in the mid-
1960s, the bipartisan progressivism of Lyndon Johnson, John
Lindsay, William Scranton, George Romney and Nelson Rockefeller was also a misleading prelude to the "Joe Sixpack" Middle American populism that precipitated the new GOP
presidential era a few years later.

This "irrelevant consensus" of outdated ideologies and com-
promises during a transitional politics about to be overtaken by
history is a recurrent phenomenon in American life. We are in
the midst of such a transition today, and serious proposals to
deal with problems churned up by the 1980s are barely in evidence. Democrats, having run out of New Deal ideas more than
twenty years ago, still don't grasp that Republicanism has been
in the White House so long that *its* ideas—from constitutional
amendments to protect the flag to further tax cuts—are them-

selves shrouded in cobwebs. So far, little about the caliber of
Democratic ideas suggests that the Republicans will soon be
hard-pressed to defend the accumulated scandals, policy mis-
calculations and economic polarization of three straight GOP
administrations.

That Washington should seem irrelevant to the average American—a sinkhole to be forgotten when the fish are biting or a
good movie is on television—means that Republicans can keep
the White House until disillusionment can no longer be avoided.
But for the Democrats—still haunted by George McGovern,
Jimmy Carter, Walter Mondale and Michael Dukakis, the four
faces on the Mount Losemore of American politics—the "irrelevant consensus" is a disaster, for it is the Democrats who
have to make Americans care about Washington again.

But Americans won't care as long as economic debate turns
on such deceptions as the bipartisan Gramm-Rudman deficit
reduction act of 1985 and the bipartisan tax reform act of 1986.
The genius of Gramm-Rudman, although it wasn't planned so
deviously, was to give Congress and the White House a deficit-
reduction game played with varying quantities of peas and wal-
nut shells, a game that preempts tougher approaches.

Democrats and Republicans collaborated on Gramm-
Rudman, as they did on the 1986 tax reform, whose proclaimed
objectives were fairness and simplification—a joke in view of
1987–89 public opinion polls that declared it less fair and more
complicated than the previous law. But, like Gramm-Rudman,
the 1986 reform was a Republican victory that trapped the
Democrats into accepting themes and rates scarcely imaginable
for the party of Franklin D. Roosevelt and Harry S. Truman.

The party of the little man and of progressive tax rates agreed
to reduce top individual tax rates for millionaires from 70 percent to 28 percent while establishing a *higher* special marginal
"bubble" rate of between 28 percent and 33 percent for the one
fifth of American households and single taxpayers with incomes
in the $45,000 to $150,000 range. In accepting these "reforms,"
Democrats not only voted for top rates contrary to their political
traditions but lost the right to criticize tax policy as a source of
both towering deficits and a concentration of wealth in which
the top 1 percent of Americans' after-tax share of U.S. income
rose from 7 percent in 1977 to a projected 11 percent in 1990.

Tax cuts certainly benefited many individuals, but at a grave price. Growing federal budget and trade deficits have forced the United States to borrow heavily from overseas, and after 1985 the value of the dollar plummeted, resulting in an extraordinary realignment of world wealth and purchasing power—and possibly standards of living. Between 1985 and 1987 the total national assets of the United States climbed from $30.6 trillion to $36.2 trillion while those of Japan, just $19.6 trillion in 1985, soared to $43.7 trillion in 1987, an almost unimaginable transfer of relative wealth and purchasing power from the United States to Japan. No wonder polls showed two thirds of Americans worried that the U.S. economy by the year 2000 will be dominated by foreign companies.

For all these reasons, the shallow and evasive political debate in the United States has been costly. Both parties have been shortsighted, but the moment of truth may not be far off. Polls show that the American people have intuited the painful truths sidestepped by the bipartisan majorities of official Washington. If reality doesn't dictate a new agenda for the 1990 elections, it should do so by 1992. And if either party can persuasively break through the failed consensus into a tough new domestic and international candor, the electorate may be ready to hand out surprising political rewards. This volume—I hope—will supply some ammunition for that candor.

This book, which I began in 1987, started out less boldly. What I had originally intended was a profile of the economic policies and speculative biases of the 1980s—and how they had produced one of U.S. history's most striking concentrations of wealth even as the American dream was beginning to crumble not just in inner-city ghettos and farm townships but in blue-collar centers and even middle-class suburbs.

Sooner or later, these tensions might help bring about a new national politics, but I was not prepared when I began this book to anticipate such a shift. Better to let the facts, statistics and historical data speak for themselves. This seemed especially fitting in light of my own background as a GOP strategist in the formative period of the current Republican cycle under Richard Nixon.

Then in late September 1989, as Congress was turning its annual autumn budget process into a greater-than-usual display of fiscal irresponsibility and shoveling out favors for influential constituencies, David Ignatius, editor of *The Washington Post* "Outlook" section, called with an idea: Could I do the lead article for that Sunday on the strategic and philosophic bankruptcy of U.S. politics? I could and would—"brain-dead" was the characterization we agreed upon—and with a deadline only forty-eight hours away and speeches to give in the meantime, I found that the piece was writing itself, that key points and themes from this book began thrusting themselves, as if of their own accord, into what amounted to an indictment of both parties.

The Outlook piece—which in essence constitutes the opening pages of this foreword—struck sparks. There was much comment and many reprints, and two weeks later, *Time* magazine took the article's thesis for its cover story, showing Gilbert Stuart's famous portrait of George Washington shedding a tear at the failure of government. *This* is the larger context in which the following chapters, assessments and supporting details should be read.

Let me say that not only do books evolve; they also represent the contribution of many persons beside the author. That certainly is true of this one. Thanks are in order to my assistants Michelle Klein and Rebecca Palmer for long days at the word processor; to my agent, Bill Leigh, and his associate Tom Neilssen for their timely counsel; to my wife, Martha, and my sons, Andrew and Alec, for two years of forbearance in what turned out to be a very time-consuming project; and in particular to my editor at Random House, Jason Epstein, for his advice, effort and invaluable assistance.

Bethesda, Maryland
October 1989

# Contents

# Introduction:
# The Triumph of
# Upper America

The 1980s were the triumph of upper America—an ostentatious celebration of wealth, the political ascendancy of the richest third of the population and a glorification of capitalism, free markets and finance. But while money, greed and luxury had become the stuff of popular culture, hardly anyone asked why such great wealth had concentrated at the top, and whether this was a result of public policy. Despite the armies of homeless sleeping on grates, political leaders—even those who professed to care about the homeless—had little to say about the Republican party's historical role, which has been not simply to revitalize U.S. capitalism but to tilt power, policy, wealth and income toward the richest portions of the population. The public understood this bias, if we can trust 1988 opinion polls; nevertheless, the Democrats shunned the issue in the election of 1988, a reluctance their predecessors had also displayed during previous Republican booms.

That discussion is now unfolding. From Congress to the executive branch, "money politics"—be it the avarice of financiers or outright corruption of politicians—is shaping up as a prime political theme for the 1990s. Class structures may be weak in the United States, but populist sensitivities run high. Wealth in this country has always been fluid, volatile and migratory. Unlike Europe, we have needed no revolutions for its redistribution. In America the reallocation of income and assets has usually followed consumer fads, population shifts and technological innovations. But politics and political ideologies have also been important keys to the cashbox. Changing popular and governmental attitudes toward wealth have always influenced who gets what. Decade after decade illustrates the point; the Reagan era was not unique.

The 1980s were a second Gilded Age, in which many Americans made and spent money abundantly. Yet as the decade ended, too many stretch limousines, too many enormous incomes and too much high fashion foreshadowed a significant shift of mood. A new plutocracy—some critics were even using the word "oligarchy"—had created a new target for populist reaction. A small but significant minority of American liberals had begun to agitate the economy's losers—minorities, young men, female heads of households, farmers, steelworkers and others. Television audiences were losing their early-eighties fascination with the rich. And many conservatives, including President George Bush himself, were becoming defensive about great wealth, wanton moneymaking and greed.

No fixed caste, class, ideology or geographic section has long governed America's lively pursuit of money and success. Sectional competition has been pursued always and everywhere, and has yielded every kind of regional advantage. Relative affluence in the United States has moved West (almost from the first days of settlement), gone North (after the Civil War) or South (with the rise of the Sunbelt). The 1980s boom in the Boston-Washington megalopolis, coupled with hard times on the farm and in the Oil Patch, produced a familiar conservative economic geography—a comparative shift of wealth toward the two coasts. *And* toward income groups already well off.

This preference was nothing new. Twice before in the last hundred years, wealth also further accumulated in the hands of those *already rich*—during the late nineteenth century, then again during the 1920s. To some extent, these buildups have also served the larger purpose of stimulating capitalist growth, entrepreneurialism and technological innovation. Avarice was only one ingredient. At other times, and also for at least partly valid public policy reasons, Washington has gone in the opposite direction and redeployed upper-income assets to fatten thinner wallets, expand low-income purchasing power and rebuild the social fabric of poorer Americans. So debtors have occasionally gained as have creditors. Farmers have outmaneuvered bankers, although rarely, but regardless of the direction it's hard to overstate the importance of American politics to American wealth—and vice versa.

Candor in these matters is rare. But in the words of an iconoclastic journalist of the Reagan era, William Greider, "Concentration of wealth was the fulcrum on which the most basic political questions pivoted, a dividing line deeper than region or religion, race or sex. In the nature of things, government might choose to enhance the economic prospects for the many or to safeguard the accumulated wealth held by the few, but frequently the two purposes were in irreconcilable conflict. The continuing political struggle across this line, though unseen and rarely mentioned, was the central narrative of American political history, especially in the politics of money." Greider's thesis is generally supported by history. Since the American Revolution the distribution of American wealth has depended significantly on *who controlled the federal government, for what policies, and in behalf of which constituencies.*

From this perspective, the Reagan era reversed what late-twentieth-century Americans had become used to. The liberal style that prevailed from 1932 to 1968 had left a legacy of angry conservatives indignant over two generations of downward income redistribution. A reorientation in the opposite direction was all but inevitable in the 1980s—and there were precedents aplenty.

In the years after 1790, when Alexander Hamilton persuaded Congress to assume debts incurred by the states during the Revolution, the result was a redistribution of wealth to bondholders, many of whom had bought the low-valued debt instruments as speculation. Then in the 1870s, restoration of the gold standard squeezed out the last vestiges of Civil War inflation, providing a similar preference to creditors over debtors. And the Harding-Coolidge tax cuts of the 1920s, in which the top individual federal income tax rate fell from 73 percent to

25 percent, furnish yet another example of realignment upward. This periodic upward bias is as much a fact of U.S. history as the liberal bias with which it alternates.

Even in this most optimistic of countries, economic individualism yields to community-minded reform on a cyclical basis as the public grows indignant over the political distribution of wealth. By the mid-1920s, and especially during the New Deal, muckraking interpretations of the economic motives of conservative governance were a dime a dozen. Historian Charles Beard became famous for his *Economic Interpretation of the U.S. Constitution* and other books arguing the premise that the Founding Fathers and their descendants had served their own class interests as well as American patriotism. Populist or progressive periods have often nurtured such materialistic views, and the 1990s are likely to regard the Reagan era as a seamless web of preoccupation with wealth and moneymaking. By 1989, after all, the statistics *were* in: once again, just as in the 1790s, the 1880s and the 1920s, conservative and upper-bracket groups had been the major gainers. As a percentage of overall national income, the shift wasn't big, of course. Yet increases of two, three and four points in the share of income held by the top 1 percent of Americans—accompanied, meanwhile, by some decline in the bottom two fifths of the population—have been the stuff of major economic and political movements.

This book is about the redistribution of power and wealth during the 1980s: who got it, who lost it and through what policies. It is also about the extent to which these changes, insofar as they reflected familiar conservative economic and demographic patterns of preferment, prepared the ground for a progressive or populist reaction. Politics is a process of movement and countermovement. Only for so long will strung-out $35,000-a-year families enjoy magazine articles about the hundred most successful businessmen in Dallas or television programs about the life-styles of the rich and famous. And the discontents that arise go well beyond lower-class envy or the anticommercial bias of academe.

A century ago established lawyers, diplomats, doctors and bank presidents—and, in particular, patrician landowners and other old-money families—seethed over the erosion of their relative wealth and importance as muddy-booted nouveau riche railroad barons and stockjobbers flourished, a frustration that foreshadowed similar public distaste in the late 1980s for corporate raiders, Wall Street inside traders and thirty-one-year-old investment bankers earning a million dollars a year. The historian Richard Hofstadter, looking at the Progressive movement as it culminated in Theodore Roosevelt's third-party bid for the presidency on the 1912 Bull Moose ticket, has argued that Progressivism drew heavily on the resentment of old money for new. How much the 1990s will follow this familiar pattern remains to be seen, but George Bush, a scion of the Eastern Establishment, for all his loyalty to Ronald Reagan, chose to echo "TR" in the 1988 campaign by deploring "this fast-buck stuff . . . I don't have great respect for just going out and stacking up money." Bush refreshed this theme in his inaugural address, for just as Ronald Reagan had replaced Richard Nixon's bias toward "Middle America" with nouveau riche ostentation, Bush represented a shift from the aggressiveness of the new rich to the defensiveness, even social conciliation, of established wealth.

Some amplifications are in order. Political terminology can be confusing, even contradictory, during these periods. The late Harvard economist Joseph Schumpeter has described how capitalism, at its zenith, is profoundly creative, profoundly destructive—and profoundly *unconservative* by any standard except its respect for market forces and moneymaking. Populists and progressives are not alone in opposing the "malefactors of great wealth." Upholders of traditional or aristocratic values, such as they are in the United States, have also been periodic critics—not just Theodore Roosevelt but also Henry Cabot Lodge and Charles Francis Adams, to say nothing of his cousins Henry and Brooks. A minor but vaguely similar dissent on the part of Southern traditionalists was also apparent during the last crescendos of the Roaring Twenties.

To be sure, historical parallels are dangerous, but history can teach certain general lessons well enough to suggest certain tentative precedents for not only what *happened* during the Reagan years but what *may occur in reaction* during the 1990s. While neither Democrats nor Republicans like to acknowledge their role in the concentration and dispersal of wealth, these roles have always been present, lurking beneath the rhetoric of individualism, market forces and free enterprise, on one side, or fairness and social justice, on the other. Excesses in one direction have always bred a countermovement in the other direction, and the Reagan era certainly had its excesses.

The shift to the right in late-twentieth-century U.S. politics—the odd mix of conservatism and populism that I described two decades ago in my book *The Emerging Republican Majority*, and that provided elements of the strategy for the 1968 GOP presidential campaign—was fading by the 1988 election. One sign that the Republican presidential cycle had reached late middle age in the 1980s was an intensified ideological focus on free markets and capitalist values. *Money and business had become fashionable—again.* History suggests that GOP cycles tend to stage capitalist blow-offs as they mature, which is what happened in the 1920s. The Reagan administration, from the beginning, was openly committed to copying the economic style and incentives of the Calvin Coolidge years, though Reagan's revival of the Roaring Twenties was more precarious and debt-dependent than the original era.

By the time of the Democratic and Republican conventions in 1988, the boosterish style of the Reagan era—from entrepreneur worship to roller-coaster stock markets—was already yielding to a more restrained, centrist tone. That was clear in *both* parties. As summer turned to autumn each groped toward a different successor politics. George Bush presented himself as a low-key activist and reformer, casting an occasional well-bred aspersion toward those who did nothing but pursue money. Both candidates eschewed the values of the glitterati. Michael Dukakis, who originally styled himself as the architect of Massachusetts' economic "miracle," assumed a more populist stance by October, but by that time it was too late for him to benefit from Democratic themes of economic discontent.

This book, then, is the portrait of what the 1988 debate largely ignored: the new political economics, intensifying inequality and pain for the poor, the unprecedented growth of upper-bracket wealth, the surprisingly related growth of federal debt, global economic realignment, foreigners gobbling up large chunks of America, the meaninglessness of being a millionaire in an era with nearly a hundred thousand "decamillionaires." Part of the portrait is international—Britain and Japan displayed a similar concentration of wealth—but mostly it is about which *American* individuals, groups, economic sectors and regions profited, and which lost.

We are talking about a major transformation. Not only did the concentration of wealth quietly intensify, but the sums involved took a mega-leap. The definition of who's rich—and who's no longer rich—changed as radically during the Reagan era as it did during the prior great nouveau riche periods of the late nineteenth century and the 1920s, periods whose excesses preceded the great populist upheavals of the Bryan era and the New Deal. Thus I shall also discuss how the political pendulum has swung back in the past, and may be ready to swing again. The 1990s could easily be another watershed decade. But this time the stakes are unusually high, in light of America's new status as a debtor nation, a situation not seen since World War I. Some relative decline in our circumstances seems inevitable—indeed, has *already* taken place. Powerful currents of global change are operating quite beyond our power to offset them.

Yet perhaps a part of America's challenge and opportunity is more traditional: as they have in the past, liberals once more favor bringing extremes of wealth, debt and inequality under control through taxation and regulation. That is the subject of my last chapter: a look at how the 1980s political and economic debate ended amid hints that America's other political-economic traditions were on the rise, with their distaste for survival-of-the-fittest economics, new talk of a "kinder, gentler nation," belief in a more activist role for government and demand for more attention to the weaker portions of society. U.S. history records significant achievements for *those* cycles, too.

*The Politics of Rich and Poor*

# Chapter

## 1

## The Best of Times, the Worst of Times: The Critical Duality of the Reagan Years

We the people. They refute last week's television commentary downgrading our optimism and idealism. They are the entrepreneurs, the builders, the pioneers, and a lot of regular folks—the true heroes of our land who make up the most uncommon nation of doers in history. You know they're Americans because their spirit is as big as the universe, and their hearts are bigger than their spirit. . . . America isn't finished, her best days have just begun.

—RONALD REAGAN
STATE OF THE UNION ADDRESS
JANUARY 27, 1987

Statistical evidence already suggests that the American dream is fading.

—THE WALL STREET JOURNAL
MARCH 31, 1989

As the Reagan years ended, the uncertain future hung like a temperature inversion over America's substantial prosperity. The economy was enjoying the century's longest peacetime recovery cycle. But economic power and riches were realigning around the world, and the two most striking economic groups of 1989 represented a stark contradiction: billionaires—and the homeless. Prophecies for the future were just as mixed.

Some pop culturists had written epitaphs for the decade right after the stock market crash of October 19, 1987. A year later, by Election Day, sentiment for new leadership, while commanding a nominal majority, had eased. Optimism was justified, in part, simply by the failure of pessimism to fulfill its prophecies. Southern California real estate prices were soaring again. Art auctions and corporate takeover bids were setting new records.

Yet, to judge by political debate and public opinion polls, the country was nervous. America's record debt levels were becoming an issue in Congress as well as in the bond markets. People felt that an era would end on that January day when the seventy-seven-year-old Reagan climbed into Air Force One for his last official flight home to California. The next president was going to be different. George Bush's postelection comments had made that clear. And possibly he would not be so lucky.

What loyalists hoped for was more of the same. The Republicans were on a roll. In their eyes, Reagan's eight-year presidency had sparked the creation of nineteen million new jobs, an exploding technology and unprecedented prosperity, and had rekindled national pride. So many Americans had been making so much money that the term "millionaire" became meaningless: in Manhattan, where midtown parking could cost fifty dollars a day, "millionaire" had come to mean only persons with yearly *incomes* over one million dollars (a level usually bespeaking assets in the $5 million to $10 million range). A Georgia marketing expert, Thomas J. Stanley, counted almost one hundred thousand "decamillionaires"—people worth over *$10 million*.[1] Back in 1960 there hadn't been that many plain-vanilla *millionaires*.

Meanwhile Reagan's critics described another country. In their eyes the eighties were a last national fling with credit-card economics, a gaudy orgy of unprecedented domestic and international indebtedness, luxury imports, nouveau riche consumption and upper-bracket tax reduction, all indulged in with the greatest recklessness while beggars filled the streets and the average family's real disposable income declined toward a dimming future. For the first time in seventy years America had even become a net international debtor. Back in 1986 this dual vision had prompted California Democratic congressman Tony Coelho, who had been chosen to reply to one of the president's Saturday radio speeches, to recall that "Charles Dickens once began a story by writing 'It was the best of times, it was the worst of times.' The same could be said of today." For the next two years, it *was* said—in many ways.

The surprise was that the 1988 presidential election—or at least the Dukakis campaign—did so little with the powerful opposition themes so many others had raised. Dukakis was too caught up in Massachusetts' own affluence and high civic culture to promote populist economics—at least until late October, when flagging polls left him no choice.* Most Republican strategists were relieved by the Democrats' failure, although a few had private doubts about having to manage the debt-ridden economy for four more years.

Back in January and February 1988, though, as the Reagan era was beginning its final year, and as the Democratic and Republican presidential nomination races were moving into their Iowa and New Hampshire killing grounds, most of the men who wanted to lead America toward the approaching millennium had begun to address these economic jitters. Jesse Jackson decried a nation "merging, purging and submerging" its workers. Missouri Democratic congressman Richard Gephardt, picturing a United States in decline, characterized the decade as "eight grey years." Robert Dole, Republican leader of the U.S. Senate, rejected his party's 1984 theme of "Morning Again in America." More accurately, he said, "it's High Noon." Even Bush, who boasted of the late 1980s economy and was careful not to attack the administration in which he served, promised to "create a more reliable prosperity."[2]

Many Americans on the lower half of the economic ladder had been losing ground. And even the affluent, enjoying their champagne and raspberries, wondered how real the good times were. For the 20 to 30 percent of citizenry in circumstances prosperous enough to grump at but pay for $7 movie tickets or to disregard restaurant prices outrunning the cost-of-living index, the eighties had been good years. Yet troubling undercurrents had begun to make it all look shaky. Perhaps the economic music *was* about to stop; maybe the eighties *were* a decade of high living on borrowed money for which the bills were about

---

* Dukakis's economic populist reluctance—as well as the astonished relief of 1988 GOP managers—is discussed on pp. 46–51.

to become due. In April, as the Democratic presidential nomination campaign moved toward its climactic showdown between Michael Dukakis and Jesse Jackson in the Wisconsin and
New York Democratic primaries, the ABC News/Money magazine poll found that only 38 percent of the public rated the
U.S. economy "excellent" or "pretty good"; 62 percent chose
to describe it as "not so good" or "poor."[3] That number would
not change much until more upbeat attitudes took over in late
summer; through August nearly 60 percent of Americans remained skeptical.

What the public was choosing to read in early 1988 mirrored
this new mood. The appearance of books like Tom Wolfe's *The
Bonfire of the Vanities* and Lewis Lapham's *Money and Class
in America* suggested growing doubts about the country's ob-
session with money. So did Texas economics professor Ravi
Batra's gloomy tome warning of a depression several years hence
because of the overconcentration of wealth. And Yale historian
Paul Kennedy's *Decline and Fall of the Great Powers* stayed on
the 1988 best-seller lists because of popular apprehension about
America's own decline, not because of some belated national
curiosity about the imperial ebb of Hapsburg Spain, maritime
Holland or Edwardian Britain.

Yet as 1988 unfolded, luxury purchases flourished as if the
crash had never taken place. Unemployment reached 5.3 percent, the lowest level in a decade and a half. Inflation was down
by two thirds from Carter administration highs. And throughout
the year the unbroken economic recovery dating back to January
1983 kept setting records—sixty-seven straight months by mid-
summer, seventy-two by December. Records keepers also sa-
luted the unprecedented 62 percent of Americans gainfully
employed, despite doubts about how many mothers were taking
jobs to salvage family purchasing power. Manufacturing rose
with resurging exports. The sales of books predicting hard times
began to fade. Ronald Reagan, on tour in the Middle West,
boasted to election-year audiences that the Rust Belt was becoming the Boom Belt.

Behind the façade of favorable monthly data, however, deeper
worries about debt had also become fashionable. Years of debate had turned the enormity of the federal budget deficit into
a cliché. Yet the headlines of 1987–88 had begun to announce

a related problem, the *international* consequences of ongoing American borrowing: not just the budget and trade deficits, but the meaning of the United States' extraordinary transformation from the world's largest creditor nation to the world's largest debtor. Conservative insistence that it really didn't matter rang increasingly hollow as U.S. international indebtedness passed $269 billion at the end of 1986, reached $368 billion at the end of 1987, and was projected to exceed a trillion dollars by 1992. One New York investment banker, Daniel Schwartz, managing director of Ulmer Brothers, had even taken unintended issue with the president of the United States over the future of the Rust Belt. He told *Fortune* magazine that Japanese purchases might turn it into the Sushi Belt.[4]

Vivid grass-roots trends fleshed out the official statistics: *Wealth within the United States had been changing hands, regions, vocations, economic sectors and income strata with a vengeance.* Magazines ran endless surveys of the new megafortunes, and of the lesser but soaring compensation packages of investment bankers and corporate chief executives. The clumsiest television producer could film the pain in boarded-up Iowa farm towns, empty Ohio steel mills and city parks full of homeless drifters—or show the BMW-thronged streets of Connecticut suburbia, retooling export plants and West Coast port cities flush with the profits of unloading and transshipping Japanese cars and Korean color televisions. Few observers doubted the rich were getting richer, while the poor were fulfilling their half of the cliché.

When Dickens wrote his novels, in economically divided mid-nineteenth-century Britain, huge fortunes were being piled up by the country's new railroad, machinery and textile magnates even as their ever more numerous wage laborers—refugees, many of them, from declining British agriculture—overflowed the squalid slums of London, Manchester and Glasgow. When Alexis de Tocqueville, the French observer of the United States, visited England in 1835, he was so struck by the same duality that confronted the creator of Oliver Twist and Ebenezer Scrooge that he prepared a "Memoir on Pauperism" for delivery to the Royal Society of Cherbourg. One sixth of Britain was on the dole versus less than 5 percent of the population in much poorer Spain and Portugal. Why? Well, for one reason, because the more highly developed the society, the more things there are to want—and to "need."[5] Welfare, he thought, might be another cause.

A third factor suggests itself to the modern observer. Nations sometimes find themselves caught up in great currents of international economic change, and the late twentieth century's enormous upheaval in finance, commerce and technology—in which old-line manufacturing and humdrum shop and office vocations yielded to high-skill service industries—ranks in scope both with the Industrial Revolution that Dickens chronicled and with the earlier Renaissance and the rising capitalism that accompanied it. Much as in those eras, the forces of the late twentieth century have required double-entry bookkeeping: new wealth in profusion for the bright, the bold, the educated and the politically favored; economic carnage among the less fortunate. In short, the United States of the 1980s.

## A BIRD'S-EYE VIEW OF AMERICAN PLUTOGRAPHICS IN THE 1980S

It is not enough to describe the United States as the world's richest nation between 1945 and 1989. The distribution of its wealth conveys a more provocative message. By several measurements, the United States in the late twentieth century led all other major industrial countries in the gap dividing the upper fifth of the population from the lower—in the disparity between top and bottom. Chart 1 displays one 1984 attempt at global comparison. Five years later economic polarization had intensified, conceivably even moving the United States ahead of France, the generally acknowledged citadel of concentrated wealth among Western nations. Calculations like these lack precision, of course, but the *generalization*, at least, seems fair: among major Western nations, the United States has displayed one of the sharpest cleavages between rich and poor. Opportunity has counted for more than equality, and in the 1980s, opportunity took on a new boldness and dimension.

By the middle of Reagan's second term, official data had begun to show that America's broadly defined "rich"—the top half of 1 percent of the U.S. population—had never been richer. Federal

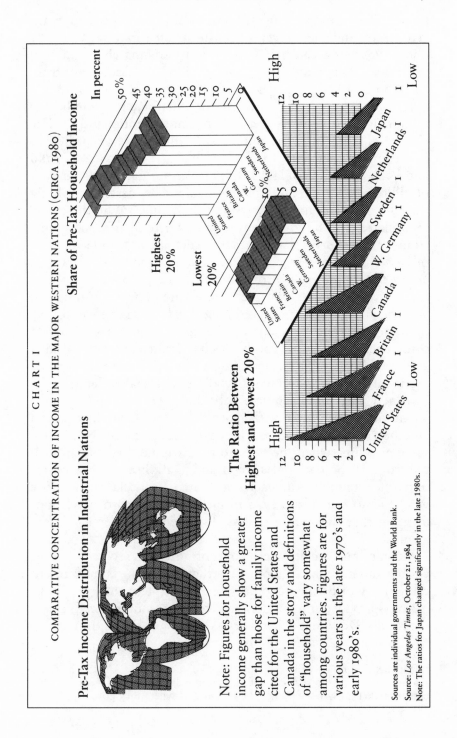

CHART I

COMPARATIVE CONCENTRATION OF INCOME IN THE MAJOR WESTERN NATIONS (CIRCA 1980)

Share of Pre-Tax Household Income

Pre-Tax Income Distribution in Industrial Nations

In percent

50%
45
40
35
30
25
20
15
10
5

Highest 20%

Lowest 20%

United States
France
Britain
W. Germany
Canada
Sweden
Netherlands
Japan

The Ratio Between
Highest and Lowest 20%

High                                    High

12
10
8
6
4
2
0

United States
France
Britain
Canada
W. Germany
Sweden
Netherlands
Japan

Low                                     Low

Note: Figures for household income generally show a greater gap than those for family income cited for the United States and Canada in the story and definitions of "household" vary somewhat among countries. Figures are for various years in the late 1970's and early 1980's.

Sources are individual governments and the World Bank.
Source: *Los Angeles Times*, October 21, 1984.
Note: The ratios for Japan changed significantly in the late 1980s.

policy favored the accumulation of wealth and rewarded financial assets, and the concentration of income that began in the
mid-1970s was accelerating. In 1988, approximately 1.3 million
individual Americans were millionaires by assets, up from
574,000 in 1980, 180,000 in 1972, 90,000 in 1964, and just
27,000 in 1953. Even adjusted for inflation, the number of
millionaires had doubled between the late seventies and the late
eighties. Meanwhile, the number of billionaires, according to
*Forbes* magazine, went from a handful in 1981 to 26 in 1986
and 49 in 1987.[6] As of late 1988, *Forbes* put that year's number
of billionaires at 52, and *Fortune*'s September assessment hung
the billion-dollar label on 51 American families. Who these new
millionaires and billionaires were and where their money came
from we will shortly examine in more detail. *No parallel upsurge
of riches had been seen since the late nineteenth century, the
era of the Vanderbilts, Morgans and Rockefellers.**

And it was equally conspicuous. Rising luxury consumption
and social ambition prompted *New York* magazine to observe
that for the third time in one hundred twenty-five years "a
confluence of economic conditions has created arrivistes in such
great numbers and with such immense wealth that they formed
a critical mass and created a whole new social order with its
own new rules of acceptable behavior." The 1980s were of a
magnitude comparable with that of the post–Civil War period
and the 1920s, and "each of these watershed eras for New York
came at a time when the need to raise capital thrust finance to
the front of the national agenda and Wall Street to the center
of public attention. And each era created a new class of wealthy
who had so much money, so much power and so much momentum that they more or less displaced the older Establishment. . . ."[7]

Incomes and wealth were concentrating for several reasons.
Global and national economic restructuring—the late twentieth
century's worldwide revolution in trade, technology and finance—provided the underlying context. Commercial chaos
is brutally Darwinian; it favors skills, enterprise and imagina-

---

* Twentieth-century wealth data are collected in Appendix A, and Chapter 6
examines in detail the sectoral and geographic distribution of 1981–88 U.S.
upper-bracket growth—who got the money and where they got it.

tion. A second circumstance was that wages—the principal source of middle- and lower-class dollars—had stagnated through 1986 even while disinflation, deregulation and commercial opportunity were escalating the return on capital. Most of the Reagan decade, to put it mildly, was a heyday for unearned income as rents, dividends, capital gains and interest gained relative to wages and salaries as a source of wealth and increasing economic inequality. By 1983, as the bull market that had begun in August 1982 kept soaring, *Fortune* magazine profiled its biggest winners: Each of fifty-three stockholders had already made profits of over $100 million! One, David Packard, cofounder of Hewlett-Packard Inc., found himself richer on paper by $1.2 billion. Nine others gained over $300 million.[8] More and bigger gains would follow in the mid-1980s, augmented by reduced tax rates on these swollen unearned incomes. In the wake of the 1978 capital gains tax reductions and the sweeping 1981 rate cuts, the effective overall, combined federal tax rate paid by the top 1 percent of Americans dropped from 30.9 percent in 1977 to 23.1 percent in 1984.[9] No other group gained nearly so much.

Wealth data, of course, always display more concentration than income statistics. Upper-income taxpayers do a lopsided share of the accumulating. In 1986 the Joint Economic Committee released Federal Reserve Board findings, overstated at first and later modified, that the share of wealth held by the naïvely labeled "super-rich"—the top one half of 1 percent of U.S. households—had risen significantly in the 1980s after falling during the prior four decades. Appendix B shows the numbers. By the JEC's revised measurement, America's top 420,000 households alone accounted for 26.9 percent of U.S. family net worth—in essence, 26.9 percent of the nation's wealth. The top 10 percent of households, meanwhile, controlled approximately 68 percent. Accumulation and concentration would be simultaneous hallmarks of the 1980s.

On the income side of the ledger, the results, while less skewed, were striking enough. Here, too, the decade's biggest advances were scored by those already doing well—the business owners, investors, financiers and service-industry professionals. "The economy," said Stanford University professor Robert Hall, "has shifted in the direction of a meritocracy," and there was no mistaking how the smart, the well-educated and the highly motivated commanded a large share of the gain.[10] Chart 2 and the accompanying table show the percentage of family money income received by each quintile of the population from 1969 to 1988. One computation grabbed most of the publicity: between 1980 and 1988, the income share taken by the upper 20 percent of Americans rose from 41.6 percent to 44.0 percent, the highest ratio since the Census Bureau began its official measurements in 1949. Parenthetically, the share of the top 1 percent climbed from 9 percent to over 11 percent during the same period, suggesting that this particularly affluent subgroup—and not those with a more middle-class position in the eightieth to ninety-ninth percentiles—took the overwhelming share of the top quintile's advance. Concentration like this is rare.

If anything, some experts argued, the Census Bureau understated the realignment of the 1980s. They contended that the Federal Reserve Board's distribution of income series offered a better profile because it included capital gains not included in standard Census Bureau income definitions. By this calculus, the income share of the top 10 percent climbed from 29 percent to 33 percent from 1969 to 1982. Liberal economist Lester Thurow observed, "That's a real earthquake if the top 10 percent of the population can add four percentage points to their total share of income. The four percentage points are a big fraction of somebody's income lower down the spectrum."[11] By the late 1980s data series including capital income were even more revealing: Experimental census income tabulations for 1986, published just before Christmas 1988, saw the top quintile's share of aggregate household income thereby expand to over 50 percent of the total. Capital gains were so concentrated at the top that their inclusion boosted the top quintile's share from 46.1 percent under the standard computation to a huge 52.5 percent.[12] Federal and state taxes brought it down to 50 percent. Another computation that included capital gains in income, this time a 1989 analysis by Brookings Institution economist Joseph Pechman, found that the top 1 percent of taxpayers in 1981 had 8.1 percent of total reported income. By 1986, with the help of soaring stock markets, that share had risen to an unprecedented 14.7 percent.

Different data series and (necessary) adjustments for inflation

CHART 2
RISING U.S. INCOME INEQUALITY

## Mean Incomes of Population Quintiles, 1954–86
### Thousands of 1986 Dollars

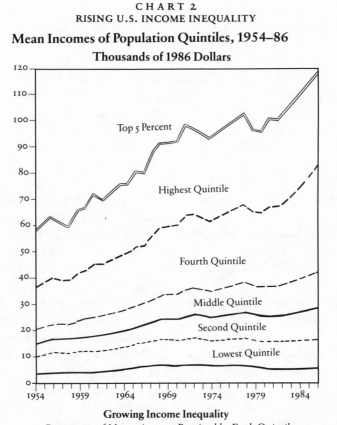

### Growing Income Inequality

*Percentage of Money income Received by Each Quintile*

| Year | Lowest | 2nd | Middle | 4th | Highest |
|------|--------|------|--------|------|---------|
| 1969 | 5.6 | 12.4 | 17.7 | 23.7 | 40.6 |
| 1974 | 5.5 | 12.0 | 17.5 | 24.0 | 41.0 |
| 1979 | 5.2 | 11.6 | 17.5 | 24.1 | 41.7 |
| 1980 | 5.1 | 11.6 | 17.5 | 24.3 | 41.6 |
| 1981 | 5.0 | 11.3 | 17.4 | 24.4 | 41.9 |
| 1982 | 4.7 | 11.2 | 17.1 | 24.3 | 42.7 |
| 1983 | 4.7 | 11.1 | 17.1 | 24.3 | 42.8 |
| 1984 | 4.7 | 11.0 | 17.0 | 24.4 | 42.9 |
| 1985 | 4.6 | 10.9 | 16.9 | 24.2 | 43.5 |
| 1986 | 4.6 | 10.8 | 16.8 | 24.0 | 43.7 |
| 1987 | 4.6 | 10.8 | 16.9 | 24.1 | 43.7 |
| 1988 | 4.6 | 10.7 | 16.7 | 24.0 | 44.0 |

### 1988 Income Range of Quintiles

Lowest: Under $15,102    Third: $26,182–38,500   Fifth: Over $55,906
Second: $15,102–26,182 Fourth: $38,500–55,906

Source: U.S. Census Bureau

can make trend analysis seem like Greek. But Ohioans Ross LaRoe and John Charles Pool put one set of comparative 1977–87 income trends in simple language for Middle America. Using data from the nonpartisan Congressional Budget Office, they wrote that "since 1977, the average after-tax family income of the lowest 10 percent, in current dollars, fell from $3,528 to $3,157. That's a 10.5 percent drop. During the same period, average family income of the top 10 percent increased from $70,459 to $89,783—up 24.4 percent. The incomes of the top 1 percent, which were 'only' $174,498 in 1977, are up to $303,900—a whopping 74.2 increase over the decade."[13]

The role played in this redistribution by Reagan's conservative economic policies will be examined more fully in Chapter 4. For the moment, suffice it to say that the concentration of income and wealth during the 1980s was unusual—the kind of buildup that occurs only once every few generations. Although distributional ratios had not quite returned to 1920s levels, favorable economic circumstances and federal policies had created an extraordinary pyramid of affluence—a record number of billionaires, three thousand to four thousand families each worth over $50 million, almost one hundred thousand with assets over $10 million, and at least one and a quarter million households with a net worth exceeding $1 million. Affluent Americans weren't thronging the Hamptons, Gold Coast Florida and California's Palm Desert area by accident. Unprecedented disposable income brought them there.

The caveat was that if two to three million Americans were in clover—and another thirty to thirty-five million were justifiably pleased with their circumstances in the late 1980s—a larger number were facing deteriorating personal or family incomes or a vague but troubling sense of harder times ahead.

## THE DOWNSIDE OF
## THE AMERICAN DREAM

By 1988 anecdotal proof abounded that the imperiled "American dream" had become an emerging battleground of national politics. The average manufacturing wage seemed to buy less. Low-income households were in trouble, especially female-headed ones. Here and there, off the main roads, large patches of small-town America were dying. Big-city poverty was on the rise. Young married couples, needing two incomes to meet bills, postponed having children and gave up buying their own homes. And in blue-collar factory towns, where a job on the production line at Ford or Bethlehem Steel had helped two generations of workers climb into the middle class, the next generation saw no such opportunity.

But if hearsay evidence was everywhere, a precise statistical portrait was a lot harder to come by—in part because there was such a confusion of numbers. Different data series gave different—and often contradictory—pictures. Take national per capita income. As figured in constant 1987 dollars, it had expanded almost automatically during the decade as a growing percentage of Americans (women especially) went to work, rising from $10,740 in 1980 to $11,301 in 1984 and $12,287 in 1987. But critics called this a deceptive measurement and pointed instead to inflation-adjusted weekly *per worker* income, which went down during the same period, dropping from $366 in 1972 to $318 in 1980 and $312 in 1987. Others preferred to cite the weakness in inflation-adjusted U.S. family median incomes.

Defenders of 1980s prosperity found family income data a problem. The average millionaire's income might be soaring, but the average family's was stagnating. In constant 1987 dollars, the median had reached $30,820 in 1973, declined slightly to $30,668 in 1979, then plummeted in the early 1980s under both Carter and Reagan. Only by 1987 did it reach $30,853, essentially recovering 1973 levels.[14] *After-tax* 1987 median family incomes were still well below those of the late 1970s. This, critics said, was the better measure of households in pain.

There were partial rebuttals. Families in 1988, having shrunk over the prior decades, were no longer comparable to earlier groupings. Families averaging 3.19 people in 1987 *did* require less consumption than those of 1970 averaging 3.58 people, which did distort comparisons of family income. Even so, the weakness in inflation-adjusted family median incomes commanded symbolic attention, as did the similar slump in real disposable (after-tax) family income. For many Middle Americans stagnant purchasing power *was* a day-to-day reality—and a stark offset to the glitter of exploding wealth in Manhattan or Beverly Hills. Appendix C illustrates the 1970–87 ups and downs of family income statistics.

There were other data, too: reams of them on both sides. And perhaps that was the most telling barometer of all. During the thirty years after World War II, when the American dream was indisputably working, no statistical profiles had really been necessary. People knew they were better off. No one could quibble.

By 1988 quibbling and ambiguity were everywhere. Too much could be made of any single broad yardstick of family, per capita or household income. As each index measured something slightly different, virtually every pundit or politician might find some statistics to document a particular case. And critics overplayed their thesis of a whole economy in decline. The Congressional Budget Office, looking for a moderate middle ground, calculated in 1987 that family income went up 11 percent from 1973 to 1986, with a meaningful percentage increase between 1981 and 1986. In many ways, though, the larger story—and the worrisome symptom—was not the slight *overall* growth in median family income. It was the comparative advances or regressions of families in different brackets. "If you look at subgroups you can see that inequality is rising more than it seems to be if you just look at the aggregate numbers," said Sheldon Danziger, a sociologist at the University of Michigan. "There's a lot more going on in the pieces than in the larger picture."[15]

Politically the economic viability of U.S. families had started to become an important issue. Academicians and politicians might be able to play ping-pong with statistics seeking to define *overall* family trends, but there was no way to argue with the official government portrait of a shift of income between 1980 and 1988 away from the bottom 80 percent of the U.S. population toward the most affluent fifth. Table 1, from the Congressional Budget Office, shows how less affluent segments of the population were slipping downward even as the top strata were enjoying a major surge of income and wealth.

Previous Republican and laissez-faire eras, periods of competitive, capitalist resurgence, have *always* produced broad ranks of losers as well as winners. And by Reagan's last year in office, evidence of a wide range of occupational declines—

TABLE I

INCOME GAINS AND LOSSES
1977–88

Changes in Average Family Income
(1987 Dollars)

| Income Decile | Average Family Income | | Percentage Change | Change in Average Family Income |
|---|---|---|---|---|
| | *1977* | *1988** | *1977–88* | *1977–88* |
| First | $ 4,113 | $ 3,504 | −14.8% | $ −609 |
| Second | 8,334 | 7,669 | −8.0 | −665 |
| Third | 13,140 | 12,327 | −6.2 | −813 |
| Fourth | 18,436 | 17,220 | −6.6 | −1,216 |
| Fifth | 23,896 | 22,389 | −6.3 | −1,507 |
| Sixth | 29,824 | 28,205 | −5.4 | −1,619 |
| Seventh | 36,405 | 34,828 | −4.3 | −1,577 |
| Eighth | 44,305 | 43,507 | −1.8 | −798 |
| Ninth | 55,487 | 56,064 | 1.0 | 577 |
| Tenth | 102,722 | 119,635 | 16.5 | 16,913 |
| Top 5% | 134,543 | 166,016 | 23.4 | 31,473 |
| Top 1% | 270,053 | 404,566 | 49.8 | 134,513 |
| All Families | 33,527 | 34,274 | 2.2 | 747 |

* CBO projection of 1988 incomes

Source: *Challenge to Leadership*, Urban Institute

for manufacturing employees, farmers, people in the oil industry, young householders and the working poor—was more or
less irrefutable. *Money* magazine's midyear polls, those in which
60 percent of Americans described the U.S. economy as "not
so good" or "poor," reflected popular disillusionments that extended far beyond much publicized Farm Belt foreclosures or
shut-down factory towns.

Previous economic dislocations in the United States during
the twentieth century could be tied to events; those of the 1980s
could not. In 1987 Frank Levy, professor of public policy at
the University of Maryland, wrote that during the Carter and
Reagan years:

. . . there was little mass unemployment [in the 1980s] and few people were forced to take money wage cuts. To the contrary, *money wages* were rising briskly, but prices were rising, too, and few people gained ground.

We knew that something was wrong, but we lacked the language to describe it. Conflict among regions, industrial sectors, and generations was clearly on the rise, and we spoke of growing inequality as if census statistics would show the income distribution splitting apart. But official income inequality increased only modestly, and the real change in inequality has been harder to measure. It involved a mixture of family arrangements, when people bought their homes, and how established they were in their careers. It involved their current income but also their outlook for the future and the likelihood of attaining their aspirations. It was an inequality of prospects in which many people who had attained the middle-class dream could ride out the period while people who aspired to the dream—people who were banking on rising living standards—saw the future shrink.[16]

White males serving as their family's only breadwinner were, as a category, particularly conspicuous. By one calculation, their median inflation-adjusted income fell 22 percent between 1976 and 1984.[17] After the 1983 recovery, many squeezed or depressed households discovered that their economic problems weren't simply recession hangovers. As domestic and global economic restructuring continued, well-paid manufacturing jobs and the purchasing power of manufacturing paychecks shrank. For *all* workers, white-collar as well as blue-collar, their real average weekly wage—calculated in constant 1977 dollars—fell from $191.41 a week in 1972 to $171.07 in 1986.[18]

But even that decline disguised the larger negative impact on men partly offset by a slight overall rise for women. Well-paid male blue-collar union members suffered the greatest loss, especially younger men and those with no more than a high school diploma. According to Marvin Kosters, a conservative economist at the Washington-based American Enterprise Institute, the median real earnings of men between the ages of twenty-five to thirty-four, measured in constant 1985 dollars, were $10.17 an hour in 1973, $9.70 an hour in 1980 and $8.85 in 1987. For men of all ages with nothing more than high school diplomas the figures were $9.90 in 1973, $9.37 in 1980 and $8.62 in

1987.[19] Frank Levy observed that "back in the early 1970s, the average guy with a high school diploma was making $24,000 in today's dollars. Today a similar guy is making about $18,000."[20]

The high-paying jobs lost in Hibbing or River Rouge had been more than just employment; they had been cultural and economic ladders to middle-class status for millions of families all across industrial America. Newspaper writers from Appalachia to the Iron Range wrote more or less the same story: "Once blue-collar sons could follow their fathers into the plants and make $13, $14 an hour. That meant the middle class, a car, maybe a little cabin on a lake, a chance for kids to go to college. Once, but not anymore." Caste and class restraints that had eased after World War II began to reemerge.

Public frustration had distinct regional accents, too. Despite a partial rebound in 1987–88 in agriculture and manufacturing, the Reagan decade favored what Democratic politicians in 1986 started calling the "bicoastal economy." Even in 1988, national income data would show the Rocky Mountains, Farm Belt and Oil Patch lagging.

Hard times in the Great Lakes factory towns were less persistent. The first half of the decade had been weak, and in 1986 wages fell in 47 percent of Illinois's manufacturing jobs, where the average reduction was 8 percent.[21] Then in 1987–88, Great Lakes manufacturing began to rebound as the falling dollar stimulated exports. What was surprising, though, was how little the rebound carried over to wages. On average, the manufacturing jobs being created in 1987–88 were not as well paid as the ones lost earlier—and the pressures of global competitiveness kept wage increases behind modestly resurgent inflation. The General Accounting Office reported the resurgence of sweatshops—businesses that regularly violate wage, child labor, safety and health laws—not just in New York, Chicago and Los Angeles but in virtually all sections of the country.

On the eve of the Democratic National Convention, Lester Thurow, dean of the Sloan School of Management at MIT, urged Dukakis to make the lack of "good jobs at good wages" the central issue of the campaign: "The real hourly wages of production or non-supervisory workers—after correcting for inflation—were no higher in the first quarter of 1988 than they had been in 1980. And in recent years, wages have been falling. In 1987, real hourly wages fell 1.1 percent. The fall continued in the first quarter of 1988. Weekly wages, a measure that takes into account both hourly pay and hours of work, were even more of a disaster. In the first quarter of 1988, they were 2.4 percent *below* where they had been in 1980 and falling at a rate in excess of 1 percent per year."[22] The political issue, Thurow contended, was that real GNP was rising despite the falling real wages, which meant that *someone's* income was going up— "and that someone has been the top 20 percent of the population."

Major 1988 contract negotiations showed that labor was still defensive. General Electric's 198,000 domestic workers settled for a 2.5 percent wage increase in the first year and 1.5 percent in each of the next two years, far below projected inflation.* But there was also another side to the story. "We concentrate on what our memberships want, and a lot of unions have decided to give up wages for guaranteed jobs and for retraining programs," said an AFL-CIO economist in Washington.[23]

Moreover, many people were not in the work force at all: members of the underclass, for example, or those no longer looking for a job. The 5.3 percent unemployment rate was misleading because definitions of the work force excluded a growing number of Americans. By the summer of 1988, 45.3 percent of New York City residents over the age of sixteen could not be counted as labor force participants because of poverty, lack of skills, drug use, apathy or other problems. Similar circumstances were reported in Detroit and Baltimore, while the ratio of uncountables for the nation as a whole was 34.5 percent.[24] Thus the paradox: *millions of jobs might be going begging, but huge numbers of Americans remained either unemployed or unemployable.* Circumstances like this resulted in the destitution and homelessness that perturbed cities and suburbs everywhere as economic polarization intensified.

Many women had also been losers. Families were not just

---

* Martin Neil Bailey, a fellow at the Brookings Institution in Washington, found it "surprising—with the current economy—that we have not seen a rise in real wages yet. What we are seeing so far is higher profits rather than higher wages." ("Pay Isn't Keeping Pace with the Economy," *Philadelphia Inquirer,* July 27, 1988).

shrinking; they were breaking down. Households headed by females ranked well down the income scale—especially those with children. In the spring and summer of 1988 polls showed that half of all men characterized the U.S. economy as "excellent" or "good," but only one third of the women did so.[25] Women preferred the Democrats largely for economic reasons, not only because of broken homes, but, as we have seen, because of the pressure on family life when wives and mothers take marginal jobs. Families were sacrificing psychic income for dollar income, a trade-off that the Census Bureau chose not to quantify, but which was probably considerable. One survey found that Americans' leisure time declined by 37 percent between 1973 and 1987—from 26.2 hours a week to 16.6 hours.[26]

By the mid-1980s a new two-tier wage system had arisen in troubled industries as senior employees kept their previous pay scales but *new* hires—from airline pilots to supermarket checkout clerks—came in at lower rates. At the same time, more people could find only part-time jobs as employers spread work and costs more carefully. This "contingent work force"—part-timers and temporaries—had doubled between 1980 and 1987, expanding to include roughly one quarter of the total work force, while the percentage of the working poor with short periods of unemployment rose.[27] Not surprisingly, given these pressures, the uncertainty and unreliability of employment also grew as an issue; a 1988 poll found "job security" reemerging as employees' number one concern. Emphasis on the low official unemployment rate was deceptive to the extent that it ignored these offsets.

Corporate chairmen and presidents as a class feasted in the 1980s, but the number of mid-level management jobs lost during those years was estimated to be as high as 1.5 million. In 1987 one survey found 41 percent of respondents acknowledging job-loss fears premised on corporate restructuring or foreign competition.[28] Blue-collar America had paid a larger price, but suburbia, where fathers rushed to catch the 8:10 train to the city, was quietly counting its casualties, too. In September 1988, Peter Drucker observed that "the cynicism out there is frightening. Middle managers have become insecure, and they feel unbelievably hurt. They feel like slaves on an auction block."[29]

Thus "downward mobility" emerged as a real fear within the

U.S. work force, white-collar and blue-collar alike. The *Los Angeles Times* reported in 1988 that "not in half a century has the United States seen so many 'givebacks' affecting so many people. But from musicians with the Honolulu Symphony Orchestra to lumbermen in the Pacific Northwest, from steelworkers in West Virginia to Greyhound bus drivers in Montana, thousands of Americans with years of experience are experiencing the vicissitudes of MAAD—middle-aged and downward."[30]

In 1986, 59 percent of the baby boomers paying Social Security taxes said they didn't ever expect to collect their benefits. At the same time, amid job switches and family breakups, *private pension* coverage also began to shrink. Between 1950 and 1980 the percentage of American workers included under retirement plans had risen from 22 percent to 45 percent. By 1986 coverage had shrunk to 42.6 percent.[31]

Many families found themselves emptying savings accounts and going in debt, often to meet the soaring price of homeownership or to put a child through college. For a family with 1985 earnings equal to the median national income, keeping a child in a four-year private college or university would have taken 40 percent of that income, up from 30 percent in 1970. Buying a house was even tougher. Homeownership had reached a record 65 percent of U.S. households in 1980, after climbing steadily from 1940, when 43.6 percent of households owned their own residences. After 1980, however, the homeownership rate would drop year by year, falling to 63.8 percent in 1986 and leveling off.[32] Young people, in particular, found that home buying was next to impossible.

In 1980, 21.3 percent of people under twenty-five owned their own homes. By 1987 that rate was down to 16.1 percent. Among those between twenty-five and twenty-nine the rate fell from 43.3 percent to 35.9 percent. For persons between thirty and thirty-four the decline was from 61.1 percent to 53.2 percent. And among those thirty-five to thirty-nine the drop was seven points—from 70.8 percent to 63.8 percent.[33] In 1988 presidential campaign rhetoric touched on the problem, but not convincingly. To more and more citizens, the American dream of homeownership was becoming just that—*a dream.*

For much of Middle America, then, the Reagan years were

troubling and ambiguous as the contrast intensified between proliferating billionaires and the tens of millions of others who were gradually sinking. Under the superficial economic glitter of *Lifestyles of the Rich and Famous* and *Architectural Digest*, powerful polarizing forces were at work.* Through much of the late spring and summer of 1988 Republican strategists couldn't understand the dissonance between strong economic statistics and the voters' doubts about George Bush, but one explanation was pervasive national uncertainty about the shape of the American dream—and suspicion that the Republicans were administering it on behalf of the few, not of the many.

## REAGANOMICS AND THE ENLARGING UPPER MIDDLE CLASS

Many upper-middle-bracket Americans found doubts about the economy hard to understand. To some ten to fifteen million families counting themselves in the top 20 percent, but below the millionaire 1 percent at the top, liberal gloom about national decline made no sense. These were the second-tier beneficiaries (and electoral foot soldiers) of the Reagan Revolution. Though sizable segments of middle-class America were losing ground, for a larger number—many of the elderly, and especially two-earner professional families, entrepreneurs and investors—the 1980s had been a decade of advancement.

Liberal politicians and writers might focus on the losers. But plenty of others were coining money from investments, rents, bonuses, businesses and highly compensated professions. To marketing and publishing executives, these were *the* new sales target; to politicians, they were the Americans most likely to vote; and to conservatives, they were also proof of 1980s economic success.

* In the late 1920s economist Stuart Chase had probed a kindred polarization in a cautionary book entitled *Prosperity: Fact or Myth* (New York: Charles Boni Paperback Books, 1929). Beneath the patina of the soaring stock market, new millionaires, two-lane highways crowded with new automobiles, and the excitement of radios, the first talking movies and Charles Lindbergh's unprecedented solo flight across the Atlantic, lots of Americans had gained little during the decade, Chase contended. Many had actually *lost* ground. By the late 1980s Reagan's critics had begun pointing to similar contradictions.

Quantifications could hardly be precise, but families making $15,000 to $50,000 in constant dollars had declined from 65.1 percent of the population in 1970 to just 58.2 percent in 1985. Low-income families with under $15,000 a year in constant dollars did expand slightly from 21.9 percent in 1970 to 23.5 percent in 1985. But America's higher-income layer—those families making $50,000 and over—jumped from 13 percent of the total in 1970 to 18.3 percent in 1985.[34] And by 1988 one study contended that thirty-six million adults—one in five—now came from households with an income of over $50,000 a year, twice as many as in 1983, a large gain, even allowing for an inflation adjustment.[35] Economic polarization and middle-class "decline" involved roughly as much *promotion* and upward mobility as *demotion*.* As Table 1 on page 17 shows, membership or graduation into the upper middle class—or even more, into the top 1 percent—was the key to significant 1977–88 improvement in average family income.

Reassurance about "Morning Again in America" might ring false in Ketchum, Idaho, or in Odessa, Texas, or in Eldon, Iowa, but seemed reasonably accurate in hundreds of booming suburbs and scores of gentrified, restored downtown neighborhoods. America in 1988 was a consumers' heaven for those on the favored side of the income charts. From a rarefied perspective, to be sure, the income gains of the thirty-odd million Americans in the $50,000- to $200,000-a-year threshhold of upper-bracket status were Coke-and-cheeseburger stuff compared with the increments registered at the true apex of the U.S. economic pyramid. Yet Reaganomics *did* have a mass constituency. Even critics of the Reagan administration acknowledged that economic woes were concentrated in the lower and middle strata; the top tenth of the country was doing very well, thank you, and the next tenth was at least holding its own.

At the ballot box, moreover, that was almost enough. Buoyed by a conservative, pro-enterprise national mood, Middle and Upper Americans were *the* power bloc of the 1980s. With just 53 percent of the eligible-age population bothering to vote in

---

* In the May 1988 *Monthly Labor-Review*, published by the nonpartisan Bureau of Labor Statistics, economists Michael Harrigan and Susan Haugen made just this point: "America's middle class has been shrinking since 1969, but mainly because more families have moved into the upper class."

the 1984 presidential election and 50 percent in 1988, the actual lever-pulling electorate was disproportionately Buick-owning and Book-of-the-Month Club. Seventy-five percent of the citizenry voted in Pacific Palisades, 25 percent in the South Bronx. Elections analysts could not be quite sure, but persons in the top-income quintile conceivably cast almost 30 percent of the total presidential ballots in Ronald Reagan's 1984 landslide, and people in the top two quintiles together probably accounted for over 50 percent of turnout—and with a disproportionately Republican effect.

Democratic strategists recognized the problem. In the 1988 words of the Texas populist Agriculture Commissioner Jim Hightower, "the greatest number of electoral drop-outs are people making less than $25,000 a year. It doesn't take a degree in sociology to figure out that these people are telling us they don't see much improvement in their lives from the economic policies of either major party. If you talk with the non-voters in any town in America, the most common sentiment you'll hear is that there is not a dime's worth of difference, to borrow George Wallace's phrase, in the two parties: the rich just get richer, and the rest get taken."[36] MIT professor Walter Dean Burnham, voicing a similar view, commented that nonvoters had become America's fastest-growing party.[37] He and other observers were struck by the economic irony: that the more politics disillusioned those Americans whose status was in decline (or had never risen), the more they gave up, leaving ballot-box decisions to those profiting from the ongoing rearrangement of American affluence.

## THE LIBERAL UNCERTAINTY:
## ECONOMIC INEQUALITY
## AS A WORLD TREND

Critics of the Reagan administration during the early and mid 1980s confronted another problem. Much of the shift taking place was a *worldwide* phenomenon, not just American, and even in the United States, rising inequality had preceded Reagan, starting under Jimmy Carter. Economists knew that during the late 1970s and 1980s the poor had been getting poorer and the rich had been getting richer virtually everywhere on the globe. The *Los Angeles Times'* exhaustive 1984 international survey found that in the Third World gaps of 20:1 and even 30:1 between the income of the richest and poorest fifths of the population were common—and widening.[38]

One popular early explanation blamed stagflation, suggesting that since the mid-1970s, equality had lost ground as the general economic slowdown convinced many voters and many governments that they could no longer afford to mitigate unfairness.[39] The result was not simply that politics and public policy became less generous, but that the triumph of conservative individualism thereupon gave *further* rein to the forces of economic inequality (and even polarization) already at work. For a decade or so, the process became something of a seamless web among the leading economic powers, so that global economic change, ascendant conservative ideology, spreading market economics and rising concentration of wealth fed off one another.

These simultaneous conservative trends in the United States, Britain, Canada, West Germany, France and Japan generated an unprecedented exchange of ideas and governmental economic collaboration—at first loosely and then formally through the Group of Seven (G-7) industrial nations. The Reagan administration and Britain's Thatcher government were the principal greenhouses of the aggressive neo-laissez-faire economics, but these views also began influencing the Japanese government of Yasuhiro Nakasone, prime minister during the rise of Japan's so-called money culture.

By then, procapitalist cooperation among the seven was unprecedented, and in many respects was a tonic—certainly for business spirit. London, Manhattan and Tokyo might have turned greedier than usual, but they also hummed with activity. More than at any other time since World War II, the major Western economic powers were dominated by conservative leaders with constituencies among their nations' business and financial elites and upper-bracket taxpayers, all of which greatly facilitated not only generally compatible economic policies but also mutual support. The United States, to be sure, was the key, both in policy leadership and as the world's most important economy and market. If the Reagan administration helped the Thatcher and Nakasone regimes, they returned the favor. Japan played such an important role in 1987 and 1988 by financing U.S. Treasury debt, stabilizing the U.S. dollar and helping the White House avoid an election-year recession that Chicago economist David Hale wryly labeled Japan's central bank as a de facto Republican political action committee.[40] The United States was the linchpin of a global realignment in which wealth was concentrating among top-income groups in the major financial and industrial nations.

By the end of the decade, however, from Tokyo to London, public sensitivity to this increasing inequality was unmistakable. Though France's mildly resurgent Socialists succeeded in reimposing a wealth tax on the nation's large fortunes, conservative governments in Britain and Japan were reducing income tax progressivity while imposing new or increased *regressive* levies—a value-added (sales) tax in Japan, a highly controversial poll tax in Britain. Coming in tandem with the stock market and real estate booms in both nations, especially Japan, conservative policies were criticized for promoting the interests of the rich.* Britain's widening gap between rich and poor emerged as a serious issue in the 1987 general election, and in early October 1988, a Gallup poll for Britain's Sunday *Telegraph* found an extraordinary 75 percent of those sampled complaining that Prime Minister Margaret Thatcher and the Conservatives "look after the rich, not ordinary people," while 66 percent of the population said the Conservatives "don't care what hardships their policies cause."[41] In Japan, meanwhile, public opinion surveys in late 1988 found the electorate's sense that their country was a middle-class society disintegrating. Critics claimed that government policy and tax reforms favored the rich, while ordinary Japanese were not sharing in the huge profits being made in real estate and the stock market. Seventy-four percent of Japanese called the economic system basically unfair in a late 1988 survey, while more than half complained that gaps in income and assets had widened over the previous decade.[42] The electoral reaction would come in 1989.

* These international parallels will be discussed in more detail on pp. 146–53.

# THE TWO FACES OF
# AMERICAN PUBLIC OPINION

Notwithstanding nagging voter uncertainties and localized hard
times in farm, energy and extractive regions, liberal economic
populism failed to develop nationwide momentum in the United
States during most of the 1980s. Nor were voters much affected
by the GOP biases that Democrats periodically emphasized: the
upper-bracket and corporate orientation of the 1981 tax cuts,
the ongoing rollback of federal programs for the poor, and even
Budget Director David Stockman's thoughtless admission that
supply-side economics was actually the latest version of old GOP
"trickle-down" theory and practice.

Yet voters perceived the administration's tilt—or said they
did. National majorities, and sometimes large ones, agreed when
pollsters asked if Reagan favored the rich. (See Appendix D.)
However, the president's personal job ratings remained high,
propped up by overall U.S. prosperity, personal affection and
public support for his "America is back" muscle-flexing,
whether it was the invasion of Grenada in 1983 or the successful
U.S. air strike against Libya in 1986.

These assessments soured in late 1986 and 1987, as revelations of the White House's gullibility in dealings with Iran's
revolutionary mullahs undercut the president with swing voters.
Within weeks his ratings tumbled ten to fifteen points, mostly
staying in the 45–55 percent range until the 1988 Republican
National Convention. Following the Iran-Contra hearings, voters let themselves think about the downside of the Reagan years
as well as the upside. October's stock market crash provided
some additional reinforcement. So did revelations early in 1988
about the White House reliance on astrology.

Concern about the economic future was part of this new
unease. In January 1988, during the week of the president's
State of the Union speech, 72 percent of Americans believed
that the rich were better off than in 1981 (only 6 percent thought
they were doing worse). The poor, almost everyone agreed, had
lost ground. As for the middle class, voters weren't sure: 31
percent saw gains, but 34 percent believed middle-class circumstances had gotten worse.[43] Presumably Democratic politicking

had fanned these doubts. In August, just before the Republican presidential convention, 73 percent of the voters identified the Republicans as doing more to help the rich; partly in consequence, they chose the Democrats by 56 percent to 28 percent as the party that would help the middle class. Still other surveys identified how closely public support for a change of direction in the White House was linked to income: upper-bracket Americans endorsed the status quo; poor people wanted a new deal.

For the first seven months of 1988, as Democratic criticisms dominated the primaries, the public seemed to agree. Back in March 1987, 65 percent had told survey takers that it was more difficult for middle-class Americans to maintain their living standards than it had been five years earlier.[44] And then in February 1988 one major national poll reported a serious rise in the worry level: "For the first time since Ronald Reagan became president more than seven years ago, Americans generally do not think the nation's future will be better than its present or its past. . . . Many of them linked their rising pessimism to the stock market collapse in October, the growing visibility of foreign imports and a general fear that America is no longer in control of its own destiny."[45] In late January the same survey detailing national belief that Reagan policies had favored the rich simultaneously revealed a larger gnawing uncertainty: in this case, doubt that the United States was better off in 1988 than it had been when the president took office. The United States was seen as being stronger *militarily* than it had been back in 1981, but weaker *economically*.

Voters also indicated that economics might be more important to national security than armaments. A midyear poll found a majority calling unfair foreign competition a threat to the U.S. economy; another survey ranked foreign investment ahead of communism as a national concern; and in a third, majorities of Americans saw a greater threat from *economic* rivals like Japan than from *military* foes like the Soviet Union.[46]

During spring and early summer, as these sentiments showed their claws in the national polls, Michael Dukakis led George Bush. In late July Democratic strategist Robert Beckel told why in explaining the results of a party poll of 601 "swing" Democrats who had voted 2:1 for Reagan in 1984: "Ronald Reagan convinced these voters that their interests were with the wealthy.

They bought into trickle-down theory." But since then, Beckel said, they have become convinced that "where they are losing out is not to poor people but to wealthy people. They believe the dollars they have lost have gone up, not down."[47] In August, however, public opinion began to shift again.

This change resulted partly from convention speeches by Reagan and Bush reminding voters how much better things were than in 1980, the gloomy high-inflation last year of the Carter administration. The electorate's new mood also reflected Dukakis's failure during the summer and autumn to indict Reagan and Bush for their economic policies. After his nomination, Dukakis produced no coherent statement to explain what had gone wrong or how to fix it. From time to time he would gingerly raise themes like runaway mergers, unfair foreign competition and the "middle-class squeeze." But until the last ten days he would invariably back off and his tough talk would tail away.

Dukakis was obviously uncomfortable with populism. Election-eve analyses in *The Washington Post, The Boston Globe* and other leading newspapers all mentioned the candidate's upper-middle-class "civic religion" that led him to reject class and cultural attacks on George Bush, refuse a campaign pledge to block increases only in low- or middle-income taxes, veto advertising invoking fears of foreign economic influence and rule out references to "country club" Republicans in his speeches.[48] Only in late October, with his campaign crumbling, did Dukakis reluctantly convert to a more traditional Democratic line. It came too late.

All too aware of George Bush's own upper-class background and presumed vulnerability to populist themes, Republican strategists could hardly believe their luck. Bush campaign manager Lee Atwater later acknowledged that he had been apprehensive, around Labor Day, when Dukakis had flirted with "us versus them" themes. After the election, Atwater stated the sociopolitical premise behind his concern: "The way to win a presidential race against the Republicans is to develop the class warfare issue, as Dukakis did at the end. To divide up the haves and have nots and to try to reinvigorate the New Deal coalition and to attack."[49] Others agreed that such a Democratic strategy from July on might have won. Vincent Breglio, director of the Republican presidential campaign's polling division, would later

disclose that even Dukakis's last-minute populist rhetoric had
made Bush survey takers nervous: "Going into the last week of
the campaign, we clearly saw that the populist message of Dukakis was having an impact. It was cutting."[50] To liberal economist Robert Kuttner, Dukakis had violated one of his party's
basic historical verities: that "Democrats do best when they
develop broad, embracing, expansive visions combining national purpose with economic advancement, and rally masses
of non-rich voters."[51]

Though the Democratic campaign failed to focus national
discontents, the Americans who went to the polls on November
8, 1988, were divided over Reagan's legacy, largely because of
apprehensions over America's economic vulnerability and the
maldistribution of national prosperity. The troubled farm and
oil states, though mostly remaining Republican, showed a disproportionate Democratic trend, while much of the booming
East Coast supported Bush at levels only slightly below Ronald
Reagan's. To Americans with long memories, the policy thrust
of the Reagan years toward inequality had not been a coincidence. Simultaneous top-bracket gains and bottom-echelon
stagnation represented a familiar politics. Other Republican political cycles and administrations had been there before.

# Chapter

**2**

## Wealth, Populism and the Genius of American Politics

In the 1980 campaign, we were able to make the establishment, insofar as it is bad, the government. In other words, big government was the enemy, not big business. If the people think the problem is that taxes are too high, and government interferes too much, then we are doing our job. But, if they get to the point where they say that the real problem is that rich people aren't paying taxes . . . then the Democrats are going to be in good shape. Traditionally, the Republican party has been elitist, but one of the things that has happened is that the Democratic Party has become a party of [rival] elites. . . .

—LEE ATWATER
1988 REPUBLICAN PRESIDENTIAL
CAMPAIGN MANAGER, 1986

Much of the new emphasis in the 1980s on tax reduction, on free market economics and on the aggressive accumulation of wealth reflected the Republican party's long record of support for unabashed capitalism. However, part of the reason that U.S. "survival of the fittest" periods of economic restructuring are so relentless rests on the performance of the Democrats as history's second most enthusiastic capitalist party.* They do not interfere much with capitalist momentum, but wait for excesses and the inevitable populist reactions.

In the United States, elections play a more important cultural and economic role than in other lands. Lacking a hereditary

* Their principal rival, Britain's Tory party, spent much of the first half of the nineteenth century favoring landed interests and opposing the new capitalism emerging under the aegis of the now virtually defunct Liberal party.

aristocracy or Establishment, our leadership elites and the alignment of wealth are more the product of political cycles than
elsewhere. Capitalism is maneuvered more easily in the United
States, pushed in new regional and sectoral directions. As a
result, the genius of American politics—failing only in the Civil
War—has been to manage through ballot boxes and electoral
votes the problems that less fluid societies resolve with party
structures geared to class warfare and even with barricades.

Because we are a mobile society, Americans tolerate one of the
largest disparities in the industrial world between top and bottom incomes as people from the middle move to the top, and vice
versa. In the United States, "circulating elites" are a reality, and
electoral politics is an important traffic controller. From the time
of Thomas Jefferson's victory, our national politics has undu-
lated in a series of twenty-eight- to thirty-six-year waves as each
watershed election puts a new dominant region, culture, ideology or economic interest (or a combination) into the White
House, changing the nation's direction. But after a decade or
two these new forces lose touch with the public, excessively em-
power their own elites and become a target for a new round of
populist outsidership and reform. Only the United States reveals
such a recurrent electoral behavior over two centuries.

The Republicans rode such a wave into office in 1969 as a
middle-class, anti-elite correction, successfully squelching social
permissiveness and disorder. But then, during the 1980s—and
not for the first time in U.S. history—Reagan's GOP became a
high-powered vehicle not only for capitalist revitalization, but
also, as we have seen, for the accumulation of wealth by a
relatively narrow elite. Twice before, the genius of the system
has generated an electoral correction to such Republican excesses, raising the possibility of another in the 1990s.


## THE REPUBLICAN PARTY
## AND HEYDAY CAPITALISM

From the formation of the Republican party in the mid-1850s
down to the 1990s, the United States has experienced successive
presidential party supremacies or waves, each lasting a long
generation. As profiled by political scientists, three have been

Republican and one Democratic: the Civil War Republican era (1860–96), the industrial Republican era (1896–1932) and the Democratic New Deal era (1932–68)—and I would add the civil-disturbance Republican era (1968 and thereafter). In each case the newly elected party has more or less dominated the White House for sixteen to twenty-four years after the pivotal election, pointing the United States in a new direction.*

In each period, wealth was redistributed regionally and from one income bracket to another. It was no fluke that the three Republican supremacies coincided with and helped generate the three major capitalist heydays in which wealth became more concentrated—the post–Civil War Gilded Age, the Roaring Twenties and the Reagan years. The Democratic era was, of course, the principal period of *downward* income redistribution, first in the 1930s, then again in the 1960s through Lyndon Johnson and his Great Society.

Notwithstanding the Republicans' ultimate economics, their rhetoric in the early stages is more broad-based. A good case can be made that Republican coalition-building has been a kind of internal "nationalism," suppressing narrow or sectional insurrections—whether by Southern slave owners in 1860, by agrarian populists in 1896 or by antiwar demonstrators, urban rioters and Southern sectionalists in 1968. Each Republican coalition began by emphasizing national themes and unity symbols while subordinating commercial and financial interests. Lincoln's struggle to maintain the Union is famous, but lesser efforts by McKinley in 1896 and Nixon in 1968 go little noticed. Even Lawrence Goodwyn, a historian of overt populist sympathies, has acknowledged the Republicans' skillful use of national-unity symbols—not least the American flag—to beat William Jennings Bryan in 1896.[1] Nixon ended slum and campus riots while co-opting George Wallace's politics of white Southern indignation.

But it is the *second* stage of presidential Republicanism, the concentration of wealth, that this book deals with. Beyond its emphasis on the politics of national unity, dynamic capitalism, market economics and the concentration of wealth are what the Republican party is all about. When Republicans are in power

* Appendix E briefly charts and explains these cycles.

long enough, that is what America gets, by the traditional Republican methods of disinflation, limited government, less regulation of business, reduced taxation and high interest rates. Over America's first two centuries, these were the same three periods that would incubate the most American millionaires (or, by the 1980s, *billionaires*).

History suggests that it takes a decade or more for the GOP to shift from broad middle-class "nationalism" into "capitalist overdrive." The lapse of twelve years between the first Nixon inauguration in 1969 and the first Reagan inauguration, which fits nicely, repeats exactly this transformation of cultural economics. Like previous Republican "nationalist" presidents— Abraham Lincoln, the small-town Illinois lawyer, and William McKinley, who campaigned from his Canton, Ohio, front porch—Nixon was an altogether middle-class figure. His empathy with insecure, postwar middle-class America had stood out in his famous Checkers speech of 1952, which blended wariness of the rich with reference to his wife Pat's "good Republican cloth coat."* Nixon had no interest in unbridled cap-

* In a short 1982 article observing the thirtieth anniversary of the Checkers speech, historian Robert S. McElvaine sketched the sharp distinctions between Nixon's imagery and Reagan's: "Most intriguing is the identification Nixon tried to make in 1952 with the 'common man,' the typical citizen who would be called during the later Nixon presidency the 'forgotten American' or part of the 'silent majority.' The people Nixon tried to identify with 30 years ago plainly were not the rich. 'I don't happen to be a rich man,' Nixon told his audience. . . . Nixon's speech stressed his humble, hard-working origins and his continuing middle-class life. 'I worked my way through college and to a great extent through law school,' he said. 'We live rather modestly,' the candidate contended." And then, citing Nixon's famous "cloth coat" sentence, McElvaine noted that "were President Reagan called upon to make a similar speech, he might say: 'Nancy doesn't have a cloth coat, but she does have a more-than-respectable sable coat and many de la Renta gowns." The professor's point was that the political culture had changed enormously by the 1980s: "The 'forgotten man' Franklin Roosevelt spoke of 50 years ago was one at the bottom of the economic pyramid. Thirty years ago Richard Nixon appealed to the middle of that structure. Today Ronald Reagan addresses himself to the pyramid's apex" ("They Don't Make 'Em Like the Checkers Speech Anymore," *Boston Globe*, September 24, 1982). Parenthetically, when he became president, Nixon also collaborated with Daniel Patrick Moynihan on a guaranteed annual income for the poor, and in 1989 the newly elected Democratic Speaker of the House of Representatives, Thomas Foley, said that the "Nixon Administration was the most important in advancing the anti-hunger fight in America" because of its efforts in the food stamp program ("A Politician Outside the Mold," *New York Times*, June 2, 1989).

italism during his 1969–74 presidency. It was Reagan who
would create another conservative economic elite and another
provocation.

## ELITES AND ANTI-ELITES IN
## AMERICAN PRESIDENTIAL POLITICS

"The love of wealth is . . . at the bottom of all that the Americans
do," Alexis de Tocqueville wrote in 1835. This is largely true
but ignores the cyclical nature of American opinion—and, most
important, the waves of anti-elite sentiment that have periodically whipped American politics.

Caste and even moderate class hostilities have always accompanied watershed politics in the United States. Occasionally
exaggerated, they are more often underestimated. Some elite or
other is *always* a target. In America's first watershed election,
Jefferson condemned the Federalist party of George Washington, John Adams and Alexander Hamilton for close ties to aristocracy and privilege, and, after leaving office, said, "I hope
we shall crush in its birth the aristocracy of our monied corporations."[2] In a campaign that reeked of cultural hostility, the
Jeffersonians pushed the losing Federalists back into what was
principally an Atlantic coastal strip of towns and counties with
cobblestoned streets, fashionable churches and prosperous commerce. Jeffersonian majorities were greatest in the homespun
hinterland, in places where farmers sent their corn to market in
whiskey barrels.

By the time Andrew Jackson won in 1828, the next watershed,
he had lashed out at the Philadelphia-based Bank of the United
States before appreciative audiences from the Monongahela to
the Mississippi. The "money power," he proclaimed, was an
evil that had to be fought.

A generation later Abraham Lincoln and his allies attacked
the "slaveocracy" of the South with such effectiveness that many
old Jacksonians forsook their party for the new Republicans,
who, not yet wholly attuned to the commercial elites of the
North, actually frightened many affluent status quo voters. Vic-
torious in the four-way race of 1860 with just 38 percent of the
national vote, the Republicans were closer to Yankee radical-

ism—the antislavery puritanism of New England Congregationalist pulpits—than to established Boston, New York or
Philadelphia commerce. Carriage-trade voters in all three cities
gave sizable support to John Bell, candidate of the Constitutional Union party, which wanted no part of a commercially
divisive antislavery crusade. Once Lincoln had won, the plantation South led Dixie into secession. After the Civil War began,
the Republicans increasingly became the party of aggressive
capitalism, not just of antislavery conscience and commitment
to saving the Union. But they began by *attacking* elites, not
parading them.

In 1896 farmers and debtors, angry at low farm prices, procreditor deflation policies and so-called Robber Baron indus-
trialism, swung behind William Jennings Bryan, the fusion
nominee of the Democratic and Populist parties. By this point,
the Republicans had a twenty-five-year record of laissez-faire
capitalism, and constituencies dating back to the Civil War were
in open revolt, particularly in the farm states where Greenback,
granger and populist third-party insurgencies were commonplace. But Bryan went too far. His attacks on Wall Street for
crucifying mankind on a "cross of gold" were effective, but
praise of prairie rusticity against urban growth and technology
offended swing voters. Besides, a conservative Democratic president, Grover Cleveland, was in power, and voters had blamed
his administration for the Depression of 1893. Anti-elite presidential politics can lose as well as win, especially when the
movements involved are premature or too primitive, as was true
of Bryan's attempt.*

Thirty-six years and another massive economic slump later,
however, Franklin D. Roosevelt did sweep the Rocky Mountain,
Great Plains and Southern states that had given Bryan his strong-
est support—the once-again-depressed centers of U.S. farming

---

* The irony is that the Republican presidential victory of 1896, coming after
two decades of tight presidential races, renewed the party hold on the White
House but obliged the GOP to handle the philosophic transitions of what
would be labeled the Populist/Progressive Era. During the administration of
Theodore Roosevelt (1901–9), a Republican chief executive was openly critical
of big business and greed and supportive of a national income tax. And even
William McKinley, the first president of the new GOP cycle, had been a
reflation-minded silver Republican with a mild reform streak in his earlier
days.

and mining. This insurgency had been partly foreshadowed in the presidential election of 1924, when third-party Progressive Robert La Follette, running against Coolidge's Eastern business-oriented Republicanism, drew 25 percent of the vote or more in eleven states. But what occurred in 1932 that had not happened in 1896 was that the Democrats also won the industrial Midwest and even much of the East. Herbert Hoover, the losing Republican, found himself squeezed back into much the same establishmentarian Eastern coastal corridor—from Du Pont–influenced Delaware to maritime Maine—that had stuck by the defeated Federalists in 1800. Roosevelt, while hardly radical, sometimes borrowed the rhetoric of radicalism, attacking "the money changers" in 1932, and in 1936 accepting confrontation with Wall Street: "They hate me, and I welcome their hatred."

There is no escaping the explanation that voters were reacting against some combination of affluence, elite status and privilege in all five upheaval years—1800, 1828, 1860, 1896 and 1932. The great corrective mechanism of U.S. national politics is the chastisement of elites at the ballot box.

Where Republican presidential cycles evolve into free-market excesses and the overconcentration of wealth, aging Democratic cycles take different forms. The Democratic-Republican party overwhelmed its Federalist opposition so completely that financial and commercial forces came within the Jeffersonian tent and took over. A generation later the Democratic party of the late 1840s and 1850s came under the thumb of the plantation South, and became the "slaveocracy" that pre–Civil War Republican orators attacked so enthusiastically. The public-sector elite that led the New Deal Democrats in their deteriorated late stages was different again, catering to big government and its economic interest-group allies.

Partly as a result, by 1964 the Republican presidential nominee, Barry Goldwater, railed against "Eastern elites" and the "Northeastern Establishment" in terms that would have been familiar to Jackson, Bryan and even Truman. By the late 1960s Washington's failures were being denounced in a ripe populist idiom of frustration with judges, bureaucrats and "social planners."

Popular rejection of liberal social policies was further aggravated by a reaction against what Tom Wolfe, a writer of populist

sentiment, would soon lampoon as "radical chic"—café society's fashionable succession of Park Avenue receptions, George-
town auctions and East Hampton beach parties in behalf of
Black Panthers, Hispanic farm workers, welfare rights, Harlem
youth gangs and campus revolutionaries. Liberalism had gone
uptown and upscale. That had begun, Wolfe observed, "in 1965
[when] two new political movements, the antiwar movement
and black power, began to gain great backing among culturati
in New York. By 1968, the two movements began to achieve
social as well as cultural prestige with the presidential campaigns
of Eugene McCarthy and Robert Kennedy. . . . The first big
Radical Chic party, the epochal event, so to speak, was the party
that Assemblyman Andrew Stein gave for the grape workers on
his father's estate in Southampton on June 29, 1969. The grape
workers had already been brought into New York social life.
Carter and Amanda Burden, the 'Moonflower Couple' of the
1960s, had given a party for them in their duplex in River House,
on East 52nd Street overlooking the East River."[3]

It's hard to overstate the electoral turnabout reflected in such
terms as "radical chic" and "limousine liberalism" as conservative ideas and politics acquired a powerful populist dimension.
At the same time, upper-bracket liberalism, though it was the
politics of only a few affluent Americans, became a telling barometer of how far progressivism had drifted from the values
of ordinary voters. As other events followed, culminating in
conductor Leonard Bernstein's famous Manhattan party for the
Black Panthers, White House aide Daniel P. Moynihan even
made l'affaire Bernstein Exhibit A in a memorandum to the
president: "You perhaps did not note on the society page of
yesterday's Times that Mrs. Leonard Bernstein gave a cocktail
party on Wednesday to raise money for the Panthers. Mrs. Peter
Duchin, the rich blond wife of the orchestra leader, was thrilled.
'I've never met a Panther,' she said. 'This is a first for me.' "[4]

"Couldn't you just see Nixon sitting in the Oval Room,"
Wolfe wrote, "and clucking and fuming and muttering things
like 'rich snob bums' as he read?"[5] Of course you could. Nixon's
"New Majority" Republicanism was middle-class and bellig-
erently antiestablishment. Its attacks on the "Eastern Establishment," liberal elites and "effete snobs" are a matter of record.
So are its populist political accomplishments, reaching beyond

suburbia to enlist Democratic Italian American union members
in South Philadelphia and George Wallace voters in piney-woods
Alabama. Republican strategists had a blueprint: cultural populism—identification with "Middle American" values—would
help the GOP transcend its traditional economic policies and
biases.

Economic sectoral shifts reinforced the transition. The Democrats' evolution into a cultural and intellectual elite was not
simply in response to the urban and Vietnam crises of the 1960s,
painful as they were. It was also a consequence of the larger
rise within the United States *and the Democratic Party in particular* of what 1970s neoconservatives and others would call
the Knowledge Elite or New Class. Reflecting the rise of the
service and information sectors of the economy—the expanding
numbers and influence of the media, academicians, think tanks,
consultants, white-collar professionals, social planners and
other kindred opinion-molding groups—the new elite was typically upper-middle-class by education and often by income. But
its politics tended to be liberal, as befitted the children of the
New Deal for whom social change had become second nature.*

In 1968 and 1972 voters whose loyalty to the New Deal
coalition had persisted as late as 1964 were now fearful of
welfare, rising crime, inflation, tax-bracket creep and federal
social engineering. They resented well-paid liberal professionals
pontificating from remote comfort. Meanwhile, as diverse observers have pointed out, party reform was institutionalizing the
power of this new class within the Democratic party. In *The
Amateur Democrat*, James Q. Wilson had described the rise of
professional-class liberals in big-city reform Democratic clubs
during the 1950s.[6] And Thomas Edsall argued that the "shift
to a more elite and affluent constituency in the [presidential]
delegate selection . . . weakens support for the interests of the
working and lower-middle class in the formulation of tax legislation, for the maintenance of government benefits to the poor
and those in the lower tax brackets."[7] The "ascendency of
upper-middle/new class Democrats within the party," Edsall

---

* By the 1980s, estimates put the information sector at 45 percent or so of
GNP. But its *political* emergence dates back to the 1960s, when the civil rights,
Great Society and Vietnam debates represented a coming-of-age for infor-
mation-sector power brokers.

added, had helped promote a fatal shift away from meat-and-potatoes economic issues toward a middle-class array of social, antiwar and environmental causes.

As the Nixon years got under way, documentation of liberal elite economic interests began to grow. In 1969 Edith Green of Oregon, ranking Democrat on the House Education and Labor Committee, observed that "probably our most enduring monument to the problem of poverty has been the creation of a poverty industry. There are more than 100 companies in Washington, D.C., alone which specialize in studying and evaluating the poor and the programs that serve them."[8] And as early as 1967, *The Wall Street Journal* showed how major U.S. corporations, particularly in the major urban centers, were finding enough profit in Democratic Great Society social programs to become an important lobbying force on their behalf.[9] Especially in America's major cities, liberalism had evolved into an important intellectual merchant class, a pervasive pro–public sector mandarinate. One consequence would be a generation of popular, even *populist*, disillusionment with government's role in social problem-solving. By the advent of the Reagan years, a "Liberal Establishment" pivoting on the new class and on "big government" and its private sector allies had become an easy elite target. And so long as it could be kept in that role, conservatism could play a more successful one—that of *anti*-elite.

During the 1968–72 period, GOP rhetoric praising "Middle America" and bashing the "Liberal Establishment" combined with liberalism's upscale transformation to break up the old Democratic presidential coalition. Huge numbers of populist Democrats shifted to the Republican column. Of the hundreds of Southern and Western counties that had voted for William Jennings Bryan in 1896, for Franklin D. Roosevelt in 1932, and for most of the other Democratic White House contenders in between, *all but a few dozen voted for Richard Nixon in 1972.* Defensive Democrats, in turn, found themselves left with the State of Massachusetts, achieving their highest percentages in the Northeastern coastal strip that has been the Atlantic Wall of aging political-economic interests. Their hollow triumph was joined by countertrending elites, from the East Side of Manhattan to participants at straw polls at the Harvard Law School and most of New England's most expensive private academies.

The same GOP insurgent demographics apparent in 1972 would substantially repeat in the elections of 1980 and 1984. Just how much the underlying Republican presidential coalition depended on anti-elite voters would become painfully clear once again in late spring 1988 as George Bush, a quintessential Establishment figure, fell ten to fifteen points behind likely Democratic nominee Dukakis. In August and September, GOP presidential election strategists found themselves scrambling to pin the fatal "elitist" label back on the Democratic donkey with "Harvard boutique" and "big government" imagery. One anonymous Dukakis adviser was widely quoted as complaining, "They're running a class war against us, saying we're a bunch of Cambridge-Brookline eccentric literature professors. We've got to fight back and say that they're the party of privilege, the party of the rich folks." But the Republicans succeeded, in part because the Democrats balked at attacking economic elites.

## RONALD REAGAN AND THE
## NEW CAPITALIST ELITE

By 1987, as the public fascination with wealth, speculation and markets had begun to peak, Ronald Reagan was not just presiding over another Republican and capitalist renaissance. He was simultaneously watching the emergence of a new conservative elite. Some left-inclined observers have minimized the change within the Republican party by theorizing that Richard Nixon, years earlier, had also promoted a kindred "cowboy capitalism"—at least until Watergate. Such analyses were unrealistic. Nixon raised some taxes in 1969, proposed a guaranteed annual income in 1970, imposed wage and price controls in 1971, and presided over a considerable expansion of environmental regulation and spending. Perhaps even more to the point, from 1969 to 1974 the index that recorded the inequality of U.S. income distribution hovered near post–World War II lows (see Chart 2, on page 13).

The supply-side economic conservatives like George Gilder and Jude Wanniski who rode to influence with Reagan in 1981 almost uniformly—and, by their measurements, correctly—insisted that *Richard Nixon did not unleash capitalism, Ronald*

*Reagan did.* The case can be made that even Jimmy Carter provided more assistance to economic change than Nixon did, in part by extending bipartisan support for economic deregulation and tight money during the late 1970s. Cynics argue further that the hapless Carter may have made his greatest contribution in a roundabout way: by losing credibility on so grand a scale as to make possible the 1980 victory of Ronald Reagan, hitherto unelectably conservative. In any event, Ronald Reagan had been a free enterprise pitchman for nearly a decade as host of the General Electric Television Theatre during the 1950s; as president of the United States during the 1980s, he would do much more—he would get to see moderate conservative politics, free-market ideas, wealth and supportive institutions become "the Establishment" again.

By the time the Dow-Jones Industrial Average took its great 508-point tumble in October 1987 resurgent capitalism had begun to redefine fashion as well as power. Entrepreneurs, heroes again as in the days of Horatio Alger and Henry Ford, were welcomed in Congress, courted by venture capitalists, coveted by investment bankers, and even transformed into civic icons by a host of new national magazines—*Inc., Venture, Entrepreneur, Millionaire* and *Success*, to name only a few. Four businessmen had even emerged as possible 1988 presidential candidates: Lee Iacocca and Ross Perot because of their national reputations, Donald Trump and William Farley because of their own paid media (Farley, in a particularly naïve gambit, targeted his company's Fruit of the Loom TV underwear advertisements on pre-caucuses Iowa). At America's universities, surveys showed that students were dominated by a single ambition—*doing something that would make money.*

Dollar signs were society's reemergent denominator. The word "Yuppie" had faded, clouded by the indictments of so many ambitious young Wall Street lawyers and investment bankers and mocked by the political collapse of Democratic "generational change" presidential candidates Gary Hart and Joseph Biden. Yet during 1987 top-bracket consumption had continued to reach new heights along with the stock market, bolstered by the sharpest reduction of top federal tax rates since the 1920s. High-income Americans shifted their income forward into 1988 to enjoy the new 28 percent top tax rate, lowest since the Coolidge years—and crossed their fingers that it would last. As the stock market moved toward its peak, luxury became increasingly conspicuous. Upscale-magazine advertising salesmen and circulation managers checked their national audit bureau numbers and counted the Rolex, Bally and Sotheby's pages. If anything, the preliminary 1985–86 federal data emerging in 1987–88 underestimated escalating upper-bracket affluence. In Greenwich, Connecticut, where the distant view of Long Island Sound from Round Hill Road was almost worth an SEC violation, average housing costs rose with the bull market, jumping from $467,000 in mid-1986 to $1.2 million as of September 1987.[10] Proliferating yacht sales brought the Atlantic and Pacific oceans their own area codes—871 and 872, respectively.[11] Glossy life-style and business magazines were flourishing even at the state and city level, turning a profit almost immediately with condominium and auto-leasing advertisements. Issue after issue broke out the ten richest suburbs, the twenty-five leading private schools, the fifty leading banks and the one hundred top local corporations. For sheer wealth, their audience had no precedent.

Indeed, rankings of all kinds became increasingly symptomatic of the commercial and success orientation of the mid-1980s. States were graded on their business climates, and the annual lists compiled by the accounting firm of Grant Thornton and others could make or break state economic development commissions. Colleges were ranked by their endowments, law firms by their net partnership profits, corporations by virtually every device imaginable. The Fortune 500 were joined by the Forbes 500 and the Business Week 1000. City magazines had their Minneapolis 100 and Tallahassee 50. America was turning into a hierarchy of wealth. Aileen Mehle, better known as Suzy, the *New York Post* gossip columnist, told Andy Warhol that "Money used to talk. Now it shrieks."[12] Certainly there were many more voices: million-dollar-a-year households more than doubled from the mid-1970s to the mid-1980s, even adjusting for inflation.

The October crash hurt, but luxury spending resumed after a nervous pause. The basic metamorphosis of the 1980s remained in place. Establishment liberalism wasn't really the Establishment anymore. Values had changed. Social causes had faded. The dominant national elite had once again become *economic*—businessmen, investment bankers, entrepreneurs, people with high incomes of almost any origin.

Even Washington was developing a new elite—beyond the Reagan White House's periodic whiffs of Versailles—around the institutionalization and excesses of *Republican* and *conservative* ambitions in place of the earlier "radical chic" and entrenched liberalism of the late 1960s. Millionaire poverty consultants, Southampton seaside benefits for Mexican grape pickers and Ford Foundation traveling grants for Democratic campaign aides were old news, the elites and perquisites of a bygone era. Now there were Southern California "kitchen cabinet" cliques, Manhattan and Capitol Hill think tanks promoting tax cuts, Republican fund-raising dinners featuring corporate raiders like Boone Pickens and Ivan Boesky, and Calvin Coolidge birthday parties hosted by parvenu GOP Washington lobbyists and consultants happy to tell attending gossip columnists the price of their new Savile Row suits.

At first, in the early 1980s, most Reagan political appointees had been capital outsiders, political insurgents from Los Angeles or Long Island. By the decade's end, however, yesteryear's outsiders had become entrenched insiders—well-paid counselors and lobbyists for domestic and foreign interests ranging from the Tobacco Institute to South Africa and Toyota, participants in a lucrative web of retainers, commissions, relationships and fees, their offices hung with framed executive commissions and two decades of ceremonial remembrances. With Republican presidents in office for sixteen years out of twenty, and with four more to come, Washington by 1989 was the seat of a new well-heeled Republican elite almost as distant from the Iowa and Idaho grass roots as their Democratic predecessors.

From the Justice Department and the Pentagon to the corruption that 1989 revealed at the Department of Housing and Urban Development, scandals and conflict of interest also recalled the dark side of previous commercial heydays—the influence buying notorious in the Gilded Age, and then again in the Teapot Dome scandals of the 1920s. By the time he resigned in mid-1988, Attorney General Edwin Meese, personal California chum of Ronald Reagan, had exceeded even Attorney General Harry Daugherty, personal Ohio chum of Warren Harding, in column inches of negative press coverage. Yet, amazingly, little of this ever figured in the 1988 Dukakis campaign; the Democrats, as election results would prove, had failed to pursue an obvious opportunity. The country's new conservative "money culture" and power structure never became an issue.

## DEMOCRATIC POLITICS AND THE CONFIRMATION OF CAPITALIST HEYDAYS

The Democrats are also a capitalist, middle-class party, if somewhat less enthusiastic and market-bewitched than the Republicans. Their reluctance to seize the populist political opportunity is an important ingredient of U.S. economic history.

Despite this reticence, America's increasing imbalance of wealth had begun to emerge as a serious political topic in 1986, after three years of economic recovery, when the Joint Economic Committee of Congress, chaired by the populist Democrat David Obey, identified a "bicoastal economy," contending that Reagan policies were serving the financial and service centers of the Atlantic and Pacific coasts at the expense of the agricultural, extractive and heavy-industry heartland. This was an old fault line in the Republican coalition, and Obey, by tapping it, helped the Democrats win the Senate in 1986.

But the committee overreached in describing a great new concentration of wealth among the "super-rich." The Federal Reserve Board data for 1983, which the Joint Economic Committee had repackaged, turned out to be flawed. The trend was not so extreme. So committee members backed down. Nor did they score better with subsequent contentions that family income was rapidly declining or that high-paying industrial jobs were disappearing in favor of low-paying service jobs. In each case, economic circumstances were more complex.

The more strongly populist Democrats in the House of Representatives also raised the issue: Speaker Jim Wright urged blocking the scheduled 1988 reduction of the top income tax rate from 38.5 percent to 28 percent; Representative Gephardt deplored the transfer of wealth from those who built cars and operated farms to paper entrepreneurs who raided corporations, speculated in foreign currencies and dreamed up new instruments of creative finance. New York senator Daniel P. Moynihan wrote:

> As for the economy, the great divide that began to open in the early 1970s separating the postwar generation from its successor continued to widen. By 1985, median family income was about what it had been in 1970; down from 1973. This would be the longest stretch of 'flat' income in the history of the European settlement of North America.[13]

But for the most part, Democrats laid little groundwork for any serious critique in 1988, leaving the issue to Jesse Jackson, whose populist appeal was limited by both race and Third World rhetoric, and to sympathetic intellectuals. The latter were vocal, but without much influence. Economist Lester Thurow proclaimed in 1986 that "we're in the midst of a real surge toward inequality, the economic equivalent of tectonic plate movements. Wherever you look, you see rising inequality."[14] And David Gordon of the New School for Social Research, said, "The most important story about the U.S. economy in the eighties is the economic warfare that the wealthy and powerful have been waging against the vast majority of Americans."[15] Ralph Nader predicted that "the gap between the rich and the poor" would become a top Democratic party issue.[16] And Lawrence Summers of Harvard, soon to be economics adviser to Dukakis, contended that "the U.S. is today in the midst of a quiet depression in living standards. The median income of the typical American family is right now the same as it was in 1969."[17]

The majority of elected Democrats, by contrast, avoided these themes, thus behaving as usual during capitalist heydays. Which is to say cowed, conformist and often supportive of the prevailing entrepreneurial, free-market mood. Indeed, one sign that a conservative cycle is moving toward its climax has been the extent to which *Democratic* politics have been cooperative. The solitary Democratic president of the Gilded Age, Grover Cleveland, was a conservative and a gold-standard supporter with close Wall Street connections and a cabinet to match. Woodrow Wilson later denied that Cleveland had been Democratic at all— "Cleveland," he said, "was a conservative Republican."[18]

During the twenties the Democratic presidential nominees in
both 1920 (Ohio newspaper publisher James Cox) and 1924
(corporation lawyer John W. Davis) were in the Grover Cleveland mold, not that of William Jennings Bryan. Even Alfred E.
Smith, in 1928, had as his principal fund-raiser John J. Raskob,
a senior adviser to the Du Pont interests.* (By 1936 Smith
himself would join the conservative Liberty League in opposition
to Franklin D. Roosevelt and the New Deal.) *When wealth is
in fashion, national Democrats have gone along.*

In the 1920s tax policy was a particularly vivid instance of
bipartisan capitalist enthusiasm. Not only did congressional
Democrats blow with the prevailing winds during the 1925–28
Coolidge stock market boom, but *competed* with Republicans
to cut upper-bracket and corporate taxes. When Furnifold Sim-
mons of North Carolina, ranking Democrat on the Senate Finance Committee, spoke about making "businessmen realize
that the Democratic Party is not bent on taxing them or their
enterprises exorbitantly," progressive Republicans chuckled.[19]
Senator George Norris of Nebraska suggested the Democrats
were owed more campaign contributions than usual for their
share in "relieving wealth from taxation," and Senator Irvine
Lenroot of Wisconsin accused them of "out-Melloning Mellon"—a reference to Republican treasury secretary Andrew Mellon.[20] Historian David Burner recalls that "in the first session
of the Seventieth Congress—the last to meet before the stock
market crashed—almost all Democrats, in company with the
United States Chamber of Commerce, continued to clamor for
reductions beyond the wishes of President Coolidge."[21]

Fifty years later, Jimmy Carter, the only Democratic president
to interrupt the long Republican hegemony after 1968, was
accused by historian Arthur Schlesinger of "an eccentric effort
to carry the Democratic Party back to Grover Cleveland."[22]
Despite his support for substantial new federal regulation,
Carter clearly deviated from the Democratic party's larger post–
New Deal norm by his candid insistence that "Government
cannot solve our problems. It can't set our goals. It cannot define

* The 1988 Dukakis parallel is not without relevance. Robert Farmer, his
extremely successful chief fund-raiser, until a few years earlier had been a
Republican businessman.

our vision. Government cannot eliminate poverty, or provide a bountiful economy, or reduce inflation or save our cities."[23] Carter built foundations that would become full-fledged conservative architecture under Reagan: economic deregulation, tax-rate reduction (for capital gains in 1978), and tight-money Federal Reserve Board policies. Federal Reserve Board chairman Paul Volcker, a high-interest-rate conservative central banker, was a nominal Democrat appointed by Carter in 1979. Congressional Democrats even echoed their policies of the 1920s by colluding in the bipartisan tax-bracket reforms of 1981 and 1986. Thus, by 1988, Democrats could hardly criticize Reagan's tax reductions, particularly those of 1986, although polls documented public unhappiness.

The prominent exception was Jesse Jackson, who called for increasing upper-income individual and corporate taxes, promised foreclosure relief to farmers, and criticized major U.S. corporations for exporting jobs to Mexico, Korea and Taiwan. In March 1988, New York governor Mario Cuomo observed that of all candidates Jackson had "the single most identifiable and attractive message: When he talks about big corporations going to Taiwan and paying low wages and then selling the goods back to us, people nod their heads in agreement."[24] Party pollster Stanley Greenberg told fellow Democrats that "many voters believe that corporate America is not sufficiently 'loyal' to the nation. U.S. corporations, many held, take their jobs and money elsewhere. America is in trouble because its own corporations refuse to make loyalty a determinate consideration in their investment decisions. We regularly encountered the belief that these institutions, which lie at the heart of the American system, have betrayed America."[25] But Jackson's ability to crystallize these issues was overstated. His race limited his influence among white workers, and so did rhetoric that seemed to put Bolivian or West African interests on a par with jobs or prosperity in Steubenville, Ohio. Jackson's populism lacked aspects of economic nationalism essential to mobilizing Middle America. He could win 20 to 30 percent of the white vote only in peripheries like small-town Vermont or rural Minnesota; by spring's later industrial-state primaries, principal rival Dukakis did not have to take his appeal to white Democratic voters seriously. Far from having to preempt Jackson's themes, he could ignore them.

Democratic contenders also minimized their criticisms of the financial markets, even though in 1987, former Arizona governor Bruce Babbitt had argued that "when Rhodes scholars are arrested for insider trading, that contributes to this populist sentiment that a privileged class is getting rich at the expense of the rest of the economy."[26] The irony was that in the wake of the stock market crash, polling had found the electorate convinced that Wall Street was a giant casino, with its insider traders and croupiers largely to blame for their own fall. Demand for tougher regulation was growing—and not just of securities-market practices but of hostile takeovers as well. By early 1988, when the takeover game was back, bigger than ever (spurred on, in part, by belief that regulatory reform lay over the horizon), public opinion surveys showed lopsided disapproval: 60 to 70 percent of Americans told Gallup, Harris and their colleagues that hostile takeovers ought to be squelched.[27]

There was also plentiful evidence of the anti-Establishment sentiments of 1988 Democratic primary electorates. For example, March NBC News/Wall Street Journal polling turned up a 47 to 35 percent plurality of Democrats indicating *more* rather than *less* inclination to vote for a presidential contender who blamed big corporations for America's economic problems. However, centrist candidates willing to rise to the populist opportunity weren't necessarily credible. Congressman Richard Gephardt's populist appeal ebbed after opponents' television advertisements cataloged his corporate political action committee contributions. When Senator Albert Gore went before the Wisconsin legislature in late March to say, "I want a chance to tell the rich and powerful their free ride is over," hardly anyone paid attention.[28]

Dukakis, as he closed in on the Democratic nomination during March campaigning in Illinois, Michigan and Wisconsin, likewise condemned corporate raiders, giant corporations and "monopoly games" on Wall Street. However, once Dukakis became the last white contender in April, sure to beat the unnominatable Jackson, he returned—as we have seen—to a relatively bland economics. A balanced-budget centrist as governor of Massachusetts during the prosperous mid-1980s, Dukakis far outdrew other major 1988 Democratic contenders in campaign contributions from businessmen, lawyers and financiers. Dependence of this kind was a major constraint, realistically barring more than a façade of populism, and in his acceptance speech Dukakis framed *competence*, not ideology, as the upcoming campaign issue. But this unwillingness to indict Republican boom economics was not just a personal preference; it was an old party tradition.

Serious discussion was left to others. In April 1988, even one national business weekly observed that the great middle class, dissatisfied with its own share of the national pie, "has suddenly become aware of the accumulating wealth of the rich."[29] But Dukakis, pushing his Massachusetts economic success and benefiting from upper-bracket fund-raising, sidestepped the issue. And even after Dukakis's last-minute decision in October to voice some mild populism, it was left for Britain's *Financial Times*—not the Democratic nominee—to muse over the trickle-down economics embraced at a November 7 GOP presidential campaign windup rally in Woodland Hills, California:

> The tone was set by Jamie Farr, who played Klinger, the male nurse in the television comedy series MASH who liked to dress up in women's clothes. He defended the ostentatious consumer spending of the Reagan years, saying that if he had a butler or a security guard for his swimming pool (which he did not) he would have created two jobs. But he had had a private pool built for himself and that had created jobs.[30]

On the surface, this was a Democratic opportunity missed. But the lesson of history is that the party of Cleveland, Cox and Davis, Carter and Dukakis has rarely rushed its anti-elite corrective role. There would be no rush again in 1988—nor, indeed, in 1989.

Nevertheless, following the Wall Street crash, the fascination of the public and the media for conspicuous opulence started to shrink, and by 1989, with a new president in the White House, the outlines of a new debate were also apparent. Discussion was beginning at least to flirt with populist themes: Had wealth accumulation, already unseemly, also become excessive and unfair? Had a relatively small American elite been favored—just as in prior Republican and capitalist heydays—by a calculated 1980s rescripting of federal economic policies?

# Chapter

## 3

# Wealth and Poverty: The Spirit of Federal Policy and Income Distribution During the Reagan Era

> What I want to see above all is that this remains a country where someone can always get rich.
>
> —RONALD REAGAN

> What the Republicans accomplished during the last 15 years was a triumph of ideas, an intellectual victory. They shifted the burden of proof onto government.
>
> —POLITICAL ECONOMIST
> ROBERT REICH, 1988

Accelerating economic inequality under the Republicans was more often a policy objective than a coincidence. But greed was rarely the motive; it was more a matter of investment theory and free-market philosophy—a case that made the new economics more salable.

When George Gilder's book *Wealth and Poverty* appeared at the time of Reagan's first inauguration, conservatives were quick to hail its celebration of enterprise, wealth and capital accumulation. Some of Reagan's theoreticians actively sought to redistribute wealth and reduce the role of government with its inflationary welfare statism. Economic renewal would mean shifting resources and power to investors and entrepreneurs. More capital, in short, for capitalists.

Within a year, this objective—like the rest of the Reagan

Revolution—was bogged down in the unanticipated 1981–82 recession, brought on by tight money and national economic restructuring, a temporary dislocation as it turned out. Unemployment peaked at 10.8 percent in December 1982, and the percentage of citizens forced to survive below the poverty level crested at 15.2 percent in 1983.

Luckily for the Republicans, the public believed that previous Democratic economic policies were partly to blame, and punished the GOP only moderately in the 1982 midterm elections. As the business cycle turned upward, conservatism renewed its philosophic and political preeminence. By mid-decade, it wasn't just Gilder's praise of Reagan's free-market approach, policies thought to have spurred capital formation, economic innovation and good times; a *wider* national consciousness was forming. Prosperity with low inflation had unnerved Democratic politicians and liberal economists, who now hesitated to emphasize such old liberal themes as economic inequality, polarization and unfairness to the working poor.

This reluctance was partly pragmatic. Market forces were fashionable again, and similar trends toward greater inequality in other major industrial nations also inhibited debate in the United States. Accelerating maldistribution seemed to be a global phenomenon. If international tides were involved, they couldn't be blamed on Ronald Reagan. Thus the experts hesitated to indict Reagan's policies, which intensified the trends underway.

Yet by 1988 many of the new patterns of wealth during the 1980s—from the increasing sales of Mercedes automobiles to the incidence of farm foreclosures in rural Iowa—could be traced to specific approaches followed by the new administration after January 1981. The catch was that the relationships between cause and effect were more complex than either loyalists or foes were willing to admit. Conservatives praised Reaganomics, pointed to the many visible signs of prosperity, and said *You see!* while progressives blamed Reagan's policies for the no less visible social ills. What each side's oversimplified rhetoric ignored was the larger historical sweep: American capitalism was moving into high gear—for better and, eventually, as debt-accumulation and corporate assets manipulation took over, for worse.

# THE SEAMLESS WEB OF
# 1980S CAPITALIST REVIVAL

Stresses of the sort that produced the gains and losses of the Reagan era had been anticipated years earlier in economist Joseph Schumpeter's description of modern capitalism as creative destruction—progress and pain at work together. The Reagan years were one of America's "capitalist blowouts," the vivid display of what Schumpeter was talking about. In the United States, transitions of this magnitude have usually coincided with new national attitudes toward wealth and poverty. Evolving policies that seem distinct are really linked. So are specific changes in the national mood. In each such transition, whether in the late nineteenth century, the 1920s or the 1980s, slowly but surely, and without real precision as to which came first, the country has witnessed, *ensemble*, Horatio Alger cultural renewal, tax reduction, entrepreneurialism, enormously popular books by the likes of Henry Ford or Lee Iacocca, stepped-up mergers and corporate restructuring, extraordinary technological innovation, disinflation, suffering in the agricultural and extractive sectors, strong financial markets, philosophic laissez-faire, economic deregulation, doubts about the role of government, and a slow further concentration of wealth and income among the already affluent. The scope of these events has been impressive—and so has their repetition, although the two heydays of the twentieth century have involved increasingly more paper manipulation and less of the raw vigor typical of late-nineteenth-century railroad and factory expansion.

The exaggerations of cyclical theorists notwithstanding, these policy shifts and mood swings *do* seem to have recurred at forty- to fifty-year intervals. There has even been a somewhat predictable sequence of outcomes: economic benefits have come first, as enterprise-oriented policies unleash latent capitalist energies; then the dislocations have followed, including speculative excesses and even market crashes. After ten to fifteen years of heyday psychology, *some* major economic or market contraction occurs.

The United States, under Republican political leadership, had arguably passed through three such commercial epochs—the

Gilded Age (cresting from 1880 or so to the mid-1890s), the 1920s and the Reagan era. In Table 2, I show the many economic and cultural parallels, from depressed commodity markets and Wall Street binges to the repetitious ethos of free enterprise unleashed. The similarities aren't all-encompassing, to be sure, but they *are* revealing—even in the way go-getter eras have always been followed by swings back to a more populist, community-minded or government-activist period. Does disinflation and prosperity bring tax cuts or vice versa? Like the chicken and egg conundrum, the question may have no answer. But it also may not really matter.

These three Republican heydays began among three roughly similar moods and circumstances. The common denominators are important. One was the great desire to curb the successive inflations following the Civil War, World War I, and then Vietnam and the emergence of the OPEC petroleum cartels. Inflation usually prods property owners and creditors to mobilize. A second factor has been a concomitant public demand for stability, for "normalcy" (as Warren Harding so pithily misphrased it in 1920) and for a return of traditional economic and cultural behavior. Traditional values, of course, are conservative, even though conservative economic policy, as Schumpeter saw, would have radical effects. A third common theme is public fatigue with overexpanded government promoted by either wartime or inflationary challenges. Disenchantment with government and renewed attention to individual enterprise have gone together. Nor should we omit the periodic, almost inbred desire of Americans to build things, to create new tastes and open new frontiers.

In all three periods of capitalist expansion, ideas were also a vital force—from the Social Darwinism of the 1870s to the supply-side theories a century later. The proponents of these ideologies have always been more deeply committed to their causes than liberal opponents have made them out to be. They were *believers* convinced of the importance of the economic forces they sought to deploy. In that sense, the supply-side stalwarts of 1981 were not unlike the Jesuits of an earlier time or Hawaii-bound nineteenth-century Congregationalist missionaries. Conviction suffused their effort, making investment, free markets and entrepreneurialism a popular cause, not just a dry

## TABLE 2

### THE TEN MAJOR CHARACTERISTICS OF REPUBLICAN BUSINESS, FINANCIAL AND POLITICAL HEYDAY PERIODS

|  | Gilded Age | Roaring Twenties | Nineteen Eighties |
|---|---|---|---|
| Conservative politics | All presidents were Republican except Grover Cleveland | All presidents were Republican | All presidents were Republican |
| Reduced role for government | Zenith of laissez-faire and limited government | Significantly reduced regulatory and antitrust enforcement | Deregulation, privatization and reduced government regulatory and antitrust enforcement |
| Difficulties for labor | Strikes and widespread labor violence | Anti-union pressures grew; the AFL-CIO and the big coal and railroad unions lost members. | Declining labor union membership and power |
| Large-scale economic and corporate restructuring | First trusts organized in 1880s; merger and consolidation wave; rise of great corporations | Merger wave; organization of first investment trusts; era of Samuel Insull and public utility holding companies | Merger wave; rise of giant pension funds; emergence of junk bonds and leveraged buyouts |

| | Gilded Age | Roaring Twenties | Nineteen Eighties |
|---|---|---|---|
| Tax reduction | End of Civil War income tax in 1872; Civil War taxes effectively removed in favor of reliance on tariff | Top personal income tax rate reduced from 73% to 25%; other taxes also reduced or eliminated | Top personal income tax rate reduced from 70% to 28%; other taxes also reduced |
| Disinflation or deflation | Hard currency and tight monetary policy; prices declined; high real interest rates | Gold standard; prices steady (but commodity prices sank); high real interest rates | Tight monetary policy; inflation reduced (commodity prices sank); high real interest rates |
| Two-tier economy | Difficult times in agricultural and mining areas; good times for emerging industry and financial centers | Difficult times in agricultural, energy and mining areas; good times in emerging industry, service and financial centers | Difficult times in agricultural, energy and mining areas; good times in emerging industry, service and financial centers |
| Concentration of wealth | Large increase in number of millionaires; 3–5% more of U.S. total income concentrated with top 1% | Zenith of 20th-century U.S. wealth concentration; top 1% of Americans had 40% of U.S. wealth | Large increase in millionaires and billionaires; 3–4% more of U.S. total income concentrated with top 1% |

TABLE 2 (*Cont.*)

## THE TEN MAJOR CHARACTERISTICS OF REPUBLICAN
## BUSINESS, FINANCIAL AND POLITICAL HEYDAY PERIODS

| | *Gilded Age* | *Roaring Twenties* | *Nineteen Eighties* |
|---|---|---|---|
| Increased debt and speculation | Major increase in individual, corporation and foreign debt; U.S. railroad bonds sold to British were that era's junk bonds | Introduction of installment buying and purchase of stocks on margin; international debt questions; massive expansion of personal debt | Ballooning of personal and corporate debt; innovative debt instruments; surge of U.S. budget deficit and emergence of large-scale U.S. trade deficit; emergence of U.S. as world's leading debtor |
| Speculative implosion | Panic of 1893 and subsequent depression | Crash of 1929 and subsequent depression | Crash of 1987, minicrash of 1989 and relevant events of the 1990s |

fiscal rationale. This periodic evangelism has been a boon to American capitalism. In each of the three great U.S. capitalist eras, although most shallowly in the commercial 1920s, genuine philosophic and cultural conviction expanded, elevated and prolonged the wave of capitalist expansion. That it ultimately encouraged excess is another part of the story, and we shall get to it before long.

The resemblance between the policy framework of the 1980s, the Coolidge era and the Gilded Age was not a coincidence. Striking similarities existed in fiscal, monetary, deregulatory and reduced-government approaches—and led to similar inequalities of wealth and income distribution. The new economics of the

1980s had gained momentum, to be sure, because of a *preexisting*, broader national conservative trend and coalition, reinforced in the late 1970s by a larger wave of inflation and popular frustration with big government. Yet it was absolutely critical that reemergent capitalism also enjoyed something more: a missionary spirit—and dedicated missionaries.

## REAGAN'S WORLDLY PHILOSOPHERS: CAPITALIST THEOLOGY AND 1980S WEALTH DISTRIBUTION

Conservatives in 1981 could not have moved public policy so far merely with a Chamber of Commerce viewpoint. No mere accountant mentality could have popularized a program almost certain to help the rich at the expense of others and to stuff more money into already fat investment accounts. But the president's theoreticians developed a greater resonance, paralleling the larger-than-ledgerdom ideas and momentum also apparent in *previous* U.S. capitalist expansions.

A century earlier, at the peak of the rip-roaring U.S. industrial expansion following the Civil War, the incumbent Republicans had their own persuasive economic and social philosophers. National growth justified concentrated wealth and public policies that resulted in inequality. What had been vices became virtues.* Avarice became achievement—a display, almost, of social fitness. Preeminent were the Social Darwinists, the men who took Charles Darwin's 1859 biological theory of evolution and transformed it into a cultural and economic thesis of the survival of the fittest. Unbridled competition, they proclaimed, was really economic nature at its most productive. Successful financiers bestriding Wall Street were like lions on the African

* The period of the Renaissance and the rise of capitalism performed much the same transformation. A 1985 SRI International analysis put it in especially blunt terms: "The seven deadly sins of the Middle Ages—pride, gluttony, avarice and prodigality, lust, sloth, anger and envy—were converted into the driving values of the Renaissance era. With the probable exception of sloth, our modern economy could not exist if people were not motivated by these values." The spirit of the 1980s certainly followed the Renaissance/Gilded Age conversion pattern.

veldt. State interference with corporations, railroad kings and
stock market buccaneers or even labor legislation seeking to
mandate an eight-hour day risked distorting the evolutionary
outcome, the natural selection of those who were fit enough to
survive. *Laissez-faire*—literally, "Leave us alone"—became the
wisdom of the day, the catchphrase of thinkers like Britain's
Herbert Spencer, whose writings became a driving force in late-
nineteenth-century industrial expansion on both sides of the
Atlantic, and America's own William Graham Sumner, professor of political science at Yale. To Sumner, the accumulation
of wealth was also a measure of progress. He argued that

> millionaires are a product of natural selection, acting on the whole
> body of men to pick out those who can meet the requirements
> of certain work to be done. . . . It is because they are thus selected
> that wealth—both their own and that entrusted to them—aggre-
> gates under their hands. . . . They may fairly be regarded as the
> naturally selected agents of society for certain work. They get
> high wages and live in luxury, but the bargain is a good one for
> society. There is the intensest competition for their place and
> occupation. This assures us that all who are competent for this
> function will be employed in it, so that the cost of it will be
> reduced to the lowest terms.[1]

This theology bore fruit. During the years that Sumner's
classes were among Yale's most popular, U.S. industry was expanding apace; harvesters were taming the prairies and railroads
were bridging the continent. The American public were, for the
most part, capitalist believers. Historian Richard Hofstadter
surmised back in 1944 that "American society saw its own
image in the tooth-and-claw version of natural selection."[2] Even
Matthew Josephson, in *The Robber Barons*, acknowledged that
"the newly rich who had so quickly won supreme power in the
economic order enjoyed an almost universal esteem for at least
twenty years after the Civil War. Their glory was at its zenith;
during this whole period they literally sunned themselves in the
affection of popular opinion. . . . The type of the successful
baron of industry now presented itself as the high human product of the American climate, the flower of its own order of
chivalry, much wondered at, envied or feared in foreign lands

whose peers had arrived somewhat earlier at coronets, garlands and garters."[3] Anticommercial conservatives came to the same reluctant conclusion. Albert Jay Nock lamented the prevailing ethos of his 1870s boyhood. "The most successful (or rapacious) businessmen were held up in the schools, the press, and even the pulpit, as the prototype of all that was making America great. . . . 'Go and Get It!' was the sum of the practical philosophy presented to America's young manhood by all the voices of the age."[4]

The 1920s, by comparison, nurtured a more sedentary, unctuous commercial spirit in which laissez-faire gave way to a new preoccupation with advertising, consumer credit and corporate public relations. Historian Merle Curti has characterized the decade as one dominated by "the cult of prosperity."[5] Successful business leaders again became folk heroes, and folk heroes were repackaged as successful businessmen, so that Jesus was portrayed as the world's first great salesman in a best-selling book by an advertising man named Bruce Barton, later a Republican congressman from Manhattan's silk stocking district. The parables, Barton wrote, were "the most powerful advertisements of all-time." And Jesus himself "picked twelve men from the bottom ranks of business and forged them into an organization that conquered the world."[6] Sinclair Lewis wrote that to businessmen "the Romantic Hero was no longer the knight, the wandering poet, the cowpuncher, the aviator, nor the brave young district attorney, but the great sales-manager, who had an Analysis of Merchandizing Problems on his glass-topped desk, whose title of nobility was 'Go-getter,' and who devoted himself and all his young samurai to the cosmic purpose of Selling—not of selling anything in particular, for or to anybody in particular, but pure Selling."[7] That image was powerful enough to become a noun: Babbittry.

The capitalist theologians of the late 1970s and 1980s could hardly ride so grand a warhorse as the Social Darwinism of the late nineteenth century. But they went beyond the Babbittry of the 1920s because Reagan's conservative theorists had a powerful premise: government, people felt, had become excessive. The overexpanded public sector was a problem not just in the United States but in most other Western democracies. From overregulation to inflation, tax-bracket creep, bloated entitle-

ments, welfare-state inertia and judicial interventionism, policy
indictment followed policy indictment. By the late 1970s free-
market counterattacks were being mounted on a half-dozen
fronts.

George Gilder's *Wealth and Poverty* was the broadest in
scope, brimful of sheer ideological enthusiasm. Liberals found
its homages to enterprise a bit silly in places—such as citations
of capitalism's essentially loving nature, or comparisons between modern commerce and the feasts and public gift giving
of primitive tribal leaders. Citations of precapitalist practices
among Kwakiutl Indians and Solomon Islanders left even conservative reviewers bemused.[8] Some historians saw in his hymns
to entrepreneurial innovation echoes of such mid-nineteenth-
century daydreams as Walt Whitman's hopes for the staggering
progress to be unleashed by the telegraph. Even so, Gilder wrote
what stands as the comprehensive theology of the Reagan era,
relating conservatism to five central objectives. First was the
importance of nurturing wealth ("a successful economy," wrote
Gilder, "depends on the proliferation of the rich"). Next was
his insistence that individual investment and production are
inherently creative, echoing the notion that *supply* (capitalism)
creates *demand*, thereby denying a Keynesian role for government ("Supply creates its own demand. . . . The importance of
Say's Law is its focus on supply, on the catalytic gifts or investments of capital. It leads economists to concern themselves
first with the motives and incentives of individual producers, to
return from a preoccupation with distribution and demand and
concentrate again on the means of production").* Gilder's third
point was the need to curb government ("Since government has
become a factor of production, the only way to diminish its
impact on prices is to economize on it"). Gilder then hailed the
unique and essential role of entrepreneurialism (entrepreneurs
"are the heroes of American life"), and finally noted the critical
importance of cutting upper-bracket taxes ("To help the poor
and middle classes, one must cut the taxes of the rich")[9].

The time was ripe for this shrewd synthesis of what conservatism was all about. Gilder's attacks on the opposition also

* Say's Law—that supply creates demand—was named for the French economist Jean-Baptiste Say (1767–1832).

helped: government was the inflationary state; New Class professionals were self-serving; languid liberal millionaires by inheritance were fearful of nouveau riche competition; and unimaginative giant corporations were locked into entangling government subsidies and alliances. All were rival elites. And rival elites made for good bogeymen.* Say's original law, propounded in the eighteenth century, that supply creates demand had been cast aside after the overproduction debacles of 1929, but in 1981 those were ancient history. *Business Week, Barron's* and *Forbes* hailed *Wealth and Poverty* as a seminal portrait of emerging Reagan era economics. It was.

By the late 1970s inflation had increased tax discontent, and several economic theorists started talking about the central role of tax rates in the rise and fall of nations. Arthur Laffer, and his journalistic Boswell, former *Wall Street Journal* editorial writer Jude Wanniski, played the decisive role—the former with his Laffer Curve, insisting that beyond a certain point increased tax rates *reduced* rather than *raised* government revenue. Wanniski in 1978 wrote a book called *The Way the World Works*, which publicized Laffer, and then proceeded to describe mankind's rise and fall so as to suggest that tax rates were the key to progress.[10] Wanniski also pursued another, more subtle goal by attempting to extricate the laissez-faire policies of the Coolidge era from the rubbish heap of 1929 by contending that the tax-cutting, entrepreneurial and speculative 1920s had really been a great and successful decade. Tax cuts *by themselves* stood unsullied and unindicted, he claimed. What had cut their underlying effectiveness short—and here Wanniski swung his pick at rocky ground—was a national depression unnecessarily brought on by protectionism and the Smoot-Hawley tariff of 1930.

Still another conservative economist, Alvin Rabushka, gave Laffer's and Wanniski's arguments a transatlantic historical twist. Circa 1840 Britain had revitalized itself, he argued, and gone on to reach its industrial heyday by cutting taxes and reducing the government's share of GNP. In the 1980s the

---

* Gilder bluntly labeled supply-side critics as rival elites. In 1982 he said, "The crucial source of opposition to supply-side economics is the media and the New Class associated with it, the upper class of the information society" (*Boston Globe*, July 25, 1982).

United States could do the same.[11] Ronald Reagan found this idea appealing. Antitax sentiment was also fanned by populist successes during the late 1970s.* California's Howard Jarvis had started a small national prairie fire in 1978 with his Proposition 13 "tax revolt." Yet even the more abstract theories of Laffer, Wanniski and Rabushka fell on receptive middle-class ears as inflationary bracket creep pulled young professionals, small businessmen and police lieutenants into brackets they had once thought reserved for corporate executive vice presidents. Tax-cutting pressure—both populist *and* elite—became a national force in the early 1980s.

Inefficient government economic regulation was another problem. Like federal tax brackets, long-standing financial regulations were being outdated by inflation. The Federal Reserve's Regulation Q, limiting the rate of interest payable on savings accounts, was a particular target until it was suspended in 1980. Bipartisan critics also began urging deregulation of specific transportation sectors. In fact, there was scarcely an industry in which theoreticians, left and right alike, failed to find some increasingly obvious regulatory inefficiency. By 1980 the message that market forces could serve consumers better than government was clearly ascendant.

Theorists committed to unrestrained market forces became more or less respectable as Carter-era cranks became Reagan-era trailblazers. The Law and Economics movement, for example, no more than a fringe group prior to Reagan's inauguration, began reshaping judicial thinking. Its strength lay in a provocative simplicity. Adherents urged courts to ignore subjective chimeras like fairness and justice in order to focus on markets—and on providing incentives for efficient competitive

---

* The importance of academicians can easily be overstated. The first national tax revolt leader was the man also in the vanguard of so many other populist causes: Alabama governor George C. Wallace. Consider this excerpt from his speech to the 1972 Democratic National Convention: "In 1968, I spoke about tax reform all over these United States. I was the only candidate that did, that said that the income tax was regressive and that the average citizen paid through the nose, while the tax free foundations went Scott-free, with their multi-billions and multi-millions of dollars. So, I am for tax reform, and I raise the issue of tax reform. But the minority plank that we will present to this platform, calls not only for reform, but calls for tax relief, because I believe there is almost a tax revolt among the average citizens."

behavior. By 1987, when movement sympathizers Robert Bork and Douglas Ginsburg were nominated for the U.S. Supreme Court, though they were ultimately defeated, the relative acceptability of this part of their lexicon—markets, efficiency, competition—bespoke the country's shift away from the egalitarian and regulatory thinking of the 1960s and its brief Indian summer following Watergate.

The new theology even had overtones of the Gilded Age. Much more overtly than the supply-siders and the antitax theorists, Law and Economics stalwarts flirted with a neo-Darwinism that echoed Herbert Spencer and William Graham Sumner in its view that commercial selection processes in the marketplace could largely displace government decision-making. One intellectual frontiersman, Richard Posner, University of Chicago law professor turned federal appeals judge—a man whose encyclopedic text *Economic Analysis of the Law* had become a familiar sight in American law schools by the mid-1980s—even briefly suggested making a market for babies so it would be easier for couples to adopt.[12] A second prominent Chicago legalist, Richard A. Epstein, leader of the movement's "economic rights" faction, deplored most government economic regulation as unconstitutional. "I oppose most of the legislation written in this century," he acknowledged in 1987.[13] Posner and Epstein defined a remote ideological periphery, but they also confirmed the power of the mainstream conservative resurgence.*

Most of the conservative theorists acknowledged their restatement of Adam Smith, but few indicated awareness of their debts to the chief thinkers of the Gilded Age. Gilder's book, for example, failed entirely to cite its forebears, Spencer and Sumner. Survival of the fittest would not have been a popular catchphrase for the 1980s. Yet many of Reagan's thinkers publicly called for recapturing the optimism and incentive economics of the 1920s. Coolidge's picture was rehung in the White House in 1981, and Treasury Secretary Donald Regan frankly ac-

---

* Some relative mainstreamers also occasionally went overboard on market economics: Campaigning for the California GOP Senate nomination in 1986, economist Arthur Laffer told an interviewer that economic incentives were even the best bet to save the state's endangered condor. Put a price on the bird's survival, he explained, and they'll be so plentiful we'll all be "eating condor cacciatore."

knowledged the prior era's inspiration: "We're not going back to high-button shoes and celluloid collars. But the President does want to go back to many of the financial methods and economic incentives that brought about the prosperity of the Coolidge period."[14] For several summers, Reagan aides even went so far as to gather in July to celebrate Calvin Coolidge's birthday. At these extremes, the commitment to wealth and enterprise simply lacked depth.

But despite these historical superficialities, Reagan's conservative thinkers helped build the foundation for a decade of reemergent enterprise, wealth and inequality. Influential new institutes and foundations were pumping new vigor into market economics not just in Washington but also in London, Bonn and other conservative capitals. To most observers, Western economies were deregulating, privatizing—*and booming*. By the time Reagan began his second term in 1985 the day-to-day guidelines of American economics were being rewritten. Free-market theoreticians, in the catbird's seat, were again making capitalism an operational and philosophic force to be reckoned with.

## THE RESURGENCE
## OF ENTREPRENEURIALISM

Support from intellectuals was one great spark, but there was a second. Resurgent entrepreneurialism was also an essential component of capitalism's new 1980s zest.* Popular impressions of leapfrogging technology, of commercial Daniel Boones pioneering suburban shopping opportunities or electronic geniuses tinkering in California garages provided the images for a new business orientation in Washington. So did a picture of

---

* One of America's most prominent economic historians had no doubt about what was happening. In 1985 Professor Alfred D. Chandler of the Harvard Business School proclaimed the United States to be in its *third* entrepreneurial period: "The first was the second Industrial Revolution of the 1880s and 1890s. The second was in the 1920s, when the great entrepreneurs, the Sloans and the Fords, put together their giant enterprises" ("Part 2: The Valley;" *Inc.*, July 1985, p. 54). But the real riches for business builders, he added, came from *exploiting* technological innovations by creating a sound organizational team: "Historically, [that was] the person who really cleaned up."

social and economic outsiders supplanting the third-generation rich of Newport, Rhode Island, or the remote corporate hierarchs of the Fortune 500.

Historically, twentieth-century liberal critics of American inequality have liked to equate wealth with stagnant, elitist, privileged inheritance. Wealth flowing from parentage rather than from merit or enterprise has never rallied electorates. Reagan-era ideologues, however, were not trumpeting inherited wealth; they were talking about self-made business success—about the success of the outsider, about anti-elitist entrepreneurialism— as the great engine of U.S. wealth creation (and, periodically, also as a guarantor of wealth's "populist" reallocation). This, they said, was exactly what was happening again in the 1980s. Most of the decade's scientific inventions, technological breakthroughs and commercial innovations reflected entrepreneurship, not inheritance. The more Horatio Alger stories in the press—the more housewives like Debbi Fields building cookie-franchise empires, the more small-town teenagers becoming computer-software millionaires—the greater the political outreach of American capitalism.

The truth fell in between. Both entrepreneurship and inheritance prospered during the Reagan era. By 1988 no one could reasonably deny that many of America's richest families had received at least *part* of their money from inheritance (see Chapter 6). Estate taxes had been cut, and so had taxation of unearned income. The so-called Idle Rich did well.

The larger characteristic, though, was that the Reagan decade, like America's earlier Darwinian eras, stimulated millions of new ventures while also encouraging a profound upheaval in business itself. Size was no guarantee against failure. Fortune 500 corporations vanished along with small Midwestern farm-equipment dealerships and Gulf Coast oil rigs. Vast amounts of new wealth were carved out by immigrants and strivers from the middle or lower classes. "Junk bonds" and other new instruments of corporate finance transferred power away from old-line firms to competitors with Bronx and Brooklyn accents. They also made instant decamillionaires out of pet-food distributors, cable TV operators and chain jewelry-store owners. New money multiplied much faster than old money. Idea mongers and arrivistes were everywhere.

Capitalism's appeal simply broadened, for Americans have always—up to a point—appreciated the accumulation of new wealth as reconfirming the economic frontier. One reason that the accumulation of riches in the late 19th century, brash and bloody as it was, failed to encourage successful political opposition for a generation after the Civil War was that *anybody* could make a fortune—and a lot of anybodies did. It was the self-made American parvenu capitalist that Gilded Age apologists trumpeted as "nature's nobleman," not some Anglophilic third-generation Virginian or Hudson Valley landowner well read in Cicero and Plutarch. The historian of the house of Vanderbilt could actually preen that "here [in the United States] the name of parvenu is the only and all-sufficient title of nobility."[15]

A century later that kind of candor was unsalable. Too much wealth *had* become multigenerational. Tributes to parvenuism acceptable at Delmonico's in 1888 would have caused smirks at the Carlyle Hotel in 1988. Nevertheless, while the full story of wealth concentration under Reagan awaits still-unpublished data, the Reagan economy was a triumph of outsider access— a cavalcade of inventors, leveragers, speculators, packagers, performers and promoters, ethnically spiced by Vietnamese-American shrimp wholesalers, Korean greengrocers and Asian high-tech entrepreneurs. Substantial fortunes were built on everything from franchised sugar wafers to lucrative new shapes in silicon and debt instruments. Most of them were largely new. Inheritance might and did provide important seed money for the 1980s. But few nonideological observers credited it as America's *dominant* form of wealth accumulation in the Reagan era.

Dozens of the entrepreneurs became billionaires; hundreds became centimillionaires; and tens of thousands became decamillionaires. Not all were traditional business builders, either, albeit two successive capital gains tax reductions in 1978 and 1981 had gone a long way to make basic enterprise more rewarding. Many were "paper entrepreneurs," as political economist Robert Reich called them, people who packaged the new financial and debt instruments proliferating on every side. Others made money by the corporate raiding and reshuffling encouraged by Reagan-era regulatory permissivism and global pressures. Moving or refinancing assets was easier than building or manufacturing them. The distinction between entrepreneurialism and debt manipulation, always a fine one in capitalist heydays, became finer than ever.

Such profiteering would ultimately become a political sore point, as we shall see. But at first, national approval of entrepreneurs was unstinted. Growth-company chief executives were hailed in visits to Congress; corporate raiders addressed prestigious forums on the renewed vitality of American capitalism.

As in the past, three "outsider" aspects of entrepreneurialism bolstered its 1980s political appeal. First, much of the new money was insurgent in an institutional sense, attacking the business and corporate establishments. Entrepreneurs insisted *they* were the key to change and growth; big business and its organizations were a bunch of dinosaurs. Adam Smith had expressed many of the same ideas two centuries earlier in trying to break down the government alliances of Britain's East India Company and great agricultural landowners. Secondly, Reagan-era enterprise drew heavily on non-Anglo-Saxon Americans, as well as Asian and Latin American immigrants. To an extent, old-stock Americans had become commercially stale. In George Gilder's words, "immigrants throng the assembly lines of Silicon Valley, and about half of the most innovative workers and engineers of American high technology firms were born abroad. Without immigrants, the U.S. would have little chance of prevailing in technological rivalries with Japan and Asian countries."[16] Past heydays, too, had drawn heavily on immigrants and the success drives of the American "melting pot." And finally, America's principal entrepreneurial eras have hummed with acknowledged surges of technological progress. Even left-leaning historian Matthew Josephson, citing Gilded Age inventions ranging from George Westinghouse's air brake to Alexander Graham Bell's telephone, allowed that "the twenty years after 1873 formed a period of unequaled material progress in the United States."[17] The 1920s were similar, and Henry Ford, in his book *Machinery: The New Messiah*, waxed fulsome about how airplanes, radios and movies, knowing no boundaries, would knit together the world.[18] Entrepreneurial theorists of the 1980s would spin similar prose around silicon chips, semiconductors and computers.

Rhetoric like this matters. As long as it is in the air, the public—and the politicians the public elects—can usually be

counted on to rally to the economic arrangements claiming
credit. The pace of invention, the surge of commercial creativity,
*did* quicken during the two capitalist heydays of the late nineteenth and early twentieth centuries. Proponents of "innovation
cycles," a presumed indicator of technological advance, have
charted three nonwartime bursts of patents granted in the United
States: in 1879–89, from 1900 through 1912, and from 1918
to 1929.[19]

But the 1980s were more complicated. Patent registration
accelerated after the 1982–83 recession's nadir, increasing
smartly through the rest of the decade, yet the percentage taken
out by foreigners kept setting records—up from 20 percent in
1966 to 47 percent in 1988. And administration critics argued
that little additional real business investment followed the 1981
tax cuts.

Liberal economist Robert Kuttner encapsulated the basic investment critique: "In 1981, before the supply-side cuts took
effect, America invested about 12.2% of its total income in new
plant and machinery. Since the big tax cut, new investment has
fluctuated narrowly, from a low of 11% in the 1983 recession
to a high of 12.6% in the 1985 recovery."[20] Harvard economist
Benjamin Friedman took the dissent a step further in his 1988
book, *Day of Reckoning*, pointing out that net business investment even during the 1983–86 recovery ran below the *average* for the nineteen fifties, sixties and seventies.[21] The public's
false sense of substantial Reagan-era business investment, he
contended, developed in two ways: First, from the statistical
illusion created by the 1983–85 uptick from the extremely depressed base of 1982 ("the worst year for net business investment since World War II") and, second, from the misperception
of business seriously "investing" when corporations were simply
buying other companies, merging, taking on debt to go private,
or otherwise reshuffling structures or assets. In the wake of the
1981 tax cuts, American business enjoyed rising profits and cash
flow, but much of what they were spending it on was an ersatz
enterprise—that apt phrase *paper entrepreneurialism*.

Something *was* missing in the equation. New production facilities often seemed to be outnumbered by new debt instruments. Yet the evidence of an entrepreneurial outlook, certainly
in services or in the moneymaking and deal-making sense, was

overwhelming. Between 1980 and 1987, venture capital investment increased 544 percent. The number of U.S. universities offering entrepreneurship programs climbed from 163 in 1981 to 250 in 1985. Incorporation of new businesses surged from 533,520 in 1980 to a record-breaking 634,991 in 1984.[22] And there was the shell burst of celebratory literature: Hundreds of books and a new breed of magazines, from *Inc., Success* and *Entrepreneur* on down. Perhaps even more than in the 1920s, popular culture gorged itself on the road-to-success stories of latter-day Thomas Edisons and Henry Fords—men like Apple Computer founder Steven Jobs, Microsoft billionaire William Gates and flamboyant real estate developer Donald Trump.

In late 1987, with national enthusiasm at its peak, publishers were plumping down six- and seven-figure bets on what amounted to a new literary genre: biographies of corporate chieftains as cult figures. One book review in 1986, lumping together five different volumes, noted that "all portray the corporate leader as teacher, mentor, exemplar and forger of values and meaning."[23] Robert Reich suggested that many of the most successful corporate leaders drew on a John Wayne or Charles Bronson imagery:

> In their contempt for bureaucracy, formal process, and intellectual abstraction—and their passion for outspoken independence, direct dealing, and charismatic leadership—these CEOs seem perfectly in tune with the anti-establishment tendencies now found on both the right and left of the political spectrum. They are cowboy capitalists.
>
> These stories therefore give comfort to Americans who harbor vague misgivings about the place of the large, sluggish corporation in American life—and about the faceless oligarchs who run them. The cumulative message of these books is that we are entering upon a new populist era in which the mavericks are in charge. They are shaking up torpid corporate bureaucracies, bringing forth a new sense of team spirit and entrepreneurship. The Henry Fords of the old world are being replaced by the Lee Iacoccas of the new. The imperious bean counters are on the run. There is no reason to question the fundamental legitimacy of big business in America, or to flirt with economic populism, because the populists already have taken over—from the inside. And they are wildly successful.[24]

Yankee inventors and technological genuises were no longer the key. Capitalism in the 1980s meant lone economic gunmen taking on saloons full of "corporados." But by the end of the Reagan era, go-it-alone or gunslinger capitalism was beginning to lose its appeal. Cowboy corporate raiders and financiers were starting to appear too unrestrained and increasingly counter-productive. The leveraged buyout tycoons had taken the re-structuring process beyond survival of the fittest to destructive profiteering, reckless expansion of corporate debt and rising bankruptcy rates.* Resurgent capitalism had been tentative in 1981, uncertain how far its emergent truths could prevail. By the late 1980s the tide had turned so far that academic biog-raphers were penning tributes to former symbols of economic ruthlessness—not just to J. P. Morgan and Andrew Mellon but also to the legendary late-nineteenth-century robber baron Jay Gould.[25] One reviewer noted that "in place of 'robber barons' roving the landscape at will, we find the business titans of Gould's generation ostensibly devoting themselves to wresting a semblance of industrial stability out of the chaos left behind by the Civil War."[26] The line between robber barons and eco-nomic statesmen began to blur. Economic biography, like the Supreme Court, follows the election returns.

By 1988 the *Harvard Business Review* had launched a series of articles suggesting that the ideal of the entrepreneur was being taken too far.[27] Rugged individualism caused problems going beyond merger wars and takeovers. Community spirit and cor-porate size also had a place in business economics. For example, the exodus from major companies of entrepreneurial fortune-seekers had begun to weaken the critical semiconductor indus-try. This kind of fragmentation, some theorized, could keep semiconductor firms from developing the size and scale needed to compete against Japan's corporate giants. In other industries

---

* "To say these guys are entrepreneurs is like saying Jesse James was an entrepreneur," observed Electronic Data Systems founder Ross Perot. "In my day, you could make lots of money creating a new product or backing a new company. But now, if you're an investment banker, you can make many times that amount of money in three or four weeks—and through the miracle of junk bonds leave all the risk with pension funds, S&Ls and banks, all of which are insured by the government . . . Now it's the taxpayer, the average citizen, who's become the entrepreneur in fact, with all the risk and very little of the reward."

the entrepreneurialism begat by deregulation was already giving way to mergers, concentration and rising prices. Benjamin Friedman cautioned that the entrepreneurial appearance of the 1980s was, in part, an illusion, based on the unprecedented shuffling of assets and funded by unprecedented debt. Greed was taking over.

What conservatives found difficult to admit, even by 1989, was that the capitalist exuberance of the 1980s—bolstered by a supportive culture and well-placed allies in Washington—had begun, inevitably, to create its own economic and social imbalances. Liberalism had not been able to recognize entrepreneurial capitalism's corrective merits in 1980; a decade later, conservatism had trouble recognizing the need for yet another pendulum swing. But Will and Ariel Durant had seen the dilemma in the study *The Lessons of History*:

> Since practical ability differs from person to person, the majority of such abilities, in nearly all societies, is gathered in a minority of men. The concentration of wealth is a natural result of this concentration of ability and regularly recurs in history. The rate of concentration varies . . . with the economic freedom permitted by morals and the laws. Despotism may for a time retard the concentration; democracy, allowing the most liberty, accelerates it.[28]

In the end, the two historians observed that "liberty and equality are like buckets in a well. When one goes up, the other goes down." During the 1980s the bucket of liberty and economic freedom rose, while the bucket of income equality fell. Upper-tier Americans significantly expanded their share of national wealth while low-income citizens lost ground, and Reagan policies were critical to this shift.

# Chapter

# 4

# Wealth and Favoritism:
## The Specifics of Federal Policy
## and Income Redistribution
## During the Reagan Era

Politics is about who gets what, especially as a result of government action. In the Reagan years, a particular social stratum has gotten a lot. . . . If Marx had been scribbling away in the Library of Congress (our equivalent of the British Museum, where Marx scribbled), in January 1981, as Reaganites marched into Washington, he would have said: The class struggle is about to intensify. During the Reagan Terror, labor will lose ground to capital.

—CONSERVATIVE COMMENTATOR
GEORGE F. WILL, 1988

The economic agenda of the past seven years produced one of the quickest and most regressive redistributions of wealth in U.S. history. For all of its impassioned rhetoric about removing government as a force in our financial affairs, the Reagan government injected itself more enthusiastically into the economy than any administration since Lyndon Johnson's Great Society. Indeed, Reagan's administration took so much money from the pockets of middle- and lower-income Americans and shoved it up to the wealthiest 10 percent in our society that a top-heavy structure now threatens to come crashing down on us.

—POPULIST TEXAS AGRICULTURE
COMMISSIONER JIM HIGHTOWER, 1987

The reorientation of federal policy from 1981 to 1988 enormously affected entrepreneurialism, investment, speculation and the creation and distribution of U.S. wealth and income, just as in previous GOP capitalist heydays. As we have seen, the largest benefits went to those already well off, so much so that one critic lamented the parallel between the distribution of wealth in the 1980s and blues singer Ray Charles's lyrics "Them that's got is them that gets, and I ain't got nothing yet."[1]

Most of the Reagan era's legislative and regulatory approaches were familiar from prior conservative periods: taxes were eliminated or reduced; discretionary federal domestic outlays for low-income and Democratic constituencies were reduced; federal regulatory agencies were restrained; federal merger law enforcement was relaxed; money was intermittently tight and real interest high, reflecting a preference for creditors over debtors. The specific directions taken were not always coherent or even compatible—for example, the troublesome mismatch in the early 1980s between a loose fiscal policy in which tax cuts were accompanied by mounting deficits and a stern survival-of-the-fittest monetarism that left too much of the burden of fighting inflation to punitive interest rates.

But this economic illogic also had a shrewd side. The benefits of these sometimes contradictory policies to GOP constituencies were long-established: tax cuts were traditional Republican economics, and the same was true of high real interest rates to protect creditors, bondholders and financial institutions. The seemingly new and tricky part lay in running up a record peacetime deficit as part of the framework.* As the Reagan era ended, however, it could be seen that even deficits had tactical pluses: they *did* help fund the tax cuts; they *did* keep real interest rates high; and they *did* squeeze discretionary federal domestic spending to a latter-day record-low percentage of GNP.

In a sense, conservatism had made debt strategic—a private sector tool, not a means of public sector expansion. Experts agreed that at some point troublesome results would almost certainly follow. But as of January 1989 the predicted calamity had *not* materialized. Meanwhile, even the most dedicated signatories of the Bipartisan Budget Appeal advertisements organized by former commerce secretary Peter Peterson could see

---

* But as we shall see on page 101, this, too, had its partial precedents. Conservative administrations have a lengthy and possibly unappreciated record of not only tolerating indebtedness but using it for political and constituency purposes.

the favorable side of the loose fiscal equation: the attractiveness of low tax brackets and high real interest rates for maid-and-chauffeur precincts like Sutton Place, Round Hill Road and Bel-Air. In dollars banked, consumed or couponed between 1981 and 1988, the amounts involved were massive.

## TAX-BRACKET REDUCTION: THE CENTERPIECE OF THE REAGAN ERA

The reduction or elimination of federal income taxes had been a goal of all three major U.S. capitalist periods, but were now a personal preoccupation for Ronald Reagan, whose antipathy toward income taxes dated back to World War II, when a top rate of 91 percent made it foolish to work beyond a certain point. Under Reagan, the top personal tax bracket would drop from 70 percent to 28 percent in just seven years. In 1987 the Congressional Budget Office (see Table 1 on page 17) showed just who was getting the cream from these reductions: the top 1 to 5 percent of the population.

In 1861 a Republican administration and Congress imposed the first U.S. income tax to finance the Civil War. After two wartime increases, the federal levy was terminated in 1872, abetting the mushrooming fortunes of the Astors, Carnegies, Morgans and Rockefellers (see Chapter 6).

Later, as postwar laissez-faire collapsed into populism and progressivism, public doubts about excessive wealth resurged, and with them came income tax pressures. In 1894, after the prior year's unnerving stock market panic, Congress passed a tax of 2 percent on incomes over four thousand dollars, which the U.S. Supreme Court declared unconstitutional in 1895. A constitutional amendment solved the problem in 1913. As Europe marched to war in 1914, joined by the United States in 1917, the demand for income tax revenue soon repeated itself. Levies climbed quickly, and by 1920, the top rate was 73 percent.

As a result, postwar federal revenues exceeded peacetime needs and discouraged peacetime enterprise. When the Harding administration took office in 1921, tax rates were quickly reduced, in four stages, to a top bracket of just 25 percent in 1925. As Reaganite theorists would recall six decades later, cutting income taxes amidst gathering commercial prosperity helped create the boom of the 1920s. The prime beneficiaries were the top 5 percent of Americans, people who rode the cutting edge of the new technology of autos, radios and the like, emerging service industries (including new practices like advertising and consumer finance), a booming stock market and unprecedented real estate development. As federal taxation eased, especially on the upper brackets, disposable income soared for the rich—and with it conspicuous consumption and financial speculation.

By the crash of 1929, striking changes had occurred in the distribution of both taxes *and* wealth. The bottom-earning 80 percent of the population, never much affected, had been cut off the income tax rolls entirely. As a result, the top 1 percent of taxpayers were paying about two thirds of what the Treasury took in. Even so, because the top rate had fallen from 73 percent to 25 percent, federal taxation was taking less and less of booming upper-bracket incomes and stock profits. By contrast, many farmers and miners, and some workers, hurt by slumping commodity prices, found themselves with lower real purchasing power than they had enjoyed in the placid decade before World War I. Tax policy was not the only source of upward redistribution, but it contributed greatly to the polarization of U.S. wealth and the inequality of income, which peaked between 1927 and 1929.*

But Democrats, soon back in control of Congress and then the White House, preferred to afflict rather than nurture concentrated wealth. Now the direction of redistribution moved *downward*. To achieve that, the top tax rate reached 63 percent by 1932, 79 percent by 1936 and soared to 91 percent during

---

* This maldistribution is often cited as a factor in the 1929 crash and subsequent depression. One scholar goes so far as to contend that the lower 93 percent of the nonfarm population actually experienced a 4 percent decline in real disposable per capita income between 1923 and 1929 (Charles F. Holt, "Who Benefitted from the Prosperity of the Twenties?" *Explorations in Economic History* 14, July 1977, pp. 277–89).

World War II, the incentiveless bracket that so offended Ronald Reagan and his Hollywood friends. Ninety-one percent remained the nominal top rate until 1964, when it fell in two stages to 77 percent and then 70 percent.

If not for the war in Vietnam, there might have been further cuts in the late sixties, but the war was costly, sustaining a high rate structure and even requiring a surtax from 1968 to 1970. More perversely, wartime outlays generated an inflation that lifted more and more middle-class citizens into what had long been *upper-class* brackets. So by the late 1970s, with the war over but with inflation still intensifying, cyclical demand for tax reduction gathered momentum. After nearly fifty years, proposals for deep rate reductions were back on the national agenda. Though Republican politicians aroused little interest in the Kemp-Roth tax cuts in 1978, this lack of support was only temporary.

Over the next two years, a new conservative outlook took shape in Washington, entrenched in 1980 by Reagan's election. The 1981 Economic Recovery Tax Act, passed by a surprisingly willing Congress, offered far more than relief for middle-class bracket creep. Supply-side proponents of individual rate cuts and business-organization lobbyists for capital formation and corporate depreciation allowances shared a half-trillion-dollar victory.* For the first time since the New Deal, federal tax policy was fundamentally rearranging its class, sector and income-group loyalties.

Corporate tax rates were reduced and depreciation benefits greatly liberalized. By 1983 the percentage of federal tax receipts represented by corporate income tax revenues would drop to an all-time low of 6.2 percent, down from 32.1 percent in 1952 and 12.5 percent in 1980. For individuals the 1981 act cut taxes across the board—by 5 percent in 1981, then 10 percent in 1982 and another 10 percent in 1983. Another highly significant change trimmed the top bracket from 70 percent to 50 percent. Taxation of *earned* income had been capped at a 50 percent top rate since 1972. Now the same treatment would be extended to *unearned* income, an enormous boon to the small percentage

---

* That was the estimated cost of the 1981 tax cuts over the next five years.

of the population deriving most of its income from rents and interest. Meanwhile, the top rate on capital gains was effectively cut to 20 percent, having earlier been dropped from 49 percent to 28 percent by the Steiger Amendment reductions of 1978. Conservative tax-reduction supporters predicted a surge in savings, venture capitalism and entrepreneurialism. Liberal economists, disheartened, prophesied more inflation and mounting inequality. Both predictions only half proved out. The savings rate didn't grow, and neither did inflation, but enterprise *and* inequality did—an old story.

Critics of emerging income polarization would eventually cite the increasingly benign treatment between 1978 and 1981 of property income (interest, dividends and rents) and capital gains, a benefit that flowed mostly to a small stratum of taxpayers. According to a 1983 Federal Reserve Board survey, families in the top 2 percent owned 30 percent of all liquid assets (from checking accounts to money market funds), 50 percent of the corporate stocks held by individuals, some 39 percent of corporate and government bonds and 71 percent of tax-exempt municipals. And applying a broader measurement of upper-income status, the wealthiest 10 percent owned 51 percent of liquid assets, 72 percent of corporate stocks, 70 percent of bonds and 86 percent of tax-exempts.[2]

The inflation of the late 1970s and then subsequent post-1981 disinflation would affect different economic strata in different ways. At first, under inflation, blue-collar wages stagnated, at least in real terms, but a fair percentage of reasonably well off property owners benefited from increased bank CD interest rates, real estate values, precious metals, jewelry, art and rents. When disinflation took over in 1981–82, the big benefit shifted to the more truly rich. Real interest rates soared, and as that happened, upper-bracket holders of financial assets—mostly stocks and bonds—chalked up the greatest gains. Data compiled by the Economic Policy Institute in 1988 spelled out the much larger 1978–86 gain in property income (up 116.5 percent) compared with wage, salary and other labor income (up 66.6 percent).[3] Lightened levies on capital gain and property income, coming just around the time when those categories were climbing, helped fuel upper-bracket wealth and capital accumulation

more or less as conservative tax strategists and entrepreneurial
theorists had hoped.

The second big redistributive spur was Washington's decision
to let Social Security tax rates climb upward from 6.05 percent
in 1978 to 6.70 percent in 1982–83, 7.05 percent in 1985 and
7.51 percent in 1988–89—a schedule originally voted in 1977
under Carter—while income tax rates were coming down. By
1987, however, Maine Democratic senator George Mitchell
complained that "as a result, there has been a shift of about
$80 billion in annual revenue collections from the progressive
income tax to the regressive payroll tax. The Social Security tax
increase in 1977 cannot be attributed to the current administration. But the response in the 1980s—to make up for a tax
increase disproportionately burdening lower-income households with a tax cut disproportionately benefiting higher-income
households—*can* be laid to the policies of this administration."[4]
Mitchell was hardly overstating the new reliance on Social Security. Between 1980 and 1988, the FICA tax on $40,000-a-
year incomes doubled from $1,500 to nearly $3,000. The portion of total annual federal tax receipts represented by Social
Security rose from 31 percent to 36 percent while income tax
contributions dropped from 47 percent to under 45 percent.
Table 3 on page 83 shows the consequent 1977–88 realignment
of effective tax rates for different groups.*

After his reelection in 1984, Reagan moved to replicate the
full reduction of the Harding-Coolidge era and succeeded in
doing so when the 1986 tax reform cut top individual rates from
70 percent in 1981 to just 28 percent as of 1988—effectively
matching the 1921–25 reduction from 73 percent to 25 percent.
Democrats were largely uncritical; as we have seen, their ac-
quiescence in such reversals is typical of capitalist heydays.

Taxpayers would not feel the final effects of the 1986 tax

---

* In December 1989 reaction against shifting the federal tax burden onto
Social Security levies would break out into open political warfare with the
proposal by New York Democratic senator Daniel Patrick Moynihan to roll
back Social Security rates. Moynihan charged that "no other democratic country takes as large a portion of its revenue from working people at the lower
ends of the spectrum and as little from persons who have property or high
incomes."

reductions until April 1989, and 1988 tax-distribution data
couldn't be officially analyzed for several years thereafter, well
past the president's departure from office. Yet the debate over
who had gained and lost under Reagan intensified. Reaganites
and their critics both had a substantial case. Supply-siders and
other advocates of bracket reduction could show that the upper-
tier rate cuts had not increased the *proportion* of taxes paid by
the poor and middle classes. During the Reagan years the percentage of total federal income tax payments made by the top
1 percent of taxpayers actually rose, climbing from 18.05 percent in 1981 to 19.93 percent in 1983, 21.9 percent in 1985
and 26.1 percent in 1986. And this could have been predicted.
As we have seen, their share of national income was increasing
by similar proportions. When wealth concentrates at the top of
the pyramid, lower rates *do* bring larger receipts than the higher
rates of the preconcentration period. Coolidge-era precedents,
invoked by supply-siders from the first, had been even more
lopsided. Because the upper-bracket rate cuts of the 1920s also
removed most lower- and lower-middle-income families from
the rolls, the percentage of total taxes paid by the top 1 percent
actually climbed from 43 percent in 1921 to 69 percent in 1926.
Early supporters of a tax rollback—not least Coolidge—were
quick to boast of this, and assigned credit to the rate cuts. The
same boasts were made in the 1980s.*

The statistical deception, of course, was that the increased
ratios of total tax payments by high-income persons were not
an increased burden. Overzealous supply-siders were way too
insistent that Reagan's tax policy "soaked the rich," promoted
"economic justice," and that "the Reagan years have been, contrary to the conventional wisdom, an age of benevolent Robin
Hoodism."[5] Claims that the tax cuts had helped promote prosperity under Coolidge and Reagan were plausible, although

---

* In his 1928 message to Congress, for example, President Coolidge observed
that tax rate cuts stimulated business production to the extent that total tax
revenues increased: "Four times we have made a drastic revision of our internal
revenue system, abolishing many taxes and substantially reducing almost all
others. Each time the resulting stimulation to business has so increased taxable
incomes that a surplus has been produced" (John D. Hicks, *Republican Ascendency, 1921–33* [New York: Harper Brothers, 1960], p. 107).

more plausibly these cuts *overlapped* rather than caused the two capitalist heydays. That the rich were "soaked" during the 1980s was, however, untrue, as anyone walking down Rodeo Drive could see. It was precisely such exaggerations that undermined supply-sider credibility.

Under Reagan, as under Coolidge, the clear evidence is that the net tax burden on rich Americans as a percentage of their total income *shrank* substantially because of the sweeping rate cuts. The surge in actual tax payments was the result of higher upper-bracket incomes. To measure the benefits, imagine a businessman who had made $333,000 in salary, dividends and capital gains in 1980, and paid $120,000 in federal income taxes. As prosperity returned in 1983, his income climbed to $500,000. Yet with the applicable rates reduced, he might well have paid, say, $150,000 in taxes, *more actual payment*, of course, but *less relative burden*. That many blue-collar and middle-class Americans had lost their jobs in 1981–82 (when unemployment briefly neared 11 percent) also helps explain why the top 1 percent of 1983 taxpayers—disproportionate beneficiaries of a surging stock market—wound up shouldering a higher portion of the overall federal income tax burden. They were gaining while the bottom half of the population was losing. "Soaked" is hardly the term to describe what happened to millionaires paying out lower percentages of sharply rising incomes.

In 1987, to plot the rearrangement of effective *overall* tax rates, the economists at the Congressional Budget Office took *all* federal taxes—individual income, Social Security, corporate income and excise—and calculated the change in their combined impact on different income strata after 1977. Families below the top decile, disproportionately burdened by Social Security and excise increases and rewarded less by any income tax reductions, wound up paying *higher* effective rates. The richest families, meanwhile, paid lower rates, largely because of the sharp reduction applicable to nonsalary income (capital gains, interest, dividends and rents).

These shifts go a long way to explain both the surge in consumption *and* the rising inequality of income. America's richest 5 percent (and richest 1 percent, in particular) were the tax policy's new beneficiaries. Nor did the CBO's 1988 projections anticipate a significant reversal from the 1986 tax reform, with

## TABLE 3

### SHIFTS IN EFFECTIVE FEDERAL TAX RATES BY POPULATION INCOME DECILE, 1977–88

| Decile | 1977 | 1984 | 1988 | Percentage Point Change in Effective Rate (1977–84) | (1977–88) |
|---|---|---|---|---|---|
| First | 8.0% | 10.5% | 9.6% | + 2.5% | + 1.6 |
| Second | 8.7 | 8.5 | 8.3 | – .2 | – .4 |
| Third | 12.0 | 13.2 | 13.3 | + 1.2 | + 1.3 |
| Fourth | 16.2 | 16.3 | 16.8 | + .1 | + .6 |
| Fifth | 19.1 | 18.5 | 19.2 | – .6 | + .1 |
| Sixth | 21.0 | 20.1 | 20.9 | – .9 | – .1 |
| Seventh | 23.0 | 21.5 | 22.3 | – 1.5 | – .7 |
| Eighth | 23.6 | 23.0 | 23.6 | – .6 | ±0 |
| Ninth | 24.5 | 23.8 | 24.7 | – .7 | + .2 |
| Tenth | 26.7 | 23.6 | 25.0 | – 3.1 | – 1.7 |
| Top 5% | 27.5 | 23.3 | 24.9 | – 4.2 | – 2.6 |
| Top 1% | 30.9 | 23.1 | 24.9 | – 7.8 | – 6.0 |

Source: Congressional Budget Office, *The Changing Distribution of Federal Taxes: 1975–1990*, October, 1987, Table 8, p. 48. (Corporate income tax allocated to labor income.) The 1988 figures were estimates.

its unusual combination of further rate reductions (down to a 28 percent top bracket) partly balanced by elimination of credits and deductions. Effective tax rates for 1988 *would* fall slightly for the bottom 20 percent relative to 1984, the CBO found, but not by enough to restore 1977's lower combined-impact levels. Middle and upper groups, in turn, would find their effective rates slightly higher in 1988 than in 1984. For these brackets, a part of the 1981 cut was recaptured. As Table 3 notes, however, the *overall* net effect of the 1977–88 tax changes would be different for *middle-class* versus *top-tier* taxpayers. For Mr. and Mrs. Middle America, the changes during Reagan's second term had the effect of canceling out the minor benefits of 1977–84 reductions. Escalating Social Security rates were a principal culprit. *Upper-echelon taxpayers alone were projected to benefit from a large net reduction in effective overall federal tax rates for the entire 1977–88 period.*

Some of the anomalies of the redesigned tax burden were

extraordinary, not least the "bubble" that imposed a marginal income tax rate of 33 percent on family incomes of $70,000 to $155,000 in contrast to the 28 percent rate that applied above these levels. In 1988 a $90,000-a-year family with two husband-and-wife breadwinners making $45,000 each found itself in a 40.5 percent marginal federal tax bracket—a 33 percent income tax rate plus a 7.5 percent Social Security levy—in contrast to the 28 percent marginal rate of a millionaire or billionaire.

Policy at the federal level wasn't unique. During 1988 a collateral thesis began to emerge that state-level tax changes during the 1980s were also aggravating the trend to inequality. Citizens for Tax Justice, a group financed by labor unions and various liberal organizations, calculated that rising state sales taxes were falling disproportionately on poor families.[6] And a 1988 study contended that half the states with income taxes had made them less fair for many low- and middle-income residents in 1986–87.[7] The 1986 federal revisions required modification of state tax laws. The complaint was that those modifications were biased. Critics, however, lacked the documentation rapidly proliferating on the federal level, and in any event, *federal fiscal policy was the main issue.*

The irony was that Democratic election-year presidential politicking did not recognize that importance. Opinion polls in April 1988—tax time—revealed public skepticism of tax reform, its fairness and its wisdom (see Appendix F). Yet Dukakis avoided the subject. Upper-bracket increases were rejected at the Democratic National Convention. Tax issues were ignored in 1988 as they had been in 1928.

What was also ignored—perhaps because of its complexity—were the data, contrary to widespread belief, showing that non–Social Security taxes for all Americans as a percentage of GNP had been significantly cut during the 1980s. Conservative insistence that the overall federal tax burden hadn't been reduced was deceptive. Certain revenue ratios *did* decline. Between 1 and 2 percent of GNP that had been gathered in taxes for *general* public sector purposes under Eisenhower and Nixon—some $40 billion to $80 billion a year in 1988 dollars—was routed back to the private sector under Reagan, enlarging the federal budget

TABLE 4

TOTAL FEDERAL RECEIPTS/OUTLAYS AS A PERCENTAGE OF GNP

| Fiscal Year | Total Social Security Receipts | Total Non–Social Security Receipts | Total Receipts | Total Outlays |
|---|---|---|---|---|
| 1945 | 1.6% | 19.7% | 21.3% | 43.6% |
| 1960 | 2.9 | 15.4 | 18.3 | 18.2 |
| 1970 | 4.5 | 15.0 | 19.5 | 19.8 |
| 1980 | 5.9 | 13.5 | 19.4 | 22.2 |
| 1981 | 6.1 | 14.0 | 20.1 | 22.7 |
| 1982 | 6.4 | 13.3 | 19.7 | 23.7 |
| 1983 | 6.3 | 11.8 | 18.1 | 24.3 |
| 1984 | 6.5 | 11.5 | 18.0 | 23.1 |
| 1985 | 6.7 | 11.9 | 18.6 | 23.9 |
| 1986 | 6.8 | 11.6 | 18.4 | 23.7 |
| 1987 | 6.8 | 12.5 | 19.3 | 22.6 |
| 1988 | 7.0 | 12.0 | 19.0 | 22.3 |

deficit, and thereby affecting federal spending and interest rate outlays, also with redistributive effects.* It was true, as Table 4 shows, that *total* federal tax receipts remained roughly constant as a percentage of Gross National Product, but Social Security receipts were rising sharply, disguising a relative decline in *other* revenues, reducing Washington's ability to fund non–Social Security programs from schools to highways.

Other postwar Republican administrations had not sought this kind of fundamental reversal in government's role. Under Eisenhower, on average, non–Social Security federal receipts—principally from personal income, corporate income and excise taxes—had represented 15 percent of GNP, enabling the gov-

* Harvard professor Benjamin Friedman reaches a similar conclusion a bit differently: "It was only in the 1980s under Reagan's new fiscal policy, that this long-standing relationship changed. Because of Kemp-Roth, the share of individuals' income paid in taxes of all kinds other than Social Security contributions *declined* between 1979 and 1986. After including the hike in Social Security, the total tax payments of individuals was still 18.2 percent. In the meanwhile, government transfer payments kept on rising in relation to income, reaching 13.4 percent in 1986. The balance left to pay for all other government services was down to just 4.8 percent of income, fully two percentage points below what it was on average from the fifties to the seventies" (Benjamin Friedman, *Day of Reckoning* [New York: Random House, 1988], p. 156).

ernment to run without deficits. By the late 1960s federal deficits were a fact of fiscal life. Ironically, bracket creep in the late 1970s was perversely helpful—non–Social Security receipts expanded to 14 percent of GNP, reducing deficits again, compared with mid-decade figures.

But the 1981 tax cuts, along with rising military outlays, tight Federal Reserve Board policy and the cost of the 1981–82 recession, sent the federal deficit soaring to 5 to 6 percent of GNP, the highest peacetime levels since the Depression. Non–Social Security revenues in the range of 12 percent of GNP simply were not enough to run the U.S. government in the late 1980s, no matter what the stimulus of tax cuts might be. Part of the slack was made up by money borrowed at home and abroad at high cost. But how long could this go on? Tax relief and incentive economics meant not only income polarization but a frightening buildup of debt.

By 1989, the question was no longer whether tax policy would have to change, but when, how much—and to whose benefit? As we shall see, pressures for redistribution were also starting to take shape.

## FEDERAL BUDGET POLICY: A SECOND FISCAL REDISTRIBUTIVE LEVER

Even as overall federal spending remained high during the 1980s, kept aloft by debt (and the collaboration of well-rewarded lenders), the allocation of federal outlays changed enormously. New priorities got funds; old priorities gave way. And not surprisingly, related alterations also soon emerged in the distribution of wealth and income.

Reagan's long-standing negative attitudes toward public sector encroachment were largely philosophic. Government isn't the solution, he insisted (both before and *after* reaching the White House): "Government is the problem." The expansiveness of the public sector during the 1970s, he charged, had burdened innovation and stifled creativity, and other conservatives like George Gilder and Charles Murray, whose book *Losing Ground* made a mid-decade splash, added an even greater outrage: that welfarism had been destroying the family, and even the fabric of society.[8] Conservative ideologists were eager to defund the welfare state. At first, libertarian-leaning Reaganites had spoken wistfully of shrinking the federal government back toward its pre–New Deal role of providing currency, police protection and national defense. These dreams failed, but conservatives did shrink many domestic programs and reversed the decline in defense, the federal role they most ardently supported.

The significance of this redirection after 1981 is best seen through two comparisons—first, by its impact on upper- and lower-income groups; and second, by the dominance of defense over domestic priorities. The unequal effect by income group was scarcely disputable—low-income families, especially the working poor, lost appreciably more by cuts in government services than they gained in tax reduction. People who needed government help and facilities would get less. The richest families, being relatively small consumers of government services, sacrificed little in exchange for lower taxes.

In 1985 the *Los Angeles Times* took Congressional Budget Office data and contrasted the impact of Reagan's fiscal policy on two families. One involved two middle-class breadwinners jointly earning in the $40,000–$80,000 range; the second, a solitary earner bringing in under $10,000 a year.[9] As of 1984 the middle-class family was $2,910 *ahead*. Its $3,080 multiyear benefit from 1981 tax cuts was only minimally eroded by $170 in benefits lost from federal spending cuts. The poor family, however, lost $390, based on a negligible $20 net gain from the tax changes and a $410 loss of benefits from federal spending reductions. Chart 2 on page 13 has already detailed how the income of the bottom quintile of Americans stagnated during the 1980s while that of the top quintile surged. The reduction in federal domestic programs intensified the basic top-bottom polarization accompanying Reagan-era tax policy.

Increased spending for defense was a prime factor in shifting dollars away from human resources. Chart 3 shows the magnitude of the 1980–87 inversion: human resources *down* from 28 percent of all federal outlays to just 22 percent, defense *up* from 23 percent to 28 percent. Of course, if many people and

CHART 3

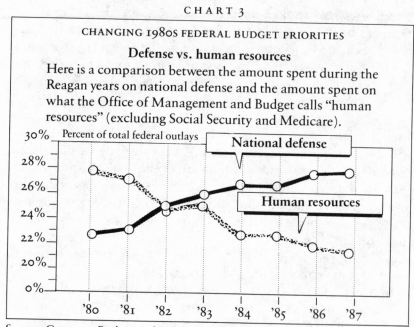

CHANGING 1980S FEDERAL BUDGET PRIORITIES

**Defense vs. human resources**
Here is a comparison between the amount spent during the
Reagan years on national defense and the amount spent on
what the Office of Management and Budget calls "human
resources" (excluding Social Security and Medicare).

Source: Center on Budget and Policy Priorities

jurisdictions dependent on housing, urban and social services
outlays suffered, other sections of the nation—and sectors
of the economy—gained. Accelerating military expenditures
brought new contracts, plants and jobs to the prime defense
contractor regions, principally the Atlantic, Gulf and Pacific
coastal states plus a few others, while favoring military bases
concentrated in similar places. Pentagon consultants and think
tanks also prospered. The overall wealth effect was considerable.

By 1989 federal spending increases in the Reagan era had
clearly benefited Republican constituencies (military producers
and defense installations, farmers and agribusiness, bondholders
and the elderly), while decreases in federal social programs
served to defund Democratic interests and constituencies (the
poor, the big cities, subsidized housing, education and many

other federal social services).* Gramm-Rudman deficit reductions worsened the pressure.

Previous capitalist heydays were different. Domestic spending had not been a major political (or redistributive) tool during the laissez-faire Gilded Age. The years 1866 to 1893, in fact, saw an unbroken series of budget surpluses.

In the 1880s and early 1890s the only war was against the Apaches—until Geronimo's surrender in 1886—and to suppress the last "ghost dance" spasms of resistance by the Dakota Sioux. The "steel fleet" launched in the 1880s was only a hint of the Great White Fleet, America's debut as a global sea power. Forty years later the 1921–29 Harding and Coolidge administrations were, if anything, less extravagant. This was a time of *disarmament*—the Washington armaments treaties were ratified in 1922. And in 1927 Coolidge vetoed the McNary-Haugen bill to subsidize troubled farmers by purchasing wheat, corn, hog, cotton and tobacco surpluses. *In prior Republican eras, realignment of large-scale federal spending was neither a problem nor a tactic.*

Reagan's willingness to implement large tax cuts despite prospective and later actual deficits in the $200 billion range was also a new development. In the 1920s yearly surpluses had made the tax cuts plausible. Former budget director David Stockman and others have admitted they anticipated large deficits in spring 1981 as they were planning their tax-reduction program. Yet in public they insisted to the contrary, lest the bracket rollbacks fail in Congress.[10]

Funding this huge deficit further realigned the nation's wealth. Under Reagan, annual federal expenditures on interest would climb from $96 billion in 1981 to $129 billion in 1983, $178

* For details, see "Background Material and Data on Programs Within the Jurisdiction of the Committee on Ways and Means, U.S. House of Representatives," March 15, 1989.

In the case of farmers, to be sure, mid-decade subsidies were anything but a from-the-beginning political strategy. Farm income support outlays *did* mushroom during the 1980s (up from $11 billion in 1981 to $25 billion in 1985 and a peak of $31 billion in 1986), but that was because farmers had been devastated during the mid-1980s by tight money and by the international trade impact of the overpriced dollar. Stepped-up federal support payments (and then 1988's costly drought aid) were less a reward than a form of reparations.

billion in 1985 and $216 billion in 1988.* No other major expense rose so sharply. Indeed, the deficit and its domino effect on other interest rates was a principal reason that property income was increasing much faster than wage income during the early and mid 1980s, which added further to upward redistribution. Not only were upper-quintile Americans collecting 80 percent of the federal interest payments made to persons, but the top tax rate applicable to these receipts was falling steadily (70 percent in 1980, 50 percent in 1982, 38.5 percent in 1987, 28 percent in 1988), so that less of the money spent on interest would come back to the U.S. Treasury as revenues. The average marginal tax rate that individuals paid on interest income fell from a peak of 38 percent in 1981 to 30 percent in 1983, worsening the pressure.[11] William Greider, in his landmark 1987 study of the Federal Reserve, wrote:

> The 1981 tax legislation proved to be regressive in a more fundamental way, hardly noted at the time. It became the pretext for a vast redistribution of incomes, flowing upward on the income ladder, through another powerful channel—interest rates. The price of money determined how the fruits of capitalist enterprise would be apportioned—the division of shares between creditors and debtors, between investors and entrepreneurs, between the old and the young, between workers and owners. The immediate consequence of the 1981 tax bill, virtually from the moment it was enacted, was higher interest rates. Paul Volcker's warnings proved correct. The division of wealth was tilted toward the top—a larger share would flow to those who already had accumulated wealth. There would be less for everyone else.[12]

This harsh assessment was not confined to populists like Greider. The conservative columnist George Will came to more or less the same conclusion:

> To pay the interest component of the 1988 budget will require a sum ($210 billion) equal to approximately half of all the personal income-tax receipts. This represents, as Sen. Pat Moynihan

---

* Part of these amounts represents interest the federal government actually paid to itself as transfers between government accounts. In 1988 *net* interest payments actually totaled $169.8 billion.

has said, a transfer of wealth from labor to capital unprecedented in American history.

Tax revenues are being collected from average Americans (the median income of a family of four is slightly under $30,000) and given to the buyers of U.S. government bonds—buyers in Beverly Hills, Lake Forest, Shaker Heights and Grosse Point, and Tokyo and Riyadh. If a Democrat can't make something of that, what are Democrats for?[13]

If the reorientation of federal domestic spending was not typical of previous conservative regimes, high interest rate payments to wealthy investors clearly were. High returns to creditors, in one form or another, have been a standby of conservative finance since Alexander Hamilton's day.

By the late 1980s, however, many of the recipients of these benefits were nervous. They worried that the deficit could ultimately mean higher taxes, a reduced standard of living, or both. High returns on bonds notwithstanding, few large investors liked Reagan's deficits, for which they thought they would eventually have to pay. And the amount of money consumed by federal debt payments and unavailable for accumulating national housing, educational and infrastructure needs was starting to seem dangerous.

## DEREGULATION:
## THE THIRD LEG OF THE STOOL

Deregulation—fewer governmental restraints on economic activity—has always accompanied the great waves of American capitalism, promoting enterprise but also leaving casualties in its wake.

The 1870s and 1880s, the high point of laissez-faire and Social Darwinism, were also a period of substantial deregulation. The U.S. Supreme Court slowly shrank the regulatory authority of the states. State acquisitions of stock in canals and turnpikes had already ended before the Civil War, and the mid-1870s saw sixteen states constitutionally prohibit state-government ownership of shares in a corporation.[14] Federal grants of land to subsidize railroad construction, heavy after the Civil War, also ended in 1872. The next fifteen to twenty years were the peak of nineteenth-century deregulation and laissez-faire, although hints of change could be seen in the establishment of the Interstate Commerce Commission in 1887 and the enactment of the Sherman Antitrust Act in 1890. Both measures foreshadowed the progressive era's regulatory tide, a decade away, but until the first decade of the twentieth century laissez-faire was an important factor in the Gilded Age's concentration of wealth and business power.

Progressive reforms exhausted themselves in the carnage, inflation and bureaucracy of World War I, and deregulatory strategies resumed in the 1920s under Harding and Coolidge—not just eliminating unnecessary federal boards and regulations left over from the Great War, but also limiting several established regulatory frameworks. For example, businessmen had never accepted the Federal Trade Commission, established in 1914 to police the perimeters of economic concentration and antitrust. By the end of the Republicans' 1921–33 reign in Washington, the FTC's primary purpose, as one New Dealer would lament, had been reduced to "preventing false and misleading advertising in references to hair-restorers, anti-fat remedies, etcetera— a somewhat inglorious end to a noble experiment."[15] Antimerger activity in the Justice Department also withered, and Herbert Hoover, first as commerce secretary and then as president, emphasized private-sector self-regulation through trade associations.* It was an alternative that came to be called Hoover Associationalism.[16] Fifty years later Reagan's approach would resemble Coolidge's.†

* Hoover was much less inclined toward laissez-faire than Coolidge. After leaving office in 1933, he complained that "the Brain Trust and their superiors are now announcing to the world that the social thesis of laissez-faire died on March 4. I wish they would add a professor of history to the Brain Trust." Hoover's term *did* represent a transition toward activism.

† By 1982 Colorado State University professor Robert R. Keller pointed out that "policies in both periods emphasize deregulating government controls over business and apply the same strategy for appointing administrators to regulatory agencies. In the Coolidge-Mellon era, and in the first stage of Reagan's term, appointments for major posts were dominated by people from the business sector, or by individuals critical of the policies of the very agency they administer" (Robert R. Keller, "Supply-Side Policies During the Coolidge-Mellon Era," *Journal of Economic Issues*, September 1982, p. 781). Nor did the 1920s analogy end there. Ronald Reagan's first-term "private sector initiative" program even bore some resemblance to Hoover Associationalism.

Reagan's economic deregulation would be far more complex and affirmative, however, than its predecessors. The tide starting in the 1970s flowed from an unprecedented, bipartisan reaction against an overextended government unimaginable in 1881 or 1921. At first the criticism was mostly academic, confined to specialized journals in which professors and dissident federal agency staffers cataloged inefficiencies, theorizing how once-logical government regulatory structures and approved monopolies were being invalidated by changing technologies. The deregulatory movement that followed would be a lot more sweeping.

As those deregulatory theses gathered momentum in the late 1970s, old ideologies had blurred. Historically, populism had been *proregulation*, but by the late 1960s this was no longer true. George Wallace's antibureaucratic rhetoric in 1968 had found a growing populist audience as he made regulators, social planners and experts a joke in the same hinterlands that had given their hearts to William Jennings Bryan and Franklin D. Roosevelt. Bureaucratic reputations were also hurt by the rising inflation of 1973–74, as government was increasingly seen to *profit* from its own ineptitude and extravagance.

Conservatives, for their part, hailed deregulation on free-market, antiregulatory and probusiness grounds. A few laissez-faire stalwarts went further, enjoying the discomfort of established Fortune 500 business-government relations. A significant minority of liberals found themselves endorsing deregulation as a means of asserting consumer interests against regulated business monopolies. Carter's election in 1976 merged some of these discordant attitudes and signaled a deregulatory coming-of-age. In March 1977 Carter promised: "One of my administration's major goals is to free the American people from the burden of over-regulation."[17] Within a year he had signed airline deregulation legislation, and by 1980 had also begun to deregulate trucking, railroad and interest rates.

Greater public disillusionment with government was still to come. The Carter interregnum merely whetted the gathering anti-Washington mood. While Carter promoted new competition in financial services and transportation, he also intensified regulation of the environment, product and occupational safety, energy, equal employment and "foreign corrupt practices."

Complaints from farmers, ranchers and business started mounting. Deregulation of a few industries notwithstanding, bureaucracy and paperwork were mushrooming. The *Federal Register*, publication place of all proposed and adopted regulations, expanded from a total of 14,479 pages in 1960 to an extraordinary 87,012 in 1980.[18] Voters' disillusionment with the welfare state and central planning, candidly acknowledged by Carter-era deregulation pioneers, made them sensitive to new regulatory dimensions. As *New Republic* editor Michael Kinsley recalled years later, about 1978 "people suddenly were bored with airbags, enraged by child-proof aspirin bottles, making jokes about the government as National Nanny."[19] The zenith of late-twentieth-century deregulation was just over the horizon.

It came with Reagan's victory in 1980, following his election with a vigor Washington hadn't seen for generations. Six years later, *Time* magazine recalled, "*Hack, chop, crunch!* were the sounds during the early 1980s as Reagan's regulatory appointees stripped away decades' worth of business restraints like so much prickly underbrush on the President's ranch. The burden of complying with federal regulations, Reagan claimed, had cost Americans between $50 billion and $150 billion a year. After only ten days in office, he put a freeze on more than 170 pending regulations."[20] The overweight *Federal Register* began to thin down again too. By 1986 it had shrunk back to 47,418 pages.

Ronald Reagan himself did little to deregulate new industries. Save for bus deregulation (1982), oil price decontrol and piecemeal dealings with telephone, electric and gas utilities, the basic framework was in place when he reached the White House. Murray Weidenbaum, the first chairman of Reagan's Council of Economic Advisers, would later volunteer that compared with his predecessors, Reagan was "extraordinarily timid in taking leadership."[21] Yet the deregulatory impetus already in motion under Carter was maintained or accelerated in transportation, financial services, telecommunications and beyond.

By mid-decade, however, some doubts were developing. The first involved safety—deregulation's contribution to reckless financial speculation, marginal airline maintenance practices, bank failures, truck highway accidents and corporate sacrifice of long-term goals to deal with raiders. The second concerned

equity and fairness. Deregulation helped some groups and regions and hurt others.

The best case for deregulation rested on general achievements—helping consumers as a class or modernizing the
economy. Academicians, many with a theoretical stake in deregulation, were especially given to calculating the favorable net
national impact. Airline deregulation was saving the public $6
billion a year, according to one study by Brookings Institution
economists. Telephone deregulation, besides bringing cheaper
long-distance rates, had opened up markets for new communications equipment and services. And other economists correctly pointed out how without deregulation financial
institutions could not have coped with the severe inflationary
wave cresting in 1979–81.

In banking, however, new regulatory flexibility was also a
problem: if banks could pay (and consumers enjoy) higher, deregulated interest rates after 1981, these same high rates deep-
ened the recession, especially in economically weak sectors. In
addition, by the late 1980s, there was evidence that deregulation
favored upper-bracket Americans. Consumers in general may
have benefited from the spread of deregulation, but critics repeatedly marshaled *specific* complaints in behalf of the poor,
small towns, farm dwellers and organized labor.

A fair consensus view was that educated, reasonably affluent
consumers able to understand the widening array of choices and
take advantage of reduced-price opportunities reaped the most
benefits, while poor people—strained by high minimum-balance
requirements at banks and steep local phone rates—fared the
worst.[22] Left-of-center critics deplored the overall effect of deregulation for redistributing income from the poor and moderate-income families to the affluent and large institutions.

Prosperous individuals and financial institutions *were* the
most obvious beneficiaries. In addition to the new services available, they gained from the high real interest rates made possible—for the first time since the Depression—by deregulation,
and they benefited, too, from the new forms of debt-backed and
speculative financial instruments used in the restructuring of
corporate America.

When Congress removed deposit and loan interest ceilings in

1980, rates rose to post–World War II records. The "small saver" cited so often in congressional debate profited, of course, but the much larger benefit, predictably, went to the wealthiest 10 percent of American families owning 86 percent of the net financial wealth. Inflation made deregulation necessary, but liberal critics complained that what the Democrats had begun reluctantly the new Reagan administration continued with relish.[23]

The result was that when the economy came out of the 1982 recession, the 1983–84 recovery became the first business cycle since the Harding-Coolidge heyday to unfold with minimal regulatory inhibition applied to interest rates. One estimate set deregulation's benefit at several hundred billion dollars of extra interest payments between 1980 and 1988.[24] But as critics pointed out, it also played havoc with marginal sectors of the economy, particularly those—from agriculture to housing— most dependent on borrowing.

Reagan's permissive approach to mergers, antitrust enforcement and new forms of speculative finance was likewise typical of Republican "heyday" conservatism. In the 1890s, the emerging oil, whiskey and tobacco trusts angered populists almost as much as deflation and tight monetary policy. In the 1920s another, if lesser, merger wave occurred as the Federal Trade Commission and the Antitrust Division of the Justice Department showed little interest in prosecutions. Consent decrees became the favored antitrust device. An estimated 1,268 mergers, involving some seven thousand firms, occurred between 1919 and 1928. Of these, only sixty were questioned by Washington— and just one was blocked.[25]

By 1988 angry Democrats leveled similar charges. Peter Rodino, the retiring chairman of the House Judiciary Committee, complained that "as record-shattering merger activity has increased, record low merger enforcement has followed in its wake. We have also seen a virtual disappearance of antitrust enforcement in entire categories of anticompetitive conduct from vertical restraints to monopoly cases."[26] Federal Trade Commissioner Andrew Strenio said the same about his commission: "Since Fiscal Year 1980, there has been a drop of more than 40 percent in the work years allocated to antitrust enforcement. In the same period, merger filings skyrocketed to more than 320 percent of their Fiscal Year 1980 level."[27] Small wonder the economy and the stock market became caught up in hostile takeovers and leveraged buyouts.

Old hands remarked on the unnerving parallels between the Wall Street raiders of the 1980s and the takeover pools of the 1920s, when high-powered operators would combine to "boom" a particular stock—appointing a pool manager, luring the public and then cashing in. Names like M. J. Meehan, Jesse Livermore, Arthur W. Cutten and Percy Rockefeller were as famous then as Carl Icahn, Boone Pickens and Ivan Boesky sixty years later.[28]

Elements of the antitrust laws *had* been outdated by the development of world markets in many industries, but the administration's tolerance, even enthusiasm, for corporate raiders and the redeployment of corporate assets had other roots, including, of course, the belief in the magic of markets and distaste for the decision-making role of government. The self-interest of important constituencies was also involved. Raiders like Pickens, Boesky, LBO magnate Henry Kravis and Sir James Goldsmith were also prominent Republican fund-raisers or conservative dinner honorees who celebrated the merits of Darwinian competition. By 1988, as we shall see in Chapter 6, a large and extremely profitable infrastructure had arisen around the economic restructuring movement, the fees from its deals, and the uplift it gave to the stock market.

Others pointed out how 1988's rapidly emerging savings and loan crisis—the projections of $100 billion to $200 billion or more that would be needed to bail out hundreds of overextended institutions—also had roots in deregulation.* Prior to 1982 federally chartered S&Ls were required to place almost all their loans in home mortgages, a relatively safe and stable class of assets. But in 1982, after soaring interest rates had made millions of low-interest mortgages into undesirable assets, new federal

---

* Edwin Gray, during the Reagan years head of the Federal Home Loan Bank Board, which regulated S&Ls, agreed that deregulation helped turn the S&L problem into a crisis because once it was enacted, there was little concern about oversight: "The White House was full of ideologues, particularly free-market types," Gray said. "They'd say 'the way to solve the problems is more deregulation—and by the way, deregulation means fewer examiners' " ("Deregulation Helped Turn S&L Problem into Crisis," *Miami Herald*, February 19, 1989).

law allowed S&Ls to invest their funds a lot more freely—100 percent in commercial real estate ventures if they so desired. Like banks in the 1920s, many S&Ls proceeded to gamble, with their (federally guaranteed) deposits, and by 1988 many had lost.

Organized labor and people in small towns and rural areas were seriously hurt by deregulation. Alfred Kahn, who promoted deregulation in the Carter administration, acknowledged in 1986 that three million union members—in airlines, telecommunications, trucking, bus transportation and others—took a severe blow. Workers in regulated industries, he explained, had often received 30 percent to 100 percent higher pay than people with comparable skills in the economy at large. "What had built up," Kahn said, "was an elite of American labor in protected industries. In a real sense, this elite of machinists and pilots and others was exploiting anyone whose average pay was much lower but who had to pay higher prices."[29] Federal and state regulation had allowed these costs to be passed along to consumers, so when competition took over, wages and permissive work arrangements in these same industries declined. Labor would have faced difficult enough times in the early 1980s without deregulation; with it, the downward or two-tier pressure on wages became painful.*

Rural areas were hurt by failures and takeovers of local financial institutions and by the way transportation and telephone deregulation gave companies the option to eliminate local services or the flexibility to charge appreciably more for them. Since survival of the fittest frequently meant survival only of what was profitable, routes and services in rural America often suffered. Byron Dorgan, the Democratic congressman from North Dakota, complained in 1983 that "there have been some benefits from deregulation, but they have gone largely to the population centers, while the costs have gone to rural areas. It's the same old economic cow—it feeds in the rural areas but is milked in the cities."[30] Other farm state officials would keep repeating the same charge.

Poorer city neighborhoods also realized little benefit from deregulation, but by 1988 the comparative statistics from the

---

* Labor has *always* lost ground during conservative deregulatory periods.

RFD precincts were especially compelling. Long-distance telephone rates, for example, were down 38 percent in five years, but some three quarters of long-distance calls were routed between eighteen large metropolitan areas. By contrast, basic local telephone service costs rose 50 to 60 percent nationwide.[31] Many farm communities complained about even sharper increases in intrastate long-distance rates, the prairie equivalent of local service.

As for air travel, during the four years following deregulation in 1978, weekly departures from large cities had risen 5 percent. Weekly departures from small towns, by contrast, had dropped 12 percent.[32] By 1988 approximately 140 small towns had lost all their air service, and in 190 others large airlines had handed over responsibility to smaller commuter carriers lacking comparable comfort, convenience and safety. Fares were high—whatever the traffic would bear.[33] No airline cared about offering supersaver flights between Billings, Montana, and Cheyenne, Wyoming. South Dakota senator Larry Pressler worried that deregulation was helping split the United States into two worlds: "There's the affluent suburbs and cities that everybody wants to serve, and then there are the rural areas."[34]

In 1986 Robert C. Byrd of West Virginia, the Democratic leader of the Senate, told a Senate hearing on transportation that he regretted only two of the votes he cast during his long career in Congress: one against the Civil Rights Act of 1964; the other in favor of the 1978 deregulation of U.S. airlines. Byrd lamented that "once there was deregulation, they [the airlines] left. Now if you want to go to West Virginia to attend a dinner, you have got to give two days to it."[35] In 1988 the *Des Moines Register* reported on a growing group of sociologists, economists and politicians who "worry that elements of deregulation may be just one more nail in rural America's coffin."[36]

If many low-income and rural Americans were deregulation's losers, the winners (beyond the financial industry) tended to be upscale—people and companies well-heeled enough to profit from new business, investment, travel and communications opportunities. That did *not*, however, include corporate America as an across-the-board category. Surveys during 1987–88 found many corporate leaders giving deregulation only qualified support. Business executives endorsed trucking deregulation because it lowered their shipping costs (although truckers themselves found the impact chaotic). As for air service, businessmen liked lower fares for advanced bookings, but complained about delays, safety and the general rise in fares for those traveling on short notice.

Reductions in health, safety and environmental regulation were also controversial within the business community. *The Wall Street Journal* had summed up the predicament in 1983 with a front-page story entitled "Federal Deregulation Runs into a Backlash, Even from Business."[37] Well-established companies often supported the status quo for a good commercial reason: having invested heavily to satisfy existing regulatory requirements, they wanted their competitors equally burdened. Officials of Vice President George Bush's Regulatory Relief Task Force admitted that there were corporate losers as well as corporate winners in most regulatory issues.[38]

The same could be said on many issues of economic deregulation. Darwinism's merits divided the business community. Retooling the economy might be desirable, but not chaos or speculation. Middle- and upper-bracket individuals and organizations launching new-niche enterprises were the greatest beneficiaries of deregulation. Many established concerns were of mixed mind.

Balancing the books isn't easy. Judgments of deregulation will probably always be in dispute because they involve so many dimensions—the overall benefit of restructuring to the national economy, social and regional fairness, consumer costs, and even physical and financial safety. But by 1989 deregulation's effect on the distribution of income—maximum profits to those well-off and frequent pain or dislocation for low-income and rural Americans—was of a piece with other Reagan-era economic policies and beginning to stir reform demands. While the economically strong thrived mounting numbers of rural poor, turned homeless, were drifting west, and the urban underclasses, also losers from Darwinian economic policies, largely stagnated. As the Reagan years ended, there were calls for new regulation of the airlines (where emerging route monopolies were raising fares), for a new regulatory framework for financial institutions, for a housing policy, and for a national policy on mergers, takeovers and leveraged buyouts to control *that* frenzy. As we shall see, academicians were already starting to discuss the possibility that the 1990s would be another of those decades in which extremes of deregulation would be followed by a regulatory wave.

## MONEY AND DEBT: THE FOURTH LEVER

With few exceptions, Republican constituency politics has supported the creditor class in a variety of ways—by securing the interests of bondholders, upholding or reestablishing the gold standard, orchestrating disinflation, shrinking the money supply or bringing about high real interest rates.

The roots of this conservative bias go back to the 1790s, when the governing Federalists, being the party of bankers and merchants, sought to ensure national financial credibility. But if the concern for financial integrity was valid, the principal policy embraced was redistributive—the decision by Congress in 1790 to honor the Revolutionary War indebtedness of both the (national) Continental Congress *and* the states. Before Alexander Hamilton drew up his plan, the $40 million in bonds and notes issued during the Revolution—selling at ten to twenty cents on the dollar because of their dubious prospects—were largely in the hands of speculators. Raising the money to pay the interest on the debt required the federal government to lay heavy taxes on the people, most of whom were farmers, not bondholders.[39]

The Federalists had also pleased America's commercial classes by setting up a national bank, initiating a controversy that would recur for over a century because national banks of that era were seen as instruments of the rich. So deep was this feeling that the rival Jeffersonians, in power when the bank's charter expired in 1811, refused to renew it, although the pressures of the War of 1812 soon forced them to establish a new bank. In 1828 Jackson was elected partly by condemning the Second Bank of the United States and the money power behind it. Jackson saw national politics as a conflict between "real people" and the financial interests, and in 1832, when he drafted a message to the U.S. Senate vetoing a charter extension for the Second Bank of the United States, Jackson fixed his complaint on the bank's benefit to a small Northeastern and foreign elite:

> The many millions which this act proposes to bestow on the stockholders of the existing bank must come directly or indirectly out of the earnings of the American people . . . of the twenty-eight millions of private stock in the corporation, $8,405,000 were held by foreigners, mostly of Great Britain. The amount of stock held in the nine Western and Southwestern States is $140,200, and in the four Southern States is $5,623,100, and in the Middle and Eastern States is $13,522,000. . . . As little stock is held in the West, it is obvious that the debt of the people in that section to the bank is principally a debt to the Eastern and foreign stockholders; that the interest they pay upon it is carried into the Eastern States and into Europe, and that it is a burden upon their industry and a drain of their currency, which no country can bear without inconvenience and occasional distress.[40]

Lincoln and the Republicans would become heirs to the Federalists and Whigs—and to their commercial loyalties and practices. By contrast, early nineteenth-century Jeffersonian and Jacksonian Democrats had been so suspicious of state finance that they opposed federal debt per se, believing that its inherent dynamics—paying interest to Eastern and international commercial and financial classes from taxes levied on land and agriculture—worked against the common man.* Jackson, as standard bearer of this philosophy, did more than veto the national bank; he also paid down the federal debt, rejoicing at its extinction, a position national Democratic platforms would restate from 1840 to 1860. Their economic alternative to borrowing was to allow state banks to print up a mildly inflationary abundance of paper currency, thereby promoting economic expansion without high-interest-bearing debt that rewarded the commercial and creditor classes allied with the political opposition.

The Civil War, of course, broke down the old Whig-Democratic party system with its overtones of economic class

---

* That thesis, ironically, would become relevant again during the Reagan era, as discussed on p. 90.

conflict, creating instead a predominantly sectional rivalry. The sectional parties that resulted—Republicans in the North, Tory Democrats in the South—restored the commercial and creditor classes to preeminence both above and below the Mason-Dixon line, a degree of control they had not enjoyed since Alexander Hamilton's day.

This was not the premise on which the new Republican era had begun. Civil War Republicanism, in fact, had displayed repeated radical overtones, unnerving genuine conservatives. Within two and a half years after Abraham Lincoln's inauguration in 1861, the new Republican administration would (1) strike a blow against property and planter wealth by freeing the slaves in the Confederate States; (2) impose the first U.S. income tax; (3) take on what would total $2.5 billion of debt to finance the Civil War; and (4) inflate prices some 75 percent from 1861 to 1864 by suspending the currency's gold convertibility and printing up huge quantities of nonconvertible greenbacks. The established order was being shaken—mightily.

Nevertheless, when the war was over, the new Republican elite quickly clarified its loyalties in ways Hamilton would have understood. First, Washington would begin paying down the massive $2.5 billion of Civil War debt in hard currency, lavishly rewarding Civil War creditors; and, second, it would shrink the huge supply of Civil War greenbacks, partially replacing them with new deflationary national bank notes and then, ultimately, with gold.

The Civil War, as historian Charles Beard observed sixty years later, confirmed Hamilton's lesson of how government debt and currency management could be applied to bind creditors to the party—earlier the Federalists, now the Republicans—which was undertaking the favorable repayment of their principal and interest. Of the mechanisms and methodologies involved, several were predictable. In 1863 the Republicans had instituted a new national banking system, and in 1865 they abolished the (inflationary) currency that state banks had printed by taxing it out of existence. Most important was the decision to strengthen the dollar and eventually redeem it in gold. The effect was to shrink the amount of currency in circulation between 1865 and the mid-1870s. Agricultural and mineral commodity prices fell;

bond prices rose; and investors redirected money in new and profitable directions—out of agriculture and into railroads and manufacturing.

Deflation's enormous redistributive impact can best be explained by an illustration. Hypothesize that a thousand farmers represent the entire population, a thousand dollars the entire national money supply and a thousand bushels of wheat the entire production of the economy. A bushel of wheat, in this situation, should sell for one dollar. If all three figures expand to two thousand over several generations, the per-bushel price should still be one dollar. However, should the population and wheat production double to two thousand while the currency was kept constant at just one thousand dollars, then the two thousand bushels of wheat would, necessarily, drop from a dollar each to sell at only fifty cents each. Farmers would find their income collapsing, while their old debts would become a hopeless burden—being repayable in dollars that had twice as much purchasing power as those originally borrowed. This is essentially what happened during the quarter century after the Civil War—a slow contraction that one historian fairly described as "a blessing to banker-creditors" but "a cruel and exploitive burden on the nation's producer-debtors."[41]

This deliberate deflation has no parallel in U.S. history. The per capita money supply, for example, fell from $30.35 in 1865 to $25.72 in 1866 (with the return of the Confederacy into the national economy) and then to $17.51 in 1876.[42] Prices, meanwhile, dropped more sharply. The general price index (using 1910–14 as 100) slid from 174 in 1866 down to 90 in 1879 and then hit a low of 68–70 in the mid-1890s. Not surprisingly, farm commodities fell even more steeply than the rest of the index. Wheat tumbled from $2.06 a bushel in 1866 to a dollar in 1876 and eighty cents by the mid-eighties. By the 1890s wheat had fallen to sixty cents, and many farmers in the Dakotas had to settle for much less. Collapsing corn prices traced a similar downcurve—from sixty-six cents a bushel in 1866 to under thirty cents in the 1890s. Prices in Kansas dipped to as low as ten cents a bushel.

Rural families agonized as the shrinking money supply forced down farm commodity prices while bankers, creditors and bondholders could fill their humidors with bigger and better cigars; bonds, in particular, climbed in value as the price index fell. Between 1850 and 1892 the number of U.S. millionaires increased by almost a hundredfold—from 50 to 4,047 (see pages 156–59)—as foreign observers marveled.

Capitalists were not the only winners. Much of the time, manufacturing wage earners profited along with bankers and factory owners. Constant (or even slightly reduced) wages wound up buying more, especially for the family dinner table. Plummeting farm prices and incomes simultaneously raised the relative economic importance of manufacturing within the United States, and the census of 1890 reported a great watershed: for the first time manufactured goods surpassed farm products in value.

For agriculture, hitherto the largest sector of the U.S. economy, America's 1866–96 internal transfer of wealth was literally devastating, especially to cultivators in the less fertile or more debt-encumbered areas. But although huge numbers of farmers were forced into liquidation, few exited gently into the economic twilight. From the early 1870s to 1896 a succession of easy-money political movements fought back in the farmers' behalf—first the Grangers and Greenbackers in the 1870s, then the Populists in the 1880s. Finally, the grand fusion of the Populists and the Democrats under William Jennings Bryan in the 1896 presidential election drew economic battle lines across the entire nation.

Four years before, in 1892, the third-party Populists had drawn a million votes running on an angry platform that decried how "the national power to create money is appropriated to enrich bondholders; a vast public debt payable in legal tender currency has been funded into gold-bearing bonds, thereby adding millions to the burden of the people."[43] Then Bryan himself, in his famous 1896 convention speech, drew the same demarcation, saying, "The question we are to decide is: Upon which side will the Democratic Party fight; upon the side of the 'idle holders of idle capital' or upon the side of the struggling masses."[44] Two decades of massive redistribution of wealth away from rural areas had made "the money issue" come alive in the United States as it never would again.

Luckily, Bryan's narrow defeat was followed by a boon for deflation-troubled farmers—new goldfields in North America

and South Africa would double the world's stock of gold by
the outbreak of World War I. Inflation rose, just as it had in
sixteenth-century Europe as Spanish treasure fleets brought
home New World gold and silver from the mines of the Aztecs
and Incas, and rising prices brought relative prosperity back to
the American countryside.

By comparison, the disinflationary policies and pressures of
the 1920s were pale stuff. Post–World War I deflation was
principally sectoral, and procreditor policies were different. During the Great War, the United States had loaned billions of
dollars to Britain and France and become a creditor nation, so
that Coolidge-era Republican policymakers' strict insistence on
repayment of debt was a matter of *external* rather than *internal*
economics—of monies being transferred to New York from
Paris and London, not from Missouri and Minnesota.

Republican economic policy during the 1920s also avoided
national bank or currency management issues, largely because
the Federal Reserve System set up in 1913 under the Democratic
administration of Woodrow Wilson assumed those responsibilities. And because the economy's boom-bust cycle had already
occurred while Democrats were in the White House—first, the
wartime inflation of 1917–19, then the collapsing prices of the
severe 1920–21 recession—the Republicans coming to power in
March 1921 weren't obliged to disinflate the economy as in
post–Civil War days. The decade's problem was mostly in agriculture, where farmers remained "trapped by deflated prices and
gutted markets" and farm families' share of U.S. national in
come dropped from 15 percent in 1920 to just 9 percent in 1928.[45]

But farm problems were less traumatic in the 1920s than they
had been a half century before, and monetary policy also provoked much less of a national debate—until the 1929 crash.
Then, as the Depression took hold, the Hoover administration
and the Federal Reserve insisted that economic weakness would
just have to work itself out without countercyclical help from
the Fed, and Republican treasury secretary Andrew Mellon
made his famous observation that the road to recovery lay in a
bitter Darwinian purgative: "Liquidate labor, liquidate stocks,
liquidate real estate . . . values will be adjusted, and enterprising
people will pick up the wreck from less-competent people."[46]

This philosophy failed, and as politics was turned on its head in 1930–32, economists began to focus on maldistribution of wealth as a cause of the great downturn. Republican prosperity, the theory went, had not spread deeply enough either to support purchasing power (especially on the farms) or to put a solid framework under the economy or the soaring, speculative stock market of 1927–29. Valid or not, the thesis was widely voiced by economists, farm leaders, and even the new chairman of the Federal Reserve Board, Utah banker Marriner Eccles:

> In the 1920s, our economy was generally prosperous, not, however, without ups and downs nor without dark spots in different industries. Agriculture was not prospering. The coal industry was sick. While the national income rose to high levels, it was so distributed that the incomes of the majority of families were entirely inadequate and business activity was sustained only by a rapid and unsound increase in the private debt structure, including ever-increasing installment buying of consumption.[47]

By the time of Franklin Roosevelt's inauguration in 1933, the peripheries of Democratic politics were once again humming with demands for inflationary money-supply expansion and wealth redistribution: Huey Long's Share the Wealth crusade; Upton Sinclair's end-poverty movement; the Townsend Plan (for old age pensions) and others. The directional change, if not the specifics, would prove irresistible. Once in power, the new Democratic administration abolished the gold standard, sharply reducing the value of the dollar and promoting some inflation. Bank interest rates came down and tax rates rose. In 1936 Roosevelt himself proposed capping incomes. But even without such measures the record share of national income and wealth the top strata of Americans had enjoyed in 1929 began a slow but steady decline that would extend some forty years.*

* Most of the decline took place by World War II. Between 1929 and 1948 the share of total U.S. personal income received by the 5 percent of Americans with the highest incomes fell from nearly a third to less than a fifth of the total. Dividends, interest and rent—the characteristic income of the wealthy—dropped from 22 percent to just over 12 percent of total family personal income. Income from wages, salaries and pensions climbed from 61 percent to 71 percent (Selma Goldsmith, George Jaszi, Hyman Kaitz and Maurice Liebenberg, "Size and Distribution of Income Since the Mid-Thirties," *The Review of Economics and Statistics*, February 1954, pp. 16, 18).

Fifty years would pass before the next enduring era of conservative finance in the 1980s. As we have seen, Carter laid the
groundwork with his appointment in 1979 of Paul Volcker as
chairman of the Federal Reserve Board, as well as his approval
of the 1980 financial deregulation that allowed interest rates—
and upper-bracket interest income—to rise so high.

But it was the Republicans who cultivated ideas that would
modify traditional conservatism as powerfully as the great post–
Civil War Republican deflation and redistribution had done.
Reagan was committed not simply to traditional conservative
politics but to right-wing economic theories and ideologies—
and *to radical combinations of these ideas.* His supply-side and
tax-reduction theories were one thing, but he also followed
Milton Friedman's monetary theology that the money supply
was the key to sound economic management. Ensure that the
money supply expands at no more than 3 to 5 percent a year,
Friedman insisted, and inflation would be minimal. A much
larger increase was what had made inflation soar under Carter.
Monetarism had the additional political appeal of precluding
yet another managerial role for government.

What conservatism needed was a way to reconcile the contradiction between supply-side tax cuts, which put more money
into the system, and simultaneous tight monetary policy, which
squeezed it out. Politically, of course, there was no problem.
Republican constituencies would benefit both from reduced
taxes and from monetarism's squeeze on inflation; the contradiction, in other words, was mainly theoretical, arising from the
assumption that fiscal looseness and monetary tightness could
not work in tandem. Enter Columbia University economics professor Robert Mundell to say "Not so": embracing the two at
the same time might actually be the key to late-twentieth-century
prosperity.

It would be Mundell's footnote in history. Back in 1971 he
had astounded an international monetary conference by chal-
lenging the "neoclassical synthesis" that the way to stop inflation was by raising taxes and cutting spending. This would bring
on a near depression, Mundell argued, and instead he proposed
a very different solution: Combine *loose fiscal policy* (through
tax cuts and large budget deficits) with *tight monetary policy.*
By 1978 Mundell's approach was politically appealing enough

to be picked up by economic publicist Jude Wanniski, whose pro-tax-reduction bible *The Way the World Works* gave Mundell a spotlight second in wattage only to tax-cut theorist Arthur Laffer's. From the point of view of GOP constituencies, the Columbia professor had provided a framework for joining three important preferences: high interest rates and tax cuts, as well as large deficits that allowed the government to spend for the benefit of favored constituencies.

By 1981–82, Mundell's abstraction had become Washington's reality. On the monetary side, the Federal Reserve Board, unnerved by the ineffectiveness of its mid-1980 actions against inflation as well as by fears of federal budget deficits, tightened with a vengeance throughout much of 1981 and early 1982. The Republicans went along reluctantly, though they complained that tight money would negate Reagan's tax cuts, and Reagan even talked about abolishing the Fed while Senate Republican leader Howard Baker threatened that Congress might seize the credit reins.[48] Overall, Ronald Reagan's commitment to Milton Friedman's theories kept him behind the Fed's tightening process. Greider recounts how the president's occasional displeasure with the Fed "conveniently overlooked the fact that the President himself—at two crucial junctures in the spring of 1981 and the winter of 1982—had personally pressured the Fed to tighten its control of money. When the Federal Reserve obliged, it inevitably made the recession worse."[49]

Part two of Mundell's equation, loose fiscal policy, became a reality after the 1981 tax cuts. To get Congress to pass the tax legislation the new administration had to hold back estimates of the exploding budget deficit. Treasury official Paul Craig Roberts admitted that "Treasury did not think Congress would pass the tax bill if it seemed that the Administration expected the deficit to grow rather than the economy." That, of course, is what happened. In 1982–83, the tax cuts, while ultimately stimulative, nevertheless cost the government $50 billion to $75 billion a year in lost revenues, and the deficit itself surged toward $200 billion. It was a Mundellian combination, but in a ghoulish context: interest rates persisted in the 10–15 percent *nominal* range and 3–8 percent *real* range, despite falling inflation, because of financial-market and Federal Reserve fears of what a string of $200 billion deficits might mean.

By 1982 tight money had quickly resumed its familiar Republican role, promoting Darwinian restructuring and redistributing wealth and income. The main effect was record federal deficits financed by extremely high real interest rates as Washington borrowed on unfavorable terms. As federal interest payments doubled from $96 billion in 1981 to some $200 billion in 1986, after-inflation interest rates paid by the Treasury reached rarely seen levels.

Historically, the general rate of real interest on U.S. government long-term Treasury bonds is assumed to be about 2 percent. During the 1981–82 recession it rose to an average of 5.2 percent, and hit 6 to 8 percent during 1983. By 1988 the real interest rate on thirty-year Treasuries was still in the 4–5 percent range, a cornucopia for bondholders. Other debt instruments were showing comparable deviations from the past. Over the three decades before the 1980s, for example, the real return on short-term business lending had been 1 percent. During the early and mid 1980s, the real rate of return was about 5 percent.[50] For high-grade long-term corporate securities, the real interest rate averaged 8.2 percent in 1983–84.[51] By 1988 it would still be near 6 percent. The real return on mortgages also moved in the 6–8 percent range from 1982 on. There had been nothing like it since the 1920s, when real interest rates had been roughly comparable—about 5 percent in long-term Treasury bonds.[52]

Returns like these, of course, made for widening income disparities. Even after inflation's back had been broken (in 1982), real interest rates stayed unusually high for several reasons: deregulation, Federal Reserve policy, the financial markets' genuine concern about deficits and foreign creditors' demand for good returns. But investors weren't complaining. The Shearson Lehman Government/Corporate Bond Index, combining interest income and price appreciation to come up with overall bond returns, calculated them at 18.5 percent per annum during 1981–85, making this the most lucrative period of the century for holders of debt securities.

As the percentage of national income represented by wages and salaries shrank during the early 1980s, the relative contribution of interest soared. In 1982 combined public and private interest payments rose to a record share of national income—$366 billion, or 14 percent, not much below the $374 billion dispensed through such income transfer payments as Social Security, veterans' pensions, welfare and the like. Almost half of the $366 billion flowed from the steep rise in interest rates between 1979 and 1982. Using a broader government measurement, by 1984 interest payments and stock dividends combined would total 20 percent of national income, up from 11 percent in 1979.[53] By 1988 even such conservatives as George Will were concerned about a "rentier" society in the making. The benefits of high interest were abetted, of course, by the declining effective tax rate on dividend and interest income. The explosion of after-tax unearned income for the top 1 percent of Americans was just that—an explosion.

Meanwhile, tight money was hurting the economy elsewhere. As personal income from interest grew by 67 percent between 1979 and 1982, industrial production was shrinking by nearly 12 percent, housing was in agony, and the extractive sectors—agriculture, timber, oil and gas, mining—were beginning what would be a 1982–86 depression.

Raw material costs fell 40 percent from their 1980 peaks. Food commodity prices peaked in early 1984, and declined by some 12 percent over the next year and a half, although government subsidy programs mitigated the impact. In 1986 the per barrel price of West Texas crude, as high as $38 in 1981, touched a low of $10. Back in the 1890s, the impact of deflation on the copper industry had prompted many mine owners to pour funds into the political campaigns of William Jennings Bryan and other easy-money Democrats. Ninety years later copper had little political reach beyond Arizona and Montana, but the oil and gas industry would become a force for reflation.

So would other sectors hurt by deflation, such as basic manufacturing (ranging from steel and textiles to machinery) and housing. All skirted disaster as tight money favored the financial sector and owners of financial assets. In 1982, at the peak of the credit crunch, home builders felt so threatened that the Kentucky Homebuilders Association distributed "Wanted" posters with photos of the seven governors of the Federal Reserve system. The charge: "premeditated and calculated cold-blooded murder of millions of small businesses." Together with the national associations of realtors and auto dealers, the home builders distributed anti-Fed lapel stickers in the shape of a hangman's noose. By 1985 national median prices for houses would be lower, adjusted for inflation, than they had been in 1979. Back in 1982, Murray Weidenbaum, chairman of the President's Council of Economic Advisers, had predicted that disinflation would bring "a major redistribution of wealth" and among the losers would be the American homeowner.[54] Across broad swaths of America, at least, that proved true.*

By 1985 Reagan's high-deficit, high-interest-rate policies had so strengthened the dollar that American industry and agriculture were in a trap. Politicians and business leaders agreed that the currency-based competitiveness of foreign products, including agricultural commodities, had gone too far. It wasn't just that foreign cars threatened Michigan or that Hong Kong textiles scared South Carolina; even the Farm Belt was being invaded by cheap foreign commodities like wheat and hogs. The dollar had to be lowered to save U.S. manufacturing and agriculture, and the devaluation that began in 1985 was precedent-shattering. First the markets, and then government strategists, drove the dollar down from a high of 262 Japanese yen in early 1985 to maximums of 202 in 1986, 159 in 1987 and 137 in 1988. By 1987–88, devaluation and reflation started the financial markets worrying about inflation again, although enough deflationary forces remained to act as a restraint.

This reflationary turnabout was important politically as well as economically. The peacetime federal budget deficits, reexpanded money supply and devalued currency of 1985–87 added up to a major break with GOP tradition. True, earlier Republican administrations had occasionally presided over oblique moves toward cheaper money—the Sherman Silver Purchase Act of 1890, the Federal Reserve's easy-money policy during 1927, Richard Nixon's decision in 1970–71 to close the U.S. "gold window" and cheapen the dollar. Yet the stimulus applied to the U.S. economy during the second Reagan administration was much larger (its best parallel was under the Democrats in 1933–37, when Franklin D. Roosevelt devalued the dollar by going

---

* In manufacturing and agricultural areas, weak housing prices provided a follow-up blow to troubled families. By contrast, in suburban, center-city and resort communities attracting the expanding financial and service elites, home prices soared. Trends in housing values became a major wealth redistributive force during the 1980s (see pp. 183–84 and Appendix I).

off the gold standard and also ran unprecedented budget deficits that were 6 percent of peacetime GNP).*

Superficially, at least, the effects of this reversal were mildly New Dealish. Money flooded the system. Agriculture, energy and basic manufacturing began recovering. Farmland values, declining since 1981, hit bottom in 1987 and began rising, and Rust Belt manufacturing surged as the falling dollar made regional products competitive again. The outlook in the Oil Patch also brightened as petroleum recovered from its 1986 low and stayed in the $15 to $20 range throughout most of 1987–88. Even so, analysts argued, much of the liquidity put in circulation was more than the weak "real economy" could use. Much of it found its way into finance—takeovers, mergers and the stock market—and then into upper-bracket life-style asset prices (housing, art). Real interest rates stayed surprisingly high, and the stock market soared—at least until October 19, 1987. So long as the financial sector boomed, much of the stimulus being fed into the economy continued to favor upper-bracket Americans.

One of the most egregious misperceptions of late twentieth-century politics is to associate only Democrats with extremes of debt and abusive debt practices. As we have seen, before 1933 it was the conservatives—Federalists, Whigs and Republicans alike—who sponsored government indebtedness and used high interest payments to redistribute wealth upward. In the late nineteenth century and again during the 1920s, Republican administrations were also responsible for two particularly notable periods of high real interest rates and innovative, ultimately precarious *private* debt expansion. In the more extreme example of the 1920s, individual, consumer and corporate debt kept setting record levels, aided by new techniques like installment purchases and margin debt for purchasing securities. Personal debt expanded by about 50 percent between 1922 and 1929,

* During the twentieth century, Republican and Democratic administrations generally have faced different economic challenges and pursued different policies. Democratic regimes, taking office when Republicans had left the economy weak, applied stimulus that often turned into inflation; Republican administrations, working to suppress inflation, have been in power for a disproportionate number of this century's recessions. Ronald Reagan, who voted four times for Franklin D. Roosevelt but hung Calvin Coolidge's portrait in the White House, broke precedent and mixed the two patterns.

and by 1930, as the Depression was getting under way, debt servicing alone accounted for nearly 10 percent of the GNP.[55]

In the kindred eighties, household debt climbed to over $3 trillion, while U.S. nonfinancial corporate indebtedness more than doubled to $2 trillion (with 25 percent of cash flow being used for debt service), following a well-worn track. And just as they had sixty years earlier, new varieties of debt became an art form. The financial community pioneered hundreds, from OIDS (original issue discount securities) to PIKS (payment in kind securities—bonds that pay additional bonds as interest). Led by Merrill Lynch and First Boston, Wall Street even turned car loans, boat loans, credit-card bills and recreational vehicle loans into "asset-backed securities," prompting one investment banker to joke that the only type of consumer credit untouched by this trend was "watches and jewelry at pawnshops."[56] Federal government fiscal strategists were equally loose. In part to avoid the deficit reduction mandates of the Gramm-Rudman-Hollings Act, they allowed federal credit programs to balloon from $300 billion in 1984 to $500 billion in 1989. The 1988–89 savings and loan bailout was more of the same.

The conservative commitment to expansive debt arises partly from a praiseworthy desire to promote commerce. Heyday capitalism requires heyday financing. But from the less flattering perspective provided by the post–Civil War period, the 1920s and the 1980s, deflation in weak sectors of the economy (agriculture, extractive industries and old-line manufacturing) has provided a convenient safety valve for an otherwise inflationary expansion of liquidity and debt in other sectors, particularly finance. Deflation in the heartland offsets expansion in finance, creating a relatively noninflationary national average. Philadelphia financial columnist J. R. Livingston, writing in 1986, had seen the parallel to the 1920s. "Then as now, banks, investment houses and brokerage firms created the debt that made money-making excursions in Wall Street possible. Money was used primarily to make money, not to produce goods and services and raise people's living standards."[57] The leveraged buyout and corporate restructuring under Reagan worked the same way. Few phenomena have been so repeatedly lucrative for Upper America as noninflationary liquidity coursing through rising stock markets.

As the Reagan era drew to a close in 1989 official statistics suggested that conservative policies had once again accelerated the concentration of income and wealth in the United States among those already favored.* However, in contrast to previous heydays, the debt strategies involved did not simply rearrange assets internally but transferred some overseas. Also, the U.S. share of world GNP had grown during the Gilded Age and again during the 1920s. The late 1980s, however, marked a significant downward movement in the United States' share of the world's industrial economies. By common measurement, the United States' share of world GNP fell from about 40 percent in the 1950s to under 30 percent in the 1970s. Currency gyrations complicated measurements during the 1980s, but in 1989 economists began predicting that the U.S. percentage of world GNP would drop to 25 percent during the 1990s for the first time since 1914. The excesses of prior heydays, whatever their effect on the distribution of wealth, had not interrupted America's rise to world economic leadership. The policies of the 1980s, by contrast, raised new questions about the role of heyday greed and the migration of wealth to other shores.

* The policies discussed in this chapter, while by far the most important, are certainly not exhaustive. Liberal economists and politicians made similar charges with respect to the massive 1988–89 savings-and-loan bailout, in which favored billionaires got to purchase bankrupt S&Ls under lucrative terms while taxpayers in general bore the costs of the bailout. By 1989 others were saying the same thing about Republican devices for harnessing the World Bank—partly supported by U.S. taxpayers—to help ensure the repayment of the roughly $100 billion of Latin American loans made by major U.S. banks.

# Chapter

**5**

## America's Shrinking Share
## of Global Wealth

They say the U.S. has had its day in the sun; that our nation
has passed its zenith. They expect you to tell your children . . .
that the future will be one of sacrifice and few opportunities. My
fellow Americans, I utterly reject that view.

—RONALD REAGAN, JULY 17, 1980

A great transfer of power is taking place in the world economy.
The center of economic power is shifting away from America,
much as it shifted from Bruges to Venice at the close of the 13th
Century or from Great Britain to the United States in this century.

—FRENCH ECONOMIC HISTORIAN
JACQUES ATTALI, 1987

When the history of this period is written, historians are going
to marvel at a great power surrendering its economic might with
so little resistance.

—HARVARD BUSINESS SCHOOL PROFESSOR
CAROL GREENWALD, 1988

America's loss of economic power accelerated during the 1980s
and was reflected in rising U.S. international debt and asset sales.
By 1989 wealth was on the move *globally*, and the domestic
consequences were profound.

Until mid-decade, most Americans hadn't paid much attention to the mildly disconcerting statistics churned out by federal
and international agencies. But by late 1987 voters had begun
to fear foreign investment and takeovers of U.S. corporations
and real estate. The future treasury secretary Nicholas Brady

blamed the October stock market crash partly on the leverage exercised by Japanese investors over U.S. capital markets. Most Americans continued to assume that their own nation was still the economic leader, but nervousness about the economic future was quickening.

Back in the autumn of 1987 Genshiro Kawamoto, architect of a billion-dollar Tokyo real estate fortune, had begun cruising the streets of Honolulu, identifying attractive properties from the backseat of a long white Rolls-Royce. Often he simply pointed. By March 1988, when he had bought 113 homes and condominiums, local radio talk-show hosts were making guesses where the "Kawamotomobile" would visit next. Press interest crested in April as Honolulu realtors gave surprised Mainland journalists an update: Kawamoto's Hawaiian holdings had jumped to 160 houses. Among them was industrialist Henry Kaiser's seaside barony of mansion, pool and tennis courts purchased for over $40 million, reputedly the highest price ever paid for a residential property in the United States.

Kawamoto seemed to think of it as petty cash. He told *The Boston Globe*, "with a chuckle," that by Japanese real estate standards, they were "almost free."[1] And reading about Kawamoto, the average American started to grasp a little better what Hawaiians confronted daily: that the United States was losing relative purchasing power on a grand scale. There might be more wealthy Americans than ever before, but foreigners—the Japanese especially—commanded greater resources, and on a scale that silenced even Manhattan investment bankers.

Table 5 shows how Japan's share of world GNP—climbing steadily in the Reagan years—accelerated during the late 1980s as the U.S. share fell. Other measurements of comparative economic size displayed similar trends. But what we are really talking about is *wealth—assets*, not income—and these yardsticks are not part of gross national product calculations. This, however, was where Japan was beginning to pull ahead. In 1987 that year's increase in the value of Japanese stocks and real estate itself exceeded the Japanese GNP. And in mid-1989 Japan's top economic daily, *Nihon Keizai Shimbun*, using figures from the U.S. Federal Reserve Board and Japan's Economic Planning Agency, proclaimed that *even in 1987* Japan surpassed

TABLE 5

THE LATE-TWENTIETH-CENTURY WEALTH REALIGNMENT

| Comparative National Assets* (trillions of U.S. dollars) | 1985 | 1986 | 1987 |
|---|---|---|---|
| U.S. | $30.6 | $34.0 | $36.2 |
| Japan | 19.6 | 28.3 | 43.7 |

* Financial assets (stocks, bonds, deposits, insurance, etc.) plus actual assets, including production facilities, housing, land and inventories. Estimated by Nihon Keizai Shimbun.

| National Shares of World GNP | 1987* | 1988* | 1990† | 1995† | 2000† |
|---|---|---|---|---|---|
| U.S. | 30% | 28% | 26.0% | 23.8% | 22.2% |
| Japan | 13% | 15% | 15.8% | 16.5% | 16.3% |

* Estimates based on tabulating individual national GNP data in the World Bank Atlas 1989, allowing for incomplete statistics from the Soviet bloc and elsewhere, and calculating the U.S. and Japanese shares.
† Projections in Nomura Medium-Term Outlook for Japan and the World (1989).

the United States in national assets with $43.7 trillion worth of land, factories, stocks and other wealth to $36.2 trillion for the United States.[2] Table 5 shows the extraordinary 1985–87 turnabout.

Another view of how far the balance had already swung was explained just after the 1988 election by Kenichi Ohmai, Tokyo manager for McKinsey & Company:

Some of America's most competitive "exports" today are land, houses and companies. But they are becoming too cheap. To realize how out of balance things are, consider this: If you collateralized a good-sized Tokyo office building, you could buy a $1 billion company in the U.S. In fact, the real-estate value of Tokyo at $7.7 trillion is so high that, once collateralized and borrowed against (at 80% of current value), it could buy all the land in the U.S. for $3.7 trillion, and all the companies on the New York Stock Exchange, NASDAQ and several other exchanges for $2.6 trillion.[3]

## TABLE 6

### DECLINING IMPORTANCE OF AMERICAN BILLIONAIRES

*Top 25 Billionaires 1989*
*(in billions of U.S.dollars)*

1. Yoshiaki Tsutsumi, Japan, $15
2. Taikichiro Mori, Japan, $14.2
3. Sam Walton, U.S., $8.2
4. Reichmann Brothers, Canada, $8
   Shin Kyuk-Ho, Korea, $8
6. Hirotomo Takei and family, Japan, $7.8
7. Kitaro Watanabe, Japan, $7+
8. Haruhiko Yoshimoto and family, Japan, $7
   Hans and Gad Rausing, Sweden, $7
10. Eitaro Itoyama, Japan, $6.6
11. Kenneth Roy Thomson, Canada, $6
12. Kenkichi Nakajima, Japan, $5.8
13. Brenninkmeyer family, Holland, $5
14. Kenneth Colin Irving, Canada, $4.5
15. Takenaka family, Japan, $4
16. Giovanni Agnelli and family, Italy, $3.7
17. Mohn family, W. Germany, $3.6
18. Warren Edward Buffett, U.S., $3.5
19. John Warner Kluge, U.S., $3.2
20. Pablo Escobar Gaviria, Colombia, $3+
    Gerald Cavendish Grosvenor, Great Britain, $3+
22. Ramon Areces, Spain, $3
    Friedrich Karl Flick, West Germany, $3
    Henry Ross Perot, U.S., $3
    Keizo Saji, Japan, $3

Source: *Forbes* magazine, July 24, 1989

At the top of *Forbes* magazine's 1989 profile of the world's billionaires were real estate and transportation entrepreneur Yoshiaki Tsutsumi ($15 billion) and downtown-Tokyo real estate magnate Taikichiro Mori ($14.2 billion).[4] Of the twenty-five richest men or families in the world as of the beginning of the year, only four were Americans, as Table 6 shows. Nine were Japanese, seven were Europeans, three were Canadians, one was a Korean, and the last, Pablo Escobar Gaviria, was the head of Colombia's Medellín cocaine cartel. In absolute numbers, the United States still had the largest number of billionaires, but on a population-adjusted per capita basis, Japan, West Germany and Canada were ahead, a far cry from the U.S. dominance of world billionaire ranks in the early 1980s. The days were long gone when Americans sitting in foreign hotel lounges could scoff at the local currency by joking, "How much is that in real money?" By 1989 a million U.S. dollars commanded a lot more respect in Wichita, Kansas—deceptively, perhaps—than in sophisticated telex-and-quotron precincts of Tokyo, Frankfurt, London, Paris and Zurich (or New York).* The realignment of global wealth was making mere dollar millionaires an outdated elite, and Washington policies bore much of the blame.

## THE SACRIFICE OF
## AMERICAN ECONOMIC INDEPENDENCE

This shift reflected the inevitable ebb of America's postwar preeminence. Yet the same Reagan policies that moved America's wealth internally also accelerated the shift of world wealth, beginning with the budget deficits of the early 1980s but intensifying after the ensuing devaluation of the U.S. dollar from 1985 to 1987.

The underlying problem was the Reagan administration's need to borrow huge sums of money at high interest rates to fund the 1981 tax cuts, the defense buildup and 1981–82 recession spending. To avert the feared inflationary effects, the Federal Reserve Board in 1981 and 1982 raised U.S. interest rates to high real levels. With U.S. bonds paying 15 percent while equivalent instruments in Germany and Japan returned only 5 percent or 6 percent, capital poured into the United States. As foreigners bought dollars to invest in U.S. debt, the dollar soared against other currencies.

Perversely, Reagan insisted that America's currency was

---

* One is reminded of circa 1950 British retirees and executives living in Tunbridge Wells or Gloucestershire on £1,500 a year—a respectable high-caste sum by 1939 standards—who could not appreciate how lower-middle-class ($4,200) their income seemed to Americans of the Korean War era.

strong again largely because America itself was strong again, ignoring the role of high interest rates. Meanwhile the strong dollar brought accumulating problems. By February 1985, with the British pound and U.S. dollar nudging parity, London merchants were besieged by credit-card-waving Americans anxious to plunder Belgravia and Savile Row. Harrods department store set up a toll-free U.S. "800" number. However, the overpriced dollar so pleasing to antiques buyers and Wedgwood collectors was also breaking the back of U.S. world trade. As we have seen, chief executives of export-dependent U.S. corporations—Eastman Kodak, Caterpillar and suchlike—visited the White House to plead for relief. Dollar-priced exports were too expensive, they said, so overseas sales were crashing. Artificially cheap imports were also capturing domestic markets, and without devaluation American manufacturing would be destroyed.

That devaluation came soon enough, as the dollar began to slide in March 1985. Six months later, a historic meeting of the Group of Five finance ministers at New York's Plaza Hotel transformed that downward slippage into policy. In the eyes of the U.S. Treasury, currency depreciation substituted for more aggressive trade policy, and within two years, as the U.S. currency had lost half its February 1985 value against the Japanese yen and the West German deutsche mark, world economic rankings began to shift. *This* was the watershed. As U.S. prices fell, international shopping traffic shifted. Foreign investors holding U.S. bonds might be losing billions as the dollar plummeted, but for many other affluent East Asians and Europeans, the United States was becoming a bargain basement.

By 1988 Harvard's Robert Reich, a sometime policy adviser to Democratic presidential candidate Michael Dukakis, suggested the possibility of a commercial Dunkirk: "With the dollar priced so low, and American companies so uncompetitive, it's as if America announced a fire sale, with everything marked forty percent off the regular price."[5] Peter Canelo, investment strategist at the New York firm of Bear Stearns, observed that "the cheapest place for a foreign industrialist to buy a plant and equipment is on the floor of the New York Stock Exchange."[6] One major Wall Street firm even rose to the opportunity by establishing a "bargain-basement committee" to identify vulnerable U.S. assets for foreign takeover.

In early 1989, shortly after Reagan left office, Democratic congressman Richard Gephardt told what a visit to Japan had shown him about the effects of dollar devaluation: "The people seemed wealthier than they were when I went in 1982," he said. "One Japanese businessman made me understand why. He said: 'Don't you understand why we're buying Honolulu and huge chunks of other American cities? You increased the wealth of Japan vis-à-vis the United States by 100% in one year—without us even lifting a *finger*."

Gephardt went on: "I had never thought of it in those terms before. Because of the Reagan Administration's failed attempt at a quick fix, our greatest economic competitor now has a lot more wealth—a vital tool to create more productivity and wealth."[7]

Meanwhile, as the dollar fell, the comparative level of U.S. wages and per capita incomes also fell. Real living standards based on local purchasing power rather than on global currency shifts showed only a minor shift, to be sure. Yet travel publications began warning Americans of a painful new truth: middle-class Japanese could live like dukes in Los Angeles; middle-class U.S. visitors to Tokyo, by contrast, could either sleep and eat like Japanese clerks or lay out a week's salary per day for thirty-dollar breakfasts and four-hundred-dollar hotel rooms.

Liberal economists echoed fears that both America's share of world wealth and Washington's ability to control ownership of American assets were being devalued along with the once mighty greenback. Lester Thurow, dean of MIT's Sloan School of Management, prophesied in late 1987 that "the epitaph of the Reagan presidency will be: 'When Ronald Reagan became President, the United States was the world's largest *creditor* nation. When he left the presidency, we were the world's largest *debtor* nation.' In 1980, we had a trade account surplus of $166 billion; by August 1987, we had an indebtedness to foreigners of $340 billion."[8] On Reagan's last day in office, that same debt calculus—which we shall revisit shortly—was approximately $500 billion. MIT economist Paul Krugman went so far as to predict that "the political issue of the 1990s is going to be the foreign invasion of the United States."[9]

Admittedly, American cities and states receiving large-scale direct foreign investment welcomed the infusion. In early 1988 the economist for the First Hawaiian Bank called heavy Japanese investment a "net positive" for the state. Local industry was humming, employment was high, and the rapid bidding up of real estate values had increased the net worth of tens of thousands of local homeowners.

The negative aspects were more subtle. Americans and U.S. Hawaiians were becoming second-class economic citizens at the Honolulu Country Club (Japanese-owned) and at yen-oriented luxury hotels. Displaced U.S. executives complained that Japanese owners of major Hawaiian firms were relegating Americans to lower management rungs. The Hawaiian bank economist warned that "it's a kind of test lab for what's facing the whole country. Because of the vagaries of the U.S. economy, this state economy is rushing willy-nilly into the arms of the Japanese...."[10]

Job-hungry Appalachia had fewer qualms because development funds were all too welcome. Tennesseans interviewed in spring 1988 were enthusiastic about Japanese investment, less intensive there than in Hawaii. Names of Japanese donor companies were proliferating on softball T-shirts, Little League uniforms and symphony programs. Newspaper racks in towns straight out of Jack Daniel's whiskey ads had begun carrying Tokyo's *Yomiuri Shimbun* next to the *Lewisburg Tribune* and *Marshall County Gazette*.[11] The immediate local benefit was unmistakable: an infusion of money. From the textile towns of South Carolina to the rolling hills of southern Ohio, foreign investors were helping declining regions of America to reverse their fate. Yet the legendary U.S. investor Warren Buffett said, "We are much like a wealthy family that annually sells acreage so that it can sustain a lifestyle unwarranted by its current output. Until the plantation is gone, it's all pleasure and no pain. In the end, however, the family will have traded the life of an owner for the life of a tenant farmer."[12]

Other skeptics noted that foreign investment created relatively few *new* jobs—about 17,500 a year between 1984 and 1986. Most of the three million Americans who worked for foreign-owned campanies in 1987 held jobs that foreigners had merely acquired, not created.[13] Foreign investment also had some outright drawbacks. Several studies showed that roughly 80 percent of the profits of foreign-owned firms were sent home from the United States to the parent company. Companies in the United States owned by foreigners also used more imported goods than did American businesses, thus increasing the trade deficit. According to a Department of Commerce report, foreign-owned companies in the United States were responsible for almost half the U.S. merchandise trade deficit in 1986 and a net $73.8 billion drain on American trade.[14]

By 1988 broader foreign ambitions were apparent. Author Daniel Burstein quoted Masaaki Kurokawa, head of Japan's Nomura Securities International, who raised with American dinner guests the possibility of turning California into a joint U.S.-Japanese economic community.[15] Japanese officials also discussed California and the U.S. Pacific coast as a potential center for Japanese retirement communities, while Japanese universities and corporations were starting to buy up U.S. colleges—Loretto Heights in Colorado, Warner Pacific in Oregon—as offshore facilities for educating their nation's young people.[16]

Dependence on overseas capital was nothing new, of course. In the late nineteenth century, when a youthful United States was borrowing to build railroads and factories, U.S. bankers welcomed foreign investors, even though foreign capital meant high interest rates, which meant pain to some sectors, particularly farmers. In his famous 1896 speech to the Democratic National Convention, William Jennings Bryan attacked British financiers, as well as America's own gold standard. But by the 1920s things were different. The United States had emerged from the war as a major international creditor, and postwar financial markets reflected this new situation.

When America's seventy-year status as a creditor nation came to an end, under Ronald Reagan, it was surprising how quickly U.S. indebtedness and foreign influence mounted to record levels. During the late 1980s the United States borrowed from abroad over 3 percent of national income, well above the prior peaks of 1866–73 (2.2 percent) and 1882–93 (1.1 percent) during America's industrial youth.[17] By 1988 U.S. manufacturing assets were over 12 percent foreign-controlled,* exceeding the pre–World War I record levels of 7 to 8 percent.[18] Still worse, late-nineteenth-century indebtedness had been undertaken to expand production, but much of what America borrowed in the 1980s was spent on consumption.

The public was concerned about America's international weakness even before Ronald Reagan's election. Voters sensed the problem in 1980, when they replaced Jimmy Carter with the more aggressive Reagan, which intensified Reagan's commitment to make the United States strong and respected again.

But for reasons we have seen, the great things promised were not delivered. Reagan was unable to reconstruct the circumstances of prior capitalist heydays, when America was rising to world leadership. Reagan would seek less to cope with U.S. world decline than to deny it by reenacting past glories. In economic policy, this included the conspicuous accumulation and display of wealth, invocation of the late nineteenth century's overseas borrowing to build U.S. industry, and mimicry of the tax cuts and stock market boom of the 1920s. It resembled what the British historian Arnold Toynbee called a Shadow Empire— the reveries of a declining nation trying to revisit the counting-houses and parade grounds of its triumphant zenith.† "America is back," Ronald Reagan would claim by 1983–84 after cutting taxes, deregulating the economy and rebuilding U.S. armed forces, and insofar as prestige and military power mattered, he was right. Yet, economically, America by 1989 was weakening in everything from chemicals and electronics to banking and capital markets. But as other nations began to take the lead, with disturbing implications for future generations, few politicians wanted to confront these portents.

---

* Broader assets tabulations also suggested a record foreign ownership in the 1980s. According to a mid-1987 Associated Press calculation from Commerce Department and Federal Reserve figures, by the end of 1986 foreigners' holdings constituted a little less than 8 percent of America's tangible assets—land, buildings, equipment and so on. Back in 1897 foreign holdings had been only half as great—a little less than 4 percent of the nation's tangible assets. In those days, foreign investors had mostly just bought bonds; they were willing to settle for paper claims.

† For a 1981 analysis of how Shadow Empire attitudes, pronouncements and politics were explicit from the beginning in the Reagan Coalition, see pp. 3–17 of my 1982 book, *Post-Conservative America*.

## GLOBAL DARWINISM AND THE
## MEASUREMENT OF AMERICAN
## ECONOMIC DECLINE

The Reagan administration's commitment to deregulated markets and free movement of capital came at a time when large numbers of American industries, hegemonies, vocations and jobs were at risk to foreign economies more youthful than America's or less in debt, principally Japan and other East Asian nations. Parts of the United States—important sectors, industries and communities—underwent commercial revitalization or at least made a lot of money. Yet the overall 1981–88 economic data seemed more negative: within the world economy the Reagan years showed at least *relative* American decline.

In 1988 the Washington-based Council on Competitiveness estimated that the U.S. standard-of-living index had increased by only 8 percent since 1972, just one fourth as much as the average gain of the other six major industrial nations (West Germany, France, Italy, Britain, Canada and Japan) and only one seventh as much as Japan. In absolute terms, as Appendix G shows, the council's estimates put the United States behind West Germany and barely ahead of the rest of Western Europe.[19]

Relative to the major industrial nations, unadjusted U.S. per capita GNP trends were even more ominous, especially as the dollar deteriorated. As the United States lost its commercial momentum, workers and executives moving toward middle age could no longer, in many industries or on average, count on the automatic economic advancement their fathers had come to expect during the 1950s and 1960s, so the price of lost domestic and international markets was not an abstraction.

Reagan supporters dismissed claims of a decline in both competitiveness and relative per capita GNP and income. The United States was *not* losing its edge; Philadelphia suburbanites were *not* falling behind. These optimists cited data prepared by the European-based Organization for Economic Cooperation and Development showing the United States slightly widening its per capita lead in the mid and late 1980s. The OECD criteria, however, sidestepped exchange-rate complications in favor of measurements based on the comparative local purchasing power of local incomes, which kept the United States ahead of Europe. Appendix G displays the OECD numbers next to the currency-sensitive figures. The problem with these alternative calculations—and most statistics do have limitations—was that *both* yardsticks mattered; relative domestic purchasing power counted, but so did the volatile exchange rates that were re-aligning international purchasing power and assets. Lester Thurow summed up the predicament: "When it comes to wealth, we can argue about domestic purchasing power. But in terms of international purchasing power, the United States is now only the ninth wealthiest country in the world in terms of per capita GNP. We have been surpassed by Austria, Switzerland, the Netherlands, West Germany, Denmark, Sweden, Norway and Japan."[20]

Some economists preferred to emphasize the role of the Reagan economy as a superb job-creation machine. MIT economist Krugman, although a Democratic campaign adviser in 1988, framed the seeming contradiction: "The U.S. share of world employment has been *rising*, not *falling*, since 1981. Total employment has increased 13 percent since then, and the unemployment rate has fallen to 5.7 percent. In every other major country except Great Britain unemployment rose over the same period. If foreigners were taking away our jobs, they were remarkably careless thieves, because they seem to have lost them on the way home."[21]

The difficulty lay in using jobs as a definitive yardstick. Warren Brookes of the *Detroit News*, Reagan's favorite economics columnist, pointed out an extraordinary statistic: that since 1981 the United States had accounted for more than 90 percent of the jobs created by the ten leading industrial democracies—hardly proof of a nation in decline.[22] But the Soviet Union also provided (service) jobs for almost all its citizens, and the primacy-of-employment yardstick fades against a larger circumstance: the other major industrial nations had been achieving better income gains and improved living standards *without* a superabundance of service jobs, most of them in low-productivity (if not always low-paying) situations. If Western Europe and Japan weren't taking away U.S. *jobs*, it nevertheless seemed that they were managing to take away American *wealth*.

The negative indexes most often cited had nothing to do with immediate per capita income but with liens on the future—the merchandise trade deficit, the current account deficit, the net U.S. international indebtedness and the burden of U.S. interest payments to foreigners, all of which set records during the late Reagan years. Through 1986–87 many conservative economists insisted on interpreting these debts as a sign of America's appeal to foreign investors. The president himself saw nothing but good news in high foreign investment levels: "We believe that there are only winners, no losers, and all participants gain from it."[23] Nobel Prize–winning economist Milton Friedman repeatedly drew attention to the fact that the United States collected more interest and dividends from abroad than were paid out. So how could we be a "debtor" nation?

But that argument began to sag in 1988. The merchandise trade deficit had fallen, thanks to the cheap dollar, to $137 billion in 1988 after peaking at $170 billion in 1987. However, the broader current account deficit, $144 billion in 1987, showed a much smaller decline to $127 billion in 1988.* The catch was that because of mounting U.S. international indebtedness, the payment of dividends, rents and interest to overseas creditors was rising. The U.S. investment-income surplus plunged from $20.4 billion in 1987 to just $2.6 billion in 1988, and economists predicted that 1989 would see a clear investment-income deficit.[24] In the second quarter, that happened. Foreigners earned $31.9 billion in their investments in the United States during that period, surpassing the $26.9 billion that Americans earned in their investments abroad. Economist Allen Sinai called it a "distressing omen of wealth migrating out of the United States."[25] And with the United States projected to add $100 billion a year or so of international debt for the foreseeable future, increasingly painful investment income deficits seemed likely if not inevitable.

Election-year estimates by the Congressional Research Service projected that U.S. net international indebtedness would surpass $1 trillion by 1991 and reach $2 trillion by 1995. Official Commerce Department estimates were predicting $50 billion net

---

* The current account covers trade in both merchandise and services. Appendix H lists the various data and deteriorations.

foreign investment income *outflows* by 1992.[26] Experts agreed on the dire implications: U.S. living standards would fall, at least relatively, as wealth was transferred to foreigners to service America's huge debt. Back in 1987 the Committee for Economic Development, a bulwark of the business establishment, warned that "as long as the United States remains a large international borrower for purposes of consumption as distinct from productive investment, it will eventually have to allocate more resources to the sectors producing exportable goods and away from those sectors catering to domestic demand. This shift will mean a decline in the potential living standards of future U.S. generations, a legacy that no previous generation has passed onto its children since the Civil War."[27]

Other great powers had let themselves slide into comparable debt—most recently, Britain after World War I. The critical difference lay in why and how the money was spent. Massive borrowing to fight a war, the usual explanation for most fading empires, was not a factor in Reagan's United States. For the first time in history, one economist noted, "an advanced industrialized nation had gone back to debtor status in *peacetime*."[28]

Conservative commentators, of course, disagreed. Presidential favorite Warren Brookes called the portrait of America as the world's leading debtor nation grossly exaggerated, and, in fact, official figures *did* exaggerate. American assets overseas, a high percentage bought decades earlier, *were* undervalued. And conservatives also noted studies by the Swiss-based Bank for International Settlements that the growth of U.S. manufacturing output during the 1980s had exceeded Europe's. But if the global-debtor thesis was overplayed, the overall debt dilemma was very real.

All over the commercial and financial map, once proud U.S. dominoes were toppling. On March 18, 1988, the Japanese Economic Planning Agency announced that Japan's per capita gross national product, the output of goods and services for each member of the population, reached the equivalent of $19,642 in 1987, surpassing the United States' $18,403—due in no small part, of course, to the 17 percent rise of the Japanese yen versus the dollar.[29] Years earlier the United States had lost its postwar position as the world's most creditworthy nation.

CHART 4A

CREDITORS AND DEBTORS:
THE CHANGING INTERNATIONAL BALANCE OF POWER, 1980–87

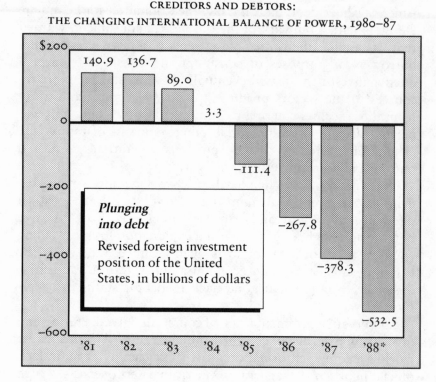

*Plunging
into debt*

Revised foreign investment
position of the United
States, in billions of dollars

By 1988 it had fallen to fourth place—behind Japan, Switzerland and West Germany.[30] Meanwhile, Japan and West Germany had *already* replaced the United States as the world's two leading creditor nations. Back in 1980 the United States had led the world in net overseas investment with over $100 billion. By 1986 reversing circumstances had turned America into a debtor, while Japan had accumulated net foreign holdings of $180 billion—more than the United States commanded at its peak. West Germany was second with $113 billion.[31] As the Reagan era closed, estimates put the late-1988 Japanese and West German positions at $300 billion and $220 billion, respectively. Charts 4A and 4B document the unprecedented size of the shift.

CHART 4B

CREDITORS AND DEBTORS:

THE CHANGING INTERNATIONAL BALANCE OF POWER, 1980–87

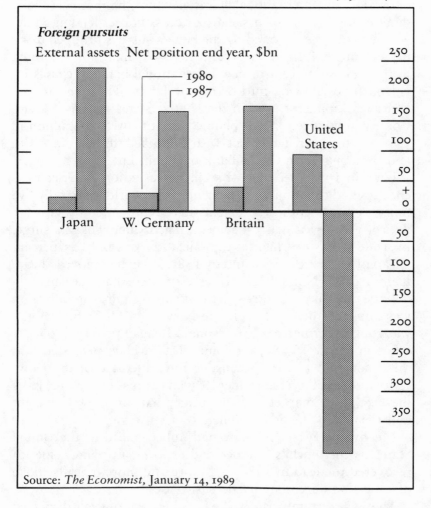

*Foreign pursuits*

External assets  Net position end year, $bn

1980
1987

Japan     W. Germany     Britain

United
States

250
200
150
100
50
+
0
–
50
100
150
200
250
300
350

Source: *The Economist,* January 14, 1989

Not surprisingly, America's eroding international economic status was also beginning to affect not just the dollar's value but its role in international commerce. Based on 1988 data, the Bank for International Settlements (BIS) reported that the "role of the dollar in international financial activity has been gradually diminishing." The dollar's share of cross-border lending in developed countries covered by the bank's surveys dropped to 53 percent in 1988 from 72 percent in 1983. In 1988, according to the BIS, 85 percent of new international banking claims involved funds flowing into or out of Japan. The trend to yen loans was apparent even in the United States, as Los Angeles County announced that it planned to borrow $100 million in yen in a ten-year agreement with Nippon Life Insurance Co. and the Long Term Credit Bank of Japan, Ltd.

Back in 1975 the value of securities listed on American exchanges had constituted 61 percent of the world total, fully five times as much as the 12 percent share represented by Japan.[32] By 1981 America had 55 percent. Then came Tokyo's surge. By 1986 U.S. stock market capitalization was only 25 percent ahead of Japanese stocks, and by 1987 Japan had moved ahead. In mid-1988, Nomura Securities estimated that, measured in dollars, the Tokyo market's share of world equity capitalization was about 42 percent, while the New York Stock Exchange's was roughly 31 percent.[33] As Ronald Reagan prepared to leave office in January 1989, economist David Hale suggested that these data mocked the ostensible huge increase of the Dow-Jones Industrial Average under Reagan because on a global basis the U.S. stock market had lost nearly half of its 1981 weight and Japan was the great winner.[34]

Meanwhile West Germany had pulled ahead of the United States as the world's number one exporter in 1986. America recovered the lead in 1989, but more and more officials spoke of American hegemony in the past tense.

That was certainly true in Japan, where top officials displayed an awareness of history that shamed their counterparts in Washington. Senior Reaganites might attend Calvin Coolidge birthday parties, but Japanese strategists reviewed Gibbon and Toynbee and pored over economic histories of the late nineteenth century and the years between the wars. They saw appealing parallels. High in the old gray Tokyo building that housed Japan's Ministry of Finance—which forty years earlier had been part of U.S. military occupation headquarters—Director General Makoto Utsumi would greet the occasional favored visitor by unfolding a gridlike chart portraying the United States, Japan, West Germany and Britain at various stages of economic power. A late 1987 *Wall Street Journal* report summarized its provocative pictography: "The U.S. now sits in the bottom corner, where Britain was from 1926 to 1944. Such nations live on past credit, suck in foreign capital and can't save enough to finance domestic investment. Two rankings higher stands Japan: a strong country with a trade surplus, saving more than it spends and sending excess money abroad. That puts Japan among other nations at the height of their strength, including the U.S. from 1946 to 1970 and Britain from 1851 to 1890."[35]

For several years, moreover, senior Japanese had also been relatively candid, semipublicly at least, about what they believed to be the principal source of U.S. decline: *imperial overreach*. In the face of ebbing resources, Washington was trying to maintain too great a global military role. Masahiro Sakamoto, chief economist of the International Trade Institute of Japan's Foreign Trade Council, had published a shrewd paper in 1986 discussing what he called "the failure to adequately share the burden of Pax Americana" and concomitant U.S. overcommitment in international security responsibilities. Using 1983 data, Sakamoto calculated that with just a 40.4 percent share of the combined GNP of the five most advanced nations (the United States, Britain, France, West Germany and Japan), the United States had simultaneously accepted a 56.7 percent share of combined defense expenditures. Western Europe's three great powers were more or less paying according to their ability, with combined GNP shares between 6.4 percent and 8.7 percent versus combined defense shares between 7.7 percent and 8.3 percent. Japan, the Tokyo-based economist acknowledged, was the unique beneficiary. In 1983 that country had enjoyed 14 percent of the combined five-nation GNP while bearing only 3.3 percent of the combined defense share because of its ability to huddle cheaply and securely under the U.S. defense umbrella.[36]

Through the mid-1980s the Reagan White House, committed to the idea that "America is back," generally ignored what

Japanese officials had begun taking for granted. Only in late 1987 and 1988 did the debate catch on in the United States, fanned by the success of books like Paul Kennedy's best-selling *The Rise and Fall of the Great Powers* reaching much the same conclusion as Tokyo's: that failure to retrench no-longer-sustainable military outlays, financed with escalating levels of debt, had been typical of past imperial declines. Post-Armada Spain, eighteenth-century Holland and early-twentieth-century Britain all displayed similar symptoms. History's lesson was simple: the United States should avoid similar excess.

In the meantime quibbles about how Japan had *not really* passed the United States—true enough with respect to ultimate national (military) power, and also in everyday living standards—served to evade the larger developing challenge. Japan's new titan status was principally *financial*. Japan had assumed the creditor role America had yielded by borrowing money from the Japanese to fund defense commitments instead of insisting that Japan help finance a common burden. Ezra Vogel, director of Harvard's East Asian program, described the basis of a major transition: "As an economic power, the United States has already been surpassed. The critical question is who has the leverage, who has the strategy, who has the critical assets that influence the course of world economic development. The key people who are able to make new loans are the Japanese. People begin to look to the rules of the game as the lender defines it."[37]

By mid-1988 Japan was rich enough for Tokyo to challenge the United States for principal influence in several international banks and monetary agencies, and former Japanese prime minister Yasuhiro Nakasone predicted in May that Japan was passing the United States as a donor of aid to the Third World.[38] On Ronald Reagan's last full day as president, the Japanese released an official 1989 budget confirming that estimate. Displacing the United States was no great achievement, of course, because after four decades American voters were sick of U.S. foreign assistance programs. The caution was that Japan was expanding its influence in East Asian nations with close ties to the United States.

Yet another transition was evident at the June 1988 seven-nation economic summit in Toronto, the last that Ronald Reagan would attend. Japanese money was beginning to speak with

TABLE 7

INTERNATIONAL BANK ASSETS, BY NATIONALITY OF BANKS

| Parent country of bank | December 1985 | | December 1986 | | December 1987 | |
|---|---|---|---|---|---|---|
| | in billions of U.S. dollars | percentage share of total assets | in billions of U.S. dollars | percentage share of total assets | in billions of U.S. dollars | percentage share of total assets |
| France | 244.0 | 9.0 | 289.6 | 8.4 | 375.5 | 8.6 |
| Germany | 191.2 | 7.0 | 270.1 | 7.8 | 347.9 | 7.9 |
| Italy | 113.3 | 4.2 | 145.1 | 4.2 | 185.0 | 4.2 |
| Japan | 707.2 | 26.1 | 1,120.1 | 32.4 | 1,552.1 | 35.4 |
| Switzerland | 109.2 | 4.0 | 152.0 | 4.4 | 196.1 | 4.5 |
| United Kingdom | 192.9 | 7.1 | 211.5 | 6.1 | 253.9 | 5.8 |
| United States | 590.2 | 21.7 | 599.2 | 17.3 | 647.6 | 14.8 |
| Other | 566.8 | 20.9 | 666.4 | 19.4 | 823.2 | 18.8 |
| Total | 2,714.8 | 100.0 | 3,454.0 | 100.0 | 4,381.3 | 100.0 |

Source: Bank for International Settlements
Source: *Grant's Interest Rate Observer*, June 24, 1988

a voice once associated with the United States: renting the best limousines and broadcast studios, insisting that the motorcycle escort for Prime Minister Noboru Takeshita be just as large as Ronald Reagan's. Reporters found themselves overwhelmed by Japan's summit presence. According to *The New York Times'* Peter Kilborn, it was "so pervasive that some of the Canadian hosts are referring to the Japanese as the next Americans."[39]

In 1981 three of the world's twenty-five biggest banks were American (a quarter century earlier, fifteen had been). By 1988 the United States could claim *just one* of the top twenty-five— Citicorp. Seven of the ten biggest were Japanese.[40] Unfamiliar names like Sumitomo and Dai-Ichi Kangyo were replacing the Bank of America and the Chase Manhattan. Table 7 shows the extraordinary 1981–87 ebb in the assets of U.S. international banks relative to their Japanese rivals.

Rankings of broader financial services remained more favorable. U.S. firms like American Express and Merrill Lynch continued to dominate, but danger signs were flashing—from the massive profits of Tokyo-based Nomura to growing Japanese domination of London's Eurobond market and the emergence of Japan Associated Finance Company (JAFCO) as the world's

largest venture capital fund.[41] Japan's great insurance companies, too, had started to reach overseas. In 1987 Nippon Life,
the country's biggest, paid $580 million for a 13 percent stake
in the U.S. investment firm of Shearson Lehman, while Yasada
Mutual Life bought 18 percent of Paine Webber. The huge
Sumitomo Bank had already bought up 12.5 percent of Goldman Sachs.

By 1988 the tide was also overrunning commercial banking
as the Bank of Ireland gobbled up the largest bank in New
Hampshire, the Royal Bank of Scotland acquired the second-
largest bank in Rhode Island, and Banca Commerciale Italiana
emerged as a white knight in the struggle for New York's Irving
Trust. In California the Bank of Tokyo took over the Union
Bank, and 1989 saw Japan's goliath Dai-Ichi Kangyo Bank take
a 4.9 percent minority position in New York–based Manufac-
turers Hanover. As of 1988, nearly 20 percent of bank assets
in the United States were already foreign-owned; roughly 14
percent were in the hands of Japan alone.* One third of California's statewide banking assets were in foreign hands, while
fully 24 percent were controlled by the Japanese.

By early 1989 only five of the world's twenty-five largest
public companies by market valuations were American (down
from seven in 1981); *seventeen were Japanese.* But this reflected
the runaway corporate valuations established by the Japanese
stock market. Better proof of the same point lay in how individual industries were succumbing to foreign dominance: consumer electronics to Asia and chemicals to Germany, for
example. In late 1987 the Dutch electronics giant Philips bought
out its North American subsidiary and took over full rights to
several famous American brand names: Norelco, Magnavox and
Philco. General Electric's sale of its consumer-electronics business to France's Thomson S.A. was a similar milestone. In January 1989 the American Electronic Association reported that
the U.S. share of overall world electronics production—from

---

* Japan's 1988 advance was particularly striking. During that year U.S. assets
held by Japanese banks grew from $232 billion to $360 billion, according to
figures compiled by the New York Federal Reserve Bank. The increase alone
was more than four times the $30 billion in assets held by U.S. banks in Japan,
and a half-dozen U.S. affiliates of Japanese banks ranked among the thirty
largest U.S. financial institutions (*Baltimore Sun*, October 29, 1989).

consumer products to telecommunications and chips—plummeted from 50.4 percent in 1984 to 39.7 percent in 1987. During the same period Japan's share rose from 21.3 percent to 27.1 percent. In the worldwide semiconductor market alone, the share of Japanese companies climbed from 28.4 percent in 1978 to 50 percent in 1988.[42] The chairman of the American Electronics Association acknowledged that "we're declining far more sharply than any of us really thought. It is obvious that American high technology is at risk."[43]

A record 47 percent of all patents issued in the United States went to foreigners, compared with just 19 percent a quarter century earlier. Japanese inventors were the leading participants, having overtaken West Germany in 1975, and by 1988 they were receiving more than twice as many U.S. patents as investors from any other country. Of the ten companies that registered the most American patents in 1988 only two—General Electric and IBM—were American. Hitachi, the Japanese electronics firm, placed first with 898 patents. Donald W. Banner, former commissioner of patents turned president of the Intellectual Property Owners Association, commented that "this shows that America's position in many technologically significant areas is decreasing, and as it decreases the number of high-paying jobs goes down and so does our standard of living. It's an unfortunate comment on America's decline in greatness."[44]

On the chemical front, a mere four decades after the Allies broke up Germany's I. G. Farben monopoly, Farben's three main remnants—BASF AG, Bayer AG and Hoechst AG—had grown to rank first, second and third in chemical sales worldwide. In the meantime, foreign companies—principally German—had also come to own roughly 30 percent of the U.S. chemical industry.[45] What's more, with the large European chemical companies on the prowl for further U.S. acquisitions—and in pharmaceuticals as well as chemicals—few analysts saw much prospect that America's embattled chemical producers would stage a global resurgence.

Even the giant U.S. defense industry began to look over its shoulder. In 1988 Daimler-Benz announced plans to absorb Messerschmitt-Bolkow-Blohm, the Federal Republic's prime aerospace and weapons concern. With estimated annual sales in the $42 billion range, the planned Daimler-MBB group would be twice the size of United Technologies, the largest U.S. aerospace firm (ahead of both Boeing and McDonnell-Douglas).[46] More or less at the same time, the Pentagon said that it would no longer necessarily object to foreign companies—*not* Japanese or German, however—buying out U.S. defense contractors. Foreign purchasers would be allowed to take over some U.S. companies to keep defense jobs from moving overseas.[47]

In October, just before the presidential election, the *Chicago Tribune* printed excerpts from a memo circulating in Tokyo which concluded that if Mitsubishi Heavy Industries, Ishikawajima-Harima and Toshiba began overseas marketing of the technology and hardware they produced for Japan's own limited military market, then in less than a decade, Japan could command 45 percent of the world's tank and motorized artillery market, 40 percent of military electronics purchases, 30 percent of the aerospace market and 60 percent of global warship manufacture, with disastrous fallout for U.S. military exports and technology.[48]

After a decade of deregulation, the pioneer U.S. international airlines—Pan American and Trans World—were in competitive difficulties. More passengers were traveling abroad in the jets of British Airways, KLM, Air France, Lufthansa, Japan Air Lines and other national-flag airlines. One aviation writer wryly noted that in 1988 "the murals depicting Pan-Am's once formidable round-the-world route system were removed from the top executive offices at Manhattan headquarters by order of the company's new chairman."[49]

Even the seed companies serving American agriculture—Funk's, Northrop King, Stauffer, Wilson Hybrids, McAllister and Garst—had also largely passed into foreign hands.[50] In February 1988 Firestone sold out to Japan's Bridgestone, leaving Goodyear as the only major American-owned tire manufacturer. "They're all foreign names now," one executive lamented.[51]

A generation earlier, Union Carbide, Chrysler, Celanese and Remington Rand had been identified with a threatened U.S. takeover of Europe, but by 1988 they were either pulling out or gone from Europe as *European* companies were mounting an unprecedented invasion of the United States. In industry after industry, according to Milton Moskowitz, foreign companies were using American acquisitions to take over global leadership.

Sweden's Electrolux became the world's largest home appliance maker by acquiring Cleveland's White Consolidated Industries (Frigidaire, Westinghouse, Kelvinator, Gibson). Switzerland's Nestle became the world's largest spirits company by scooping up Heublein. British Petroleum became the world's largest producer of animal feeds by acquiring Purina Mills from Ralston Purina. Germany's Bertelsmann became the world's largest publishing company by taking over Doubleday. London's Saatchi & Saatchi became the world's largest advertising agency complex by acquiring a clutch of American shops: Compton, Ted Bates, Backer & Spielvogel.[52]

In 1986 takeovers of U.S. corporate assets by foreign investors totaled $23.3 billion; by 1987 that had climbed to $40 billion—and Merrill Lynch international economists estimated the 1988 figure at $60 billion.[53] Corporations and individual investors from Japan were cautious, at least through 1987, but British companies readily attempted hostile takeover attempts. "Britain Buys Back the Colonies," screamed Dun's *Business Month* in November 1987. Two months earlier, after $1.5 billion had changed hands in ten days, British firms had won control of Hilton International and the international network of Holiday Inns, thereby replacing the United States as the world's largest owner and operator of quality hotels. Grocery, supermarket and retail publications also chronicled Britain's emergence in those industries.

Throughout the first half of 1988, the sale of what might be called "corporate Americana" was a regular media sidebar. Smith & Wesson, whose pistols helped tame the American West, became British. Brooks Brothers, the Establishment tailor, and J. Press, clothier to generations of affluent Yale and Harvard undergraduates, were now in British and Japanese hands.[54] *Time* magazine also noted that "the question of what constitutes a truly American icon has become befuddling. A Sohio gasoline station? British Petroleum owns that company now. An Allis-Chalmers farm tractor? The West Germans manufacture those. Ball Park franks are owned by a British conglomerate; so is French's mustard. The take from Las Vegas' Dunes Hotel and Country Club, one of the best-known American gambling and entertainment centers, will soon go to its new Japanese owner.

The latest hit recording by Country Singer Kenny Rogers is a foreign-owned product; his record label, RCA, is now West German property. And what about breakfast (or a diamond ring) at Tiffany, or drinks in the rarefied atmosphere of Manhattan's Algonquin hotel? Those vintage landmark buildings are now Japanese possessions."[55]

Changes in the publishing and entertainment sectors were particularly notable. One 1989 survey noted that since 1985 overseas investors had laid out over $14 billion to acquire American-made movies (and movie libraries), record companies, song catalogs and book publishers. United Artists and Twentieth Century-Fox passed into Australian hands. In publishing, foreigners now owned such venerable imprints as Harper & Row, Doubleday, Bantam Books, Dell, Viking, E. P. Dutton, Delacorte, Grolier and Charles Scribner & Sons. Of the five largest record companies in the United States, four were in European hands— Polygram (Dutch), RCA (German), CBS (Japanese) and Capitol (British). Only Warner/Elektra remained in American hands.[56] While entertainment was becoming one of America's major exports, a diminishing percentage of the firms involved remained under U.S. control.

During the late Reagan years, the U.S. commercial real estate market also showed large-scale national ownership changes. A Canadian company, Olympia & York, had quietly become New York City's biggest office-building landlord. And in early 1988 the Coldwell Banker Real Estate Group reported a stunning set of figures: Foreigners owned 46 percent of downtown Los Angeles's commercial real estate, 39 percent of downtown Houston's, 32 percent of Minneapolis's and 21 percent of Manhattan's.[57] The tallest building in Texas—at seventy-five stories also the highest west of the Mississippi—was sold to a group of investors led by Lebanese businessman Rafik B. Hariri.[58] In 1988 Japan's Sumitomo Life bought Atlanta's tallest building, the IBM Tower. In Los Angeles, Japan's Shuwa Investments Corporation announced plans for what would be that city's tallest building—an eighty-four-story tower.[59] And in Chicago, Japanese investors were interested when the Sears Tower, the world's tallest building, was put on sale in 1988, but decided not to buy.

As foreign investment grew, it raised the percentage of U.S.

corporate assets owned by foreigners (during a period when most other major industrial nations' ratios of outside ownership declined). As of 1988, foreigners owned 12 percent of America's manufacturing base, setting a twentieth-century record; back in 1980 the figure had been a negligible 3 percent. Individual figures for the United Kingdom, the lead acquisitor of U.S. companies, were particularly striking. By the end of 1987 British direct investment in U.S. manufacturing plants, banks, real estate and corporations stood at $75 billion, up 431 percent from 1980.[60] A year later the total had climbed to nearly $100 billion. By contrast, the grand total of U.S. direct investment in Britain as of 1988 came to only $50 billion.* People in South Hertfordshire and East Surrey were beginning to live off business in New York and California, not vice versa.

Parallel trends were at work between the United States and Canada. As Canadian investment in the United States rose, American corporations were pulling back. Between 1971 and 1985, the share of Canadian nonfinancial corporate assets owned by U.S.-controlled companies slipped from 27 percent to 17 percent.[61] Estimates put the 1988 figure in the 16 percent range.

Cumulative foreign direct investment in the United States— in corporations and real estate—rose from $83 billion in 1980 to $184.6 billion in 1985, $209.3 billion in 1986, $249.9 billion in 1987 and $304 billion in 1988.[62] By this time foreign investors in the United States had organized two national lobbies—the Association of Foreign Investors in America and the Association of Foreign Investors in U.S. Real Estate, with such members as Japan's Mitsubishi Bank and the pension fund of Philips, the Dutch electronics giant.

Not only did America's relative net indebtedness—via huge foreign ownership of bonds and securities as well as corporations and real estate—represent an appreciably higher percentage of national income in 1988 than it had back in the late nineteenth century, but the United States continued to permit free inflow and outflow of investment. That was an important

* The one-year transatlantic imbalance of investment in 1988 was extraordinary. According to a survey by the accounting firm of KPMG Peat Marwick, British companies bought 420 U.S. firms valued at $32.7 billion, while U.S. corporations in turn bought 71 British companies at a total cost of $4.0 billion.

distinction because many nations did not. For example, as it became obvious during the mid-1980s that Latin American nations couldn't pay their enormous international debts, creditors—including U.S. banks—proposed to swap the debt they held, at a discount, for ownership positions in local banks, companies and productive assets. As Benjamin Friedman pointed out, most of the debtors rejected the idea as threatening their national patrimony. Only the United States left itself open:

> What is happening in America's open markets amounts to exactly this kind of exchange. Foreign investors holding deposits in U.S. banks or U.S. Treasury securities or the debt of most other American borrowers can liquidate these assets at any time. They are then free to use the proceeds to buy stocks or whole companies or blocks of American real estate. No official permission is necessary.[63]

As a result, the Reagan years, and especially the president's debt-ridden second term, saw an indisputable shift of comparative wealth and economic leverage away from the United States: assets began to migrate along a pathway blazed by debt. Friedman and other economists acknowledged that the implications for the future might have looked different if Americans had productively invested most of these foreign borrowings. But much of the borrowed money wound up in financial restructuring, paper entrepreneurialism and lavish consumption, as well as in millions of attendant low-productivity service jobs. These and other dislocations within the late-1980s U.S. *domestic* economy only aggravated the global redistribution of wealth.

## A PARTIAL EXPLANATION: AMERICAN SECTORAL SELF-INTEREST

For important American regions, sectors and vocations—especially in trade and finance—the global restructuring of the 1980s produced lucrative, even unprecedented, rewards. Accountants, lawyers, merger experts, business consultants, investment bankers, stock brokers, economic journalists, publishers, real estate brokers, international economists and consultants, trade experts, importers, people in port cities, elements of the transportation industry, freight handlers and longshoremen were all beneficiaries. Tens of thousands of Americans profited even more directly as lobbyists, lawyers, brokers or advisers for foreign economic interests. Most of them lived in the coastal states, the recurrent home of U.S. Establishment politics and finance (and, as Chapter 6 will discuss, again the predominant locus of 1980s U.S. income gains).

There was a substantial overlap between those who gained from the free international flow of investments and those who also benefited from Reagan's tax, budget and monetary policies. Defense and aerospace contractors enjoyed a unique position because with the United States paying a disproportionate share of Western defense bills, sales that might have gone to Mitsubishi and Messerschmitt went to Boeing, Grumman and McDonnell-Douglas. But even here, U.S. military exports plummeted during the 1980s—from $22 billion in 1982 to just $9 billion in 1987, though commercial aircraft remained one of America's largest export successes.[64]

The geography of trade was also a major factor in free-market sentiment and profits. America's port cities were important collective beneficiaries of both the globalization of the economy *and* the huge trade deficit, which was predominantly a function of swollen imports. Major cities like Boston, Baltimore, Norfolk and Seattle were in the vanguard, but lesser ports like Wilmington, North Carolina, and Long Beach, California, also cashed in on growing positions as freight handlers or at least container transshippers to the world.

Fewer beneficiaries were found in America's heartland. The high dollar of 1985—which stunned Iowa pork producers with home-state competition from cheap Canadian hogs and Minnesota wheat farmers with competitive Argentine and Australian wheat pouring into Twin Cities grain elevators—was painful but brief. A longer-term problem lay in the fundamental changes overtaking world agriculture. Third World nations like India, China and Brazil were no longer U.S. agricultural export markets; buoyed by high U.S. prices, they had become *competitors*. Successful new Asian competitors also threatened Rust Belt industry.

But the deflationary damage done in 1984–86 was partially

reversed during Reagan's last two years. By 1987–88, as the
dollar fell, the United States rejected global laissez-faire to rescue
agriculture and basic manufacturing. Farmland values bounced
back somewhat in 1987 and 1988, and so did industries like
steel and machine tools.

By 1988, then, no one still talked about American manufacturing dying. *But under whose ownership and for whose profit
would it flourish?* Lawrence Brainerd, chief international economist for Manhattan's Bankers Trust, said, "By the end of this
century, the U.S. may have the most modern manufacturing
sector in the world, but it won't own it."[65] Lester Thurow
speculated that the workers would still be American, but that
top-level executive positions would be lost to foreigners. The
upshot was that as the Reagan era ended, the Darwinian forces
of the 1980s had undergone an important transformation.
Americans would continue to farm, to make automobiles and
pour into their downtown office buildings, but in whose behalf?
The same dollar devaluation that made U.S. commodities and
products competitive again had also put U.S. plants and real
estate properties on the block at bargain discounts while American budget and trade deficits had given foreigners the money
to buy them.

The challenge of the 1990s was becoming clear. How much
in property and then in profits, dividends and rents would have
to be deeded over or flow abroad to foreign creditors? What
parts of America would they buy up? Because of the enormous
brokerage and management fees being generated, more and
more influential Americans found their high incomes linked to
foreign interests and purchasers. With unusual candor, one
newsweekly observed in the autumn of 1987 that "the buying
of America has virtually turned into an industry of its own."[66]
And that was just one dimension of the new relationship. Much
more was involved than lucrative fees for finance teams huddling
with investment bankers in Tokyo and London or blue-chip law
firms constantly drafting reams of tender offers, prospectuses
and sale documents.

Stockbrokers, investment bankers, bond salesmen and realtors found that surging foreign demand for U.S. assets—at prices
that seemed cheap in yen, marks, francs or pounds—was raising
volume and prices in real estate and financial markets alike,

enabling other deals, properties and securities to hitch a ride. Prices that were already inflated kept increasing. In cities like Los Angeles, New York, Chicago and Boston, where foreign ownership of downtown office buildings rose to 30 to 50 percent levels by 1988, real estate turnover soared, and prices climbed 35 to 45 percent during the 1983–88 period.[67] Japanese real estate investment—rising by $16 billion in 1988 alone—was a particularly powerful market force. Shuwa Investment Corporation's $620 million purchase of the ARCO Plaza in downtown Los Angeles was the biggest all-cash real estate deal in U.S. history. Dai-Ichi Real Estate paid the highest price per square foot ever recorded in North America when it bought Manhattan's Tiffany Building.[68]

By 1989 the Japanese were providing powerful support of the U.S. stock and bond markets and leveraged buyout explosion. Financiers in New York and Tokyo indicated that Japan—with its low domestic interest rates and $350 billion a year of surplus cash—was the source of one third of the cash funding Wall Street's corporate buyout boom.[69] Yukuo Takenaka, chairman of Peat Marwick Japan, told *Business Tokyo* magazine that the real LBO-related opportunity for Japanese buyers would come when the cash-hungry new owners spun off parts of their new companies to raise money for debt service. Then, he said, "the bid prices will increase, and more offers will come to Japan from U.S. corporations whose biggest concern will be to resell divided pieces of company assets at as high a price as possible."[70] In Los Angeles the financial establishment, embracing a Pacific Rim strategy for success, welcomed Japanese money for enabling the burgeoning local financial-services industry to pass both Chicago and San Francisco in asset size and prepare a challenge to New York.[71]

By the end of the Reagan era, in short, foreign investors' dollars—the ironic consequences of U.S. budget and trade deficits—had become a massive, even essential, cause of high-flying valuations in the real estate and financial markets, propping up the shift of wealth within the United States to the investment-oriented upper stratum. But the global economic realignment and "one-world" capitalism so popular with large segments of Upper America soured many other people, and Democratic congresswoman Marcy Kaptur of Ohio charged Americans serving as agents or lobbyists for foreign purchasers with "economic treason."

In 1988 Richard Gephardt had discovered a responsive audience in the early Democratic primaries when he charged that lawyers, financiers and trade consultants were part of a mostly Eastern Establishment that saw profit-making opportunities from "an America in decline."[72] During the general election campaign, Michael Dukakis would only hint at similar themes, but Gephardt had named one of America's most troubling redistribution dynamics.

## INTERNATIONAL WEALTH WAVE: THE SHARED DYNAMICS OF BRITISH, JAPANESE AND U.S. INEQUALITY TRENDS

By the late 1980s the polarization of wealth was emerging as an important factor in both rich and poor nations around the world. The rich nations were mostly getting richer, while impoverished continents and regions lost ground, especially Africa and Latin America. Economic polarization was also intensifying inside Third World nations, as local elites sent hundreds of billions of dollars of flight capital from the soft-currency Mexicos, Brazils and Nigerias to the security of Miami, New York, London and Switzerland while the rest of the population languished. In Latin America, for example, real per capita income was 9 percent lower in 1988 than in 1980, and in Africa, things were worse. Within the leading financial countries, by contrast, global and ideological circumstances were ballooning upper-bracket wealth that had no need to flee to safer or more hospitable climes. It was free to display itself, to escalate stock and real estate prices, and to become a political issue.

Which is just what was happening—most strikingly in the case of Britain, Japan and the United States, seats of the world's major financial markets and all dominated during the 1980s by entrenched conservative governments. In 1989 a survey by *The Economist* of the wealth of corporate chief executives found those in the United States, Japan and Britain—the financial centers—outgaining those in France and West Germany. Rising stock markets, soaring real estate values and financial deregulation were all factors. To an extent, heyday conservatism was developing transnational characteristics and values.

In Britain, where Charles Darwin was born in 1809, Margaret Thatcher's conservatism, harsher and more controversial than Reagan's, sought to rehabilitate the economy by making Darwinism come alive again. But in 1985, six years after Thatcher came to power, a report by the International Monetary Fund found the average Briton poorer than the average Italian. *The Sunday Times* of London compared working-class Liverpool to Turin, two cities whose fans had just clashed at a bloody football match in Brussels, and the contrast was startling: a car for every 2.14 people in Turin, one for every 6.2 in Liverpool; one baby in thirteen born illegitimate in Turin versus Liverpool's one in three. "England has grown much poorer than the rest of Europe," observed University of Liverpool professor of politics Fred Ridley. "People here still haven't caught on to the extent to which they have been excluded from prosperity."[73]

Thatcher's remedies enjoyed a significant national success by 1988, but largely by ignoring the Liverpools and the lower classes and rewarding the stronger parts of the British economy—notably finance and the capital markets—that either already worked or could be made to. Division within the country widened accordingly.

By the general election of 1987 wealth and inequality were central issues. Unemployment was three times as high as it was when Thatcher took office, causing critics to talk about the split between a prosperous, greedy south and a bleak, depressed north. Labour party leader Neil Kinnock accused Thatcher of trying to re-create Victorian extremes of wealth and poverty, and proclaimed, "Charles Dickens, thou shouldst be alive at this hour."[74] Even Conservatives remarked on Thatcher's apparent indifference to the underclass.

A few days before the June 1987 election a report claimed that because of Thatcher's "two nations" policy, inequalities between rich and poor had grown sharply between 1979 and 1985. Poor families with children experienced a drop in real income, depending on their size, of some 15.7 percent to 27.2 percent between 1979 and 1985. The bottom tenth of Britons had seen their real incomes slip by an average of 9.7 percent during the same period while the top quintile of wage earners enjoyed real gains of 22 percent. The report asserted that "the policy of two nations has been pursued remorselessly since 1979. The government has exacerbated changes in the distribution of industry and employment and the increasing segmentation of the labor market, rather than attempting to ameliorate them as previous governments have done."[75] The less biased *Financial Times* agreed: "The increase in inequality since 1979 is beyond dispute. This is not only a consequence of lower taxation of the rich; it also follows from the more rapid rise in incomes of those in work as against benefits paid to those who are dependent upon the state."[76]

The general election followed the "two nations" patterns. Thatcher won a large parliamentary majority with 43 percent of the total popular vote against a divided, multiparty opposition. Her success was based on the rich south of England. In the poorer north, the Labour party enjoyed a 5.4 percent trend, and Conservatives failed to win or keep a single parliamentary seat in Manchester, Bradford, Liverpool, Leicester and Newcastle. In egalitarian Scotland the Conservatives lost eleven of their twenty-one seats, and even prosperous Edinburgh joined the trend.

However, if victory cautioned the Conservatives, defeat demoralized Labour. Party deputy leader Roy Hattersley argued the reverse side of the new political economics: Labour, he thought, had to realign to the right "to persuade the newly prosperous, newly emergent middle classes that we want their vote as well."[77] And Margaret Thatcher, seeing little reason to change, proposed new policies in the same, established directions. By 1988 the programs she was offering to Parliament were almost revolutionary in their attack on Britain's established welfare state. In April the Anglican Bishop of Durham denounced as "wicked" Thatcher's cuts in social services to the poor, reduction of housing benefits and elimination of free school lunches for the children of low-income workers.[78]

Her government's 1988 tax proposals were equally controversial. One set requested only two rates of income tax (25 percent and 40 percent) in lieu of a previous range for six rates from 27 percent to 60 percent. *The Economist* agreed that this was "a budget for the rich and high earners," and noted that a family breadwinner on average earnings (£12,600 a year, or roughly $22,000) would keep only £250, or $440, more of that money, whereas a senior executive making £125,000 ($225,000) would get to keep an additional £19,000 ($35,000).[79] Her second proposal was to replace the (local) property tax as a means of financing local government with a flat fee or poll tax that would average about $350 per person nationally but could range up to $1,500 in some big cities. Former Conservative prime minister Edward Heath joined the Labour opposition in opposing the tax as blatantly unfair to low-income people, and critics pointed out that Thatcher herself would pay $3,600 a year less in poll taxes than she currently paid in property taxes on her retirement home in Dulwich.[80] By the end of the year, opinion surveys in disaffected areas like Scotland indicated that 40 percent of the population supported nonpayment of the poll tax when it first came due in March 1989.[81]

Yet another major new factor in wealth polarization involved the sharp 1980s upsurge not just in the high-flying stock market but also in British residential housing prices, especially those in and around London. By 1986–88 increases were running 15 to 25 percent a year—far, far above inflation.[82] The result was trebled house prices from 1977 to 1988, further concentrating wealth among the more affluent homeowning half of the population.* The *Evening Standard* newspaper predicted that "the house price spiral is on the point of ushering in a major social revolution in this country, a revolution which will do more to transform the lives of people in the next 20 or 30 years than any amount of political initiatives or trade union militancy."[83]

For most foreign observers, and to many Britons, the country *was* in better shape after Thatcher's first decade. Tax cuts, privatization of hitherto mismanaged state industry, deregulation of the financial markets (London's so-called Big Bang), revitalization of British management techniques, legislation curbing the power of the trades unions, all made a difference. Yet greed had become a byword. One of London's most popular 1987 entertainments was a play, *Serious Money*, attacking the City—

---

* But, as in the United States, the boom ended in 1989. That year, housing prices in the south of England actually declined 10 to 20 percent from their 1988 peak ("Voters' Vertigo," *The Economist*, September 23, 1989, p. 67).

London's Wall Street—for youth-driven avarice; its climax came with a bevy of would-be transatlantic Ivan Boeskys singing Thatcher's praises in a song called "Five More Glorious Years." Another frequent term heard was "Loadsamoney," after a character popularized by a British comedian lampooning Thatcherism. The liberal *Guardian* newspaper caricatured the prime minister rolling on the ground with a button reading "Money Is God," and Craig Brown in *The Times*, a newspaper generally supportive of Thatcher, joked that if the Conservatives were to rewrite the ten commandments, the new rules would include "Thou Shalt Not Whimper. Shoplifters Will Be Prosecuted. Don't Come Running to Me. Never Knowingly Undersold."[84] But upper-bracket Britons were doing so well that at the spring 1988 steeplechase championships at Cheltenham, dozens of arrivals came by helicopter, causing an air jam over rural southwest England's Cotswold Hills.[85] Nobody had heard of such a thing before.*

In Japan, too, old conceptions of economic fairness were breaking down, largely the result of the surging Tokyo stock market and real estate prices, which not only magnified Japan's wealth but concentrated the benefits among a small elite while squeezing the middle class. Chart 5 illustrates the extraordinary dimensions of Japanese riches during the 1980s. The increase in financial and real estate values actually exceeded the country's GNP in 1987, greatly favoring the rich, and Tokunosuke Hasegawa, author of two books on the land issue, noted that "a vacant lot barely big enough for a tiny house costs 40 times an average salaryman's average income. It is absolutely insane, and it is wreaking social havoc. A relatively small number of people are becoming land billionaires, while the rest of the people—especially younger people—are locked out."[86] In early 1988 the press began carrying reports of how middle-class self-perceptions in Tokyo were starting to break down along the lines of who owned land and who didn't. Those who did found themselves multimillionaires in Western currency terms; those who didn't faced dreary lives and rooms (with three-bedroom apart-

---

* Upper-income ranks were increasing even faster than in the United States. *The New York Times* (May 2, 1989) reported that Inland Revenue authorities officially listed four times as many pound millionaires as five years earlier.

CHART 5

THE 1983-89 EXPLOSION OF JAPANESE FINANCIAL AND REAL ESTATE WEALTH

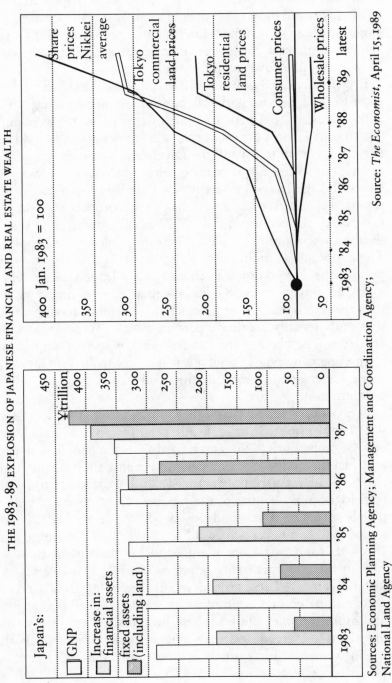

400  Jan. 1983 = 100

Share prices Nikkei average
Tokyo commercial land prices
Tokyo residential land prices
Consumer prices
Wholesale prices

350

300

250

200

150

100

50

1983  '84  '85  '86  '87  '88  '89  latest

Source: *The Economist*, April 15, 1989

Japan's:

☐ GNP
Increase in:
☐ financial assets
▨ fixed assets (including land)

¥trillion
450
400
350
300
250
200
150
100
50
0

1983  '84  '85  '86  '87

Sources: Economic Planning Agency; Management and Coordination Agency; National Land Agency

ments in good districts going for $7 million to $9 million).
"Tokyo's population is being polarized," said Akinobu Maeda,
a metropolitan government land-planning official. "Until a year
ago, most people considered themselves solidly middle-class.
Now, you either own land or you don't."[87]

Even as George Bush prepared to take over the U.S. presidency
from Ronald Reagan with talk about reorienting policy toward
a "kinder, gentler America," more intense pressures were building around Japan's governing conservatives of the Liberal Democratic Party. In late 1988 the government Economic Planning
Agency lamented an increasing sense of division between the
haves and the have-nots. Its *White Paper on the National Life*
reported that a record 74 percent of Japanese were telling poll-
takers that the economic system is basically unfair, and that "a
feeling of economic injustice is growing among the people."[88]
The Economic Planning Office also reported that soaring stock
prices—the Tokyo Stock Exchange Index leaped 48 percent in
1987, 40 percent in 1988—had eliminated small investors, limiting them to bank or post office savings accounts paying modest
dividends usually in the 3 percent range. These factors had
created a new class of the "super-rich," who represented only
a small percentage of society, but who controlled its most val-
uable assets and enjoyed the bulk of its rising luxury
consumption.

"People used to feel that if they worked hard, they would live
well," said Satoko Tanaka, head of the Tokyo League of Wom-
en's Organizations. "Now even hard-working people with good
jobs feel themselves to be poorly off because they cannot attain
the types of security that matter." And Wakako Hironaka, a
sociologist and member of the Japanese Diet, observed that "if
people give up saving and buy a BMW simply because they
know they can never afford a home, that is not genuine affluence—that is frustration. We used to say that owning a house
was an integral part of the Japanese dream. Now we say it is
just a dream."[89] These attitudes worsened in late 1988 and into
1989 as the Recruit Corporation bribery scandal enmeshed more
and more leading politicians and business leaders in a web of
illegal bribes, greed and easy-money stock market deals that
began nurturing increasingly widespread public doubts about
Japan's "money culture."

Takamitsu Sawa, professor of econometrics at Kyoto University, linked Japan's accelerating preoccupation with wealth to global trends promoted by the rise of neo-laissez-faire in the United States. Before then, money was less respected, but by 1988 money was "no longer a dirty word in Japan. In fact, you hear many people using the English terms 'money' and 'money game.' The Nineteen Eighties saw the rise of neoconservatives like Margaret Thatcher, Ronald Reagan and Yasuhiro Nakasone. Their hallmark was deregulation, privatization and 'small government.' "[90] Even more, their shared ideological and constituency values, as well as the close collaboration between the United States and both Japan and Britain, promoted the financial sector—and with it, stock market, housing and art prices, as well as wealth concentration and inequality—in all three nations.

Few decades have seen more confusing crosscurrents. Swiss investors, Japanese creditors and nervous Mexicans might be pouring money into the United States during the 1980s, but Americans' actual ownership share of global wealth was declining. Behind the fanfares of worldwide free-market economic triumph, other nations were gaining or taking over financial, commercial and industrial advantages that had been American for almost a half century. This new global interface of the U.S. economy—be it the migration of old-line manufacturing from Pennsylvania to Korea or the floodwaters of liquidity sloshing around the financial and real estate sectors and the willingness of so many influential people to help mortgage America so long as they could take broker's fees—had a twofold wealth effect. Within the United States, the rich got richer, but at the cost of a major decline in comparative U.S. world assets and purchasing power and a squandering of the nation's future. So the portrait of American wealth in the Reagan era—to which we now turn— was an extraordinary one, and not just because of the unprecedented size of the new fortunes but also because of their new origins, distribution and significance. Unlike prior heydays when the country as a whole was getting richer, many of the new fortunes of the 1980s reflected a nation consuming, rearranging and borrowing more than it built.

# Chapter

# 6

## *The New Plutography of 1980s America*

In January 1985, it was estimated that there were 832,602 American millionaire households. In January 1987, the level had reached 1,239,713. In both percentage and number, this change is the largest in the past 15 years. The number of households in America increased during the same time at an annual rate of only 1.5 percent. The millionaire population has increased at a rate almost 15 times faster than the household population in America.

—THOMAS J. STANLEY, 1987

This is a television nation. Maybe it's time for a mini-series about the *second* American Civil War. This time it would not be North versus South. This time it would be the haves versus the have-nots: Harlem against the Yupper East Side, Beverly Hills against Compton, the suburbs against the inner cities, the displaced against the entrenched. This time it would not be neat and territorial. This time it would be guerrilla war, in neighborhoods, in cities, with block against block until people walked across the gulf and discovered the unique idea of sharing.

—BENJAMIN J. STEIN
COLUMNIST AND FORMER REPUBLICAN
WHITE HOUSE AIDE, 1987

Society matrons, Wall Street arbitrageurs, Palm Beach real estate agents and other money-conscious Americans picking up the newspaper *USA Today* on May 22, 1987, must have been first bewildered and then amused by that day's lead story. In describing a new Louis Harris & Associates survey of the attitudes of upper-bracket citizens, reporter Martha Moore summed up the typical interviewee as "rich. Very. He's part of the thinnest economic upper crust: households with incomes of more than

$100,000 a year. Only 1.2 million households in the USA have that kind of dough, 1.9% of the population."[1]

Statistics like these clouded the true peaks of wealth in the polarized late 1980s. So did talk about eliminating Social Security benefits for the $50,000-a-year "rich." Households with annual incomes of $100,000 and net worths of $500,000—the threshold for Louis Harris's study—were only the upper-middle class of late-Reagan-era America, commercial and professional cupbearers to the genuinely monied. In Wichita, Kansas, or Beaufort, South Carolina, they would have been local gentry— of a sort. In high-priced Manhattan, though, they might have been a young accountant and his teacher wife, reluctantly planning to sell their cramped cooperative apartment and move to the suburbs. Yet a surprising number of late-1980s polls and comments contributed to what was a truly flawed perception— that circa 1988 "rich" somehow started at $50,000 or $100,000 a year, and that gradations above that were somehow less important. The truth was that the critical concentration of wealth in the United States was developing at *higher* levels—centimillionaires, half-billionaires and billionaires—provocative enough to resummon the spirits of American populism.

## THE NEW MAGNITUDE OF RICHES
## IN THE REAGAN ERA

For the first time in U.S. history, millionaires were economic nobodies as mega-wealth ballooned out of sight. By the late 1980s a person couldn't be a serious millionaire with just $1 million in *assets*; $1 million in annual *income* was what it took. As for *rich*, old-line money managers and private bankers generally agreed that $10 million in assets or two or three successive years of several million dollars in annual income was at least entry-level.[2] *Over a hundred thousand Americans still qualified.*

Economic change had rendered the term "millionaire" all but meaningless, something that median-income families earning $30,000 a year rarely understood. The price explosions of the Carter years in agricultural commodities, oil and farmland had minted millionaires out of Idaho potato growers, Oklahoma oil wildcatters and Ohioans with three hundred fifty fertile acres, and then the Reagan years finished the process by reestablishing a more familiar wealth boom in financial assets and professions. Bare-bones millionairedom, its ranks fattened from six hundred thousand Americans in 1981 to roughly one and one half million in 1989, was becoming no more than middle-class. Purchasing power was deteriorating along with status. To replicate the over-the-counter clout of $1 million in 1913 required progressively larger sums: $2.02 million in 1920, $1.38 million in mid-Depression 1935, $2.43 million in 1950, $3.18 million in 1965, $8.32 million in 1980, and almost $12 million on Election Day, 1988.[3]

The contrast was even greater with the decades before the Civil War, when the label "millionaire"—just then coming into real use—meant genuine wealth. Gustavus Myers, in his *History of the Great American Fortunes*, observed that "in 1847, millionaires were so infrequent that the very word was significantly italicized."[4] Back in 1831 banker Stephen Girard had died the richest man in America, boasting an estate of some $8 million. The next great millionaire—John Jacob Astor—was worth about $25 million when he died in 1848, which made him by far the richest man in the pre–Civil War United States. Newspaper surveys taken during the 1847–52 period gave the number of millionaires at twenty-five in New York City and nine in Philadelphia.[5] The Mississippi River plantations of the Deep South housed another dozen or two. Few boasted more than one or two million dollars; none compared with Astor. Among a nation of twenty-five million people, there might have been fifty or sixty millionaires.

Astor's 1848 fortune would have been $330 million in 1988 by a rough purchasing-power calculus. But in *relative* wealth and importance, he was a colossus dwarfing any late-twentieth-century U.S. billionaire. According to Myers, "Statistics issued in 1844 of manufactures in the United States showed a total gross amount of $307,196,844 invested. Astor's wealth, then, was one-fifteenth of the whole amount invested throughout the territory of the United States in cotton and wool, leather, flax and iron, glass, sugar, furniture, hats, silks, ships, paper, soap, candles, wagons—in every kind of goods which the demands of civilization made indispensable."[6]

Riches must be judged in the context of their times. More

TABLE 8

| Year | Millionaires | Decamillionaires | Centimillionaires | Billionaires |
|------|-------------|------------------|-------------------|--------------|
| 1981 | 600,000 | | | ? |
| 1982 | | 38,855 | 400 | 13 |
| 1983 | | | 500 | 15 |
| 1984 | | | 600 | 12 |
| 1985 | 832,602 | | 700 | 13 |
| 1986 | | | 900 | 26 |
| 1987 | 1,239,000 | 81,816 | 1200 | 49 |
| 1988 | 1,500,000 | 100,000 | 1200 | 51 |

than inflation is involved. If the country's wealth has grown, so has what a rich man can do with it.

Besides increasing the enjoyment of wealth, new technology and leisure time also spur *further* wealth creation. Economist Milton Friedman has pointed out that "historically, rising income has transformed what one generation thought of as a luxury into what the next sees as necessity."[7] Meanwhile, this process of turning former luxuries into everyday commodities also becomes a vehicle of watershed changes in new fortunes— from John Jacob Astor's beaver hats and Henry Ford's model T automobiles to the computers, cable systems, videocassettes, gourmet foods, fashions and luxury real estate developments of 1980s mega-money.

The 1980s were another of these watersheds in which, at first, public understanding and perceptions trailed far behind the new magnitudes of wealth accumulation. Table 8 plots the extraordinary escalation of all four relevant asset-holding classifications: millionaires, decamillionaires, centimillionaires and billionaires. (Fuller historical data are available in Appendix A).

Predictable precedents can be found in the two prior heydays, which also saw new magnitudes of riches, mostly from finance, land development or entrepreneurship, outpace public comprehension. The Gilded Age, for its part, was almost certainly the gaudiest economic escalator of American history. Relative to the economy Stephen Girard and John Jacob Astor had known, the Civil War years beginning in 1861 unloosed an enormous surge in currency, government contracts, new factories, financial liquidity, moneymaking chances and inflation. Railroad builders, war contractors, industrialists and Wall Street financiers found themselves gorging on economic opportunities that literally dwarfed those of sugar planters, fur traders and shipowners only a generation earlier.

Politics and wealth distribution realigned together. By 1865 the Southern planters were mostly ruined; even the established mercantile and landowning classes of the North found themselves overshadowed by the nouveaux riches. But the great fortunes were only *beginning* to emerge. They would lead at first to admiration but then to distrust, anger and finally into a populist explosion.

During the 1870s and 1880s, change was roughly on the level seen again during the 1980s. The wealth of Cornelius Vanderbilt, the richest man in post–Civil War America, mushroomed from $15 million in 1862 to a stunning $105 million by his death in 1877.[8] Astor's fortune had been a wonder; Vanderbilt's was four times greater. By 1883 his son, William H. Vanderbilt—enjoying an income of $10,350,000 a year—claimed that he had nearly doubled his father's fortune to $194 million, and said, "I am the richest man in the world."[9] By the mid-1880s, dozens of other Americans were worth $50 million or so.

The world took note, and these awesome accumulations propelled American heiresses into Europe's rich and titled clans by the hundreds. Bourbons, Braganzas and Churchills replenished their banklines from the marriage settlements made by rich Chicagoans, New Yorkers and Clevelanders. By 1888 the English observer Lord Bryce was remarking that "sixty years ago, there were no great fortunes in America, few large fortunes, no poverty. Now there is some poverty . . . many large fortunes, and a greater number of gigantic fortunes than in any other country in the world."[10] Poor Americans, by contrast, were outraged. The Farmers' Alliance, livid over the upper-bracket biases of both deflation and the protective tariff, charged that thirty-one thousand businessmen had become millionaires, largely at agriculture's expense.[11]

That figure of thirty-one thousand was wild talk. But the best statistics—compiled as part of an 1892 *New York Herald Tribune* study involving fifteen hundred field researchers over an eighteen-month period—proved staggering enough. There had been fifty to sixty millionaires in the pre–Civil War decade. A half century later there were 4,047. Inflation, moreover, might have been a factor back during the 1861–66 period, but not in the deflationary seventies, eighties and nineties, when money was mostly *gaining* value. Price levels, in fact, were not much different in 1892 from what they were in 1850.

That hundredfold increase in millionaires was politically explosive because part of this concentrated wealth among the top 1 percent of Americans was being withdrawn from an agricultural sector that had hitherto provided a living for two thirds of the population. William Jennings Bryan spoke for millions in 1896, when he attacked "the few financial magnates who, in a back room, corner the money of the world."[12] Bryan lost in 1896, but populist arguments changed the economic culture of America. Conspicuous consumption found itself increasingly defensive. As Matthew Josephson recounted in *The Robber Barons*:

> Finally, a costume ball given by Bradley Martin, a New York aristocrat, in 1897, reached the very climax of lavish expenditure and 'dazed the entire Western world.' 'The interior of the Waldorf-Astoria Hotel was transformed into a replica of Versailles, and rare tapestries, beautiful flowers and countless lights made an effective background for the wonderful gowns and their wearers. . . .' One lady, impersonating Mary Stuart, wore a gold-embroidered gown, trimmed with pearls and precious stones. 'The suit of gold inlaid armor worn by Mr. Belmont was valued at ten thousand dollars.' The affair, reported in the new 'yellow' press of Pulitzer and Hearst, caused a general storm among the citizens of New York, and its sponsors felt obliged to take sudden refuge in England.[13]

Public policy also changed. Laissez-faire slowly gave way to regulation of business concentration and practices. Relative prosperity returned to the countryside, and the Federal Reserve System was established in 1913 to prevent a recurrence of post–Civil War monetary contraction. The concentration of wealth slowed, and pressure for reestablishing the income tax grew— by 1909 Congress had passed a corporation tax and sent to the states for ratification a constitutional amendment authorizing a federal income tax.

By the late 1920s the concentration of wealth had again become politically provocative. By some calculations, the country got its first billionaire in Henry Ford; other estimates gave John D. Rockefeller the honor. Millionaires were becoming common, if not commonplace. In 1892 there had been approximately four thousand, and probably five thousand by 1910. The World War provided another spur, and by 1918 ten thousand Americans were thought to be millionaires. The popular economist Stuart Chase cited estimates of fifteen thousand millionaires by 1927 and at least twenty thousand by 1929, at which point "there were probably six times as many millionaires in the United States . . . as there were in 1914."[14] Once again the rapid growth in millionaires reflected an imbalance in the economy—the rampant expansion of financial speculation and debt—so that when the economy crashed, Upper America lost its hold on economic policy and fashion. The collapsed stock market was followed by large-scale new business regulation and income-tax-bracket increases under the New Deal, and by the mid-1930s there were only half as many millionaires as in 1929.

In the 1980s the emergence of four dozen U.S. billionaires, some virtually overnight, with a supporting cast of a hundred thousand decamillionaires, represented a plutographic revolution comparable to that of the late nineteenth century. From 1981 to 1988 the ranks of the "rich" jumped by factors of three, six and even ten, duplicating the leading indicators of the Gilded Age and the twenties.

So unprecedented were the asset bases involved that brief market movements created and lost paper fortunes that would have been unbelievable a generation earlier. In 1983, roughly a year after the 1982–87 bull market in stocks began, *Fortune* magazine featured the enormous gains made in just one year by individuals and families with large corporate shareholdings. Four years later *Forbes* would carry a similar portrait of the losses in the October 19 stock market crash.

From 1927 to 1929 the richest individuals' gains and losses were principally in the $25 million to $100 million range. Greater ups and downs began in the 1970s and intensified in the 1980s. Taking the *Fortune* and *Forbes* surveys together, and also including the lesser (but *over* $200 million) shareholders named by the magazines but not listed above, some hundred and fifty Americans owned so much publicly traded corporate

TABLE 9A

INCREASE IN STOCK MARKET VALUATION OF CORPORATE
SHAREHOLDINGS, AUGUST 12, 1982—JULY 1,1983*

| Name | Company | Gain In $ Millions | In Percent |
|------|---------|--------------------|-----------|
| David Packard | Hewlett-Packard | $1,212 | 134% |
| George P. Mitchell | Mitchell Energy | 624 | 203 |
| William R. Hewlett | Hewlett-Packard | 599 | 134 |
| Jane B. Cook | Dow Jones | 515 | 175 |
| Kirk Kerkorian | MGM Grand Hotels | | |
| | MGM/UA Entertainment | 443 | 213 |
| Leslie H. Wexner | The Limited Inc. | 440 | 505 |
| H. Ross Perot | Electronic Data Systems | 412 | 171 |
| David B. Shakarian | General Nutrition | 360 | 299 |
| An Wang | Wang Labs | 357 | 220 |
| Sam Walton | Wal-Mart Stores | 301 | 216 |
| Alice L. Walton | Wal-Mart Stores | 297 | 216 |
| Jim C. Walton | Wal-Mart Stores | 297 | 216 |
| John T. Walton | Wal-Mart Stores | 297 | 216 |
| S. Robson Walton | Wal-Mart Stores | 297 | 216 |
| James L. Knight | Knight-Ridder | 290 | 106 |
| Steven P. Jobs | Apple Computer | 265 | 272 |
| Warren E. Buffet | Berkshire Hathaway | | |
| | Blue Chip Stamps | 248 | 110 |
| K. Philip Hwang | TeleVideo Systems | 247 | 49 |
| William J. Pulte | Pulte Home Corp. | 239 | 556 |
| John W. Kluge | Metromedia | 230 | 176 |
| Carl H. Lindner | Penn & Central | | |
| | Gulf & Western | 222 | 76 |
| A. C. Markkula, Jr. | Apple Computer | 222 | 243 |
| Leon Levine | Family Dollar Stores | 220 | 311 |
| Milton Petrie | Petrie Stores | 219 | 86 |
| Irving Gould | Commodore International | 217 | 307 |

* The basis and methodology of Fortune's calculations appear on p. 240.

stock that major surges or collapses in the Dow-Jones Industrial
Average could add or subtract centimillions of their net worth.
Roughly as many large fortunes resided in *privately* held firms,
beyond easy calculation, but weighing almost as heavily on the
scales of overall U.S. wealth.

TABLE 9B

DECLINES IN NET WORTH, SEPT. 15, 1987–OCT. 23, 1987

| Name | Source of Wealth | Decline | |
|------|------------------|---------|--|
| | | In $ Millions | In Percent |
| Sam Walton | Wal-Mart Stores | 2,598 | 31% |
| Leslie Wexner | The Limited | 1,046 | 50 |
| Rupert Murdoch | Publishing | 981 | 47 |
| David Packard | Hewlett-Packard | 914 | 32 |
| Ted Arison | Cruise Ships/Banking | 717 | 40 |
| Bob Magness | Cable TV | 450 | 61 |
| William Hewlett | Hewlett Packard | 426 | 29 |
| Ewing Kauffman | Marion Laboratories | 406 | 30 |
| Donald Fisher | The Gap | 386 | 67 |
| Kirk Kerkorian | Investments | 375 | 39 |
| Warren Buffett | Stock market | 370 | 18 |
| Milton Petrie | Petrie Stores | 345 | 27 |
| Roy Speer | Home Shopping Network | 344 | 57 |
| Robert Naify | Movie theaters, cable TV | 339 | 68 |
| Marshall Naify | Movie theaters, cable TV | 339 | 68 |
| Jane Cook | Dow Jones | 326 | 36 |
| Edgar Bronfman | Seagram Co. | 319 | 18 |
| Carl Icahn | Financier | 313 | 60 |
| Leon Hess | Amerada Hess | 276 | 44 |
| Katharine Graham | Washington Post Co. | 269 | 31 |
| An Wang | Wang Laboratories | 237 | 33 |
| William Kelly | Kelly Services | 226 | 46 |
| Lowell Paxson | Home Shopping Network | 221 | 58 |
| William Ford | Ford Motor Co. | 218 | 24 |
| Saul Steinberg | Financier | 215 | 33 |

Middle Americans began to appreciate the size of this vast wealth with the 1989 revelation that investment banker Michael Milken, the pioneer of high-yield, high-risk "junk bonds," received $550 million in salary and bonuses for 1987, making him the highest-paid employee in history. *The Wall Street Journal* noted that Milken might have fallen short of the inflation-adjusted gross take of Chicago crime boss Al Capone in 1927, but that he overshadowed two other financial legends, J. P. Morgan and John D. Rockefeller. The latter's earnings, at his

1910–13 peak, were $400 million a year in 1989 dollars (much less in the currency of the day).[15]

At the end of the Reagan era, as the national mood began to shift, the nation's unprecedented hierarchy of wealth can be summed up as follows. First, fifty billionaires headed by down-home Arkansawyer Sam Walton of Wal-Mart and ex–deputy defense secretary David Packard of Hewlett-Packard. Then another seventy-five to one hundred fifty half-billionaires. And below them, another thousand lesser centimillionaires—men and women whose wealth had its genesis in everything from inheritance to nursing-home chains, teddy bears and the invention of "fuzz-buster" radar. In 1980 there had been only three hundred centimillionaires, and in 1970 not quite one hundred fifty. Late-nineteenth-century wealth increases might have been sharper, but lesser sums were involved. Further down the upper rungs of the U.S. economic ladder, the roughly one hundred thousand Americans enjoying decamillionaire status in 1988, with $10 million or more in assets, included many regional and local real estate developers, media owners, people with midsized businesses, cousins of large family fortunes, lucky investors, successful deal-making lawyers, multiple fast-food franchisers, the occasional doctor, and senior corporate executives enriched by bonuses, stock options or the right "golden parachute."

Overall, two hundred thousand to four hundred thousand people in the United States—roughly one or two tenths of 1 percent of the total population—belonged to immediate families that, having at least $10 million, could assuredly be called rich. These were the Americans overrepresented in places like Park Avenue, Greenwich, Southampton, Locust Valley, Lyford Cay, Upperville, Palm Beach, Beverly Hills and Bel-Air.

Estimates projected well over a million other Americans as millionaires or better. Seven hundred fifty thousand or so fell into the $1–1.999 million prosperous upper-middle-class range; some three hundred thousand found themselves in the $2–4.999 million category, and two hundred thousand were in the $5–9.999 million range. Large numbers of this latter group could also be classified as "rich," especially if they lived outside the large metropolitan centers. So the total number of "rich" Americans, including immediate families, may have totaled four hundred thousand to seven hundred thousand persons. Here is where the economic polarization of the 1980s left its most striking mark—on the record share of postwar U.S. affluence that was being enjoyed not so much by the top quintile of the population as *by the top 1 percent or even one half of 1 percent.**

Similar concentrations in the past had eventually invited attack. If history held true to past form, the 1990s could see a cultural and economic countertrend like the one symbolized by Thorstein Veblen's attack on "conspicuous consumption" in his 1899 book, *The Theory of the Leisure Class*, or by the resentful demands for economic redistribution voiced in the early 1930s by Huey Long's Share the Wealth clubs, which registered five to eight million adherents nationally.

The realignment of wealth in the 1980s appears to have been almost as pronounced as in earlier heydays. From 1866 to 1896, the share of national income passing into the hands of the top 5 percent of the country appears to have risen—not that any official tabulations exist—by 4 to 8 percentage points, principally at the expense of the traumatized agricultural sector. The shift during the 1920s was comparable. One tabulation shows the concentration of wealth in the hands of Americans making over twenty-five thousand dollars a year—a very small group then—rising by 4 percentage points.[16] Change in the Reagan era was not much less. The top 5 percent of Americans appear to have increased their share of the nation's income by some 3 to 4 percent, aided by federal policies ranging from economic deregulation to upper-bracket tax reduction and high real interest rates. Even so, 3 to 4 percent of a $4 trillion economy represented a movement of $120 billion to $160 billion a year, enough over a decade to swell hundreds of thousands of new fortunes and to reduce the circumstances of tens of millions of other citizens. In prior decades transfers of this magnitude eventually made their beneficiaries targets of an emerging national resentment, although not until the economy entered some crisis. Excessive concentration of wealth was then seen to be part of the problem.

---

* By 1989 Congressional Budget Office projections showed the percentage of family income in the hands of the top 1 percent of Americans rising from 9 percent in 1980 to nearly 12 percent in 1988.

TABLE 10

HOW DIFFERENT GROUPS FARED IN THE REAGAN YEARS

*Increases in index, 1976 equals 100.*

| Year | CEOs | Workers | Retirees | Investors | Homeowners | CPI |
|------|------|---------|----------|-----------|------------|-----|
| 1979 | 100  | 100     | 100      | 100       | 100        | 100 |
| 1980 | 109  | 107     | 116      | 132       | 112        | 113 |
| 1981 | 123  | 116     | 131      | 126       | 119        | 123 |
| 1982 | 139  | 121     | 143      | 153       | 122        | 127 |
| 1983 | 148  | 128     | 150      | 187       | 126        | 132 |
| 1984 | 165  | 133     | 157      | 199       | 130        | 137 |
| 1985 | 183  | 136     | 163      | 263       | 136        | 142 |
| 1986 | 200  | 138     | 166      | 312       | 144        | 144 |
| 1987 | 226  | 142     | 174      | 326       | 154        | 150 |

Source: Scott Burns, *Dallas News*, August 21, 1988. Data from Towers, Perrin, the National Association of Realtors and official economic indicators.

# THE WINNERS: BUSINESS, FINANCE AND THE PROFESSIONS

Not everyone in the upper one half of 1 percent, 1 percent or 5 percent of the country prospered under Reagan. Scores of the Fortune 500 companies of 1981 no longer existed in 1988, having been acquired or gone bankrupt. A half-dozen Texas centimillionaires had flirted with insolvency, and several lost. Hundred of thousands of managers and entrepreneurs had failed—and not just in agriculture or the oil business.

But in the main the 1980s saw upper-bracket America pull farther ahead of the rest of the nation. In August, just after the GOP convention, conservative economics columnist Scott Burns said, uncharacteristically: "The facts suggest that the '80s will be known as the decade of the fat cats, a time when entrepreneurial pieties were used to beat the average worker into cowed submission while America's corporate elite moved yet higher on the hog"[17] Tough words? Burns allowed as much, but then supported his case with the data presented above in Table 10. From 1981 on, workers barely kept up with inflation and home-

TABLE 11

THE FORBES 400 DURING THE REAGAN YEARS:
THE VERY RICH OUTGAIN INFLATION
(INDEX: JULY 1982 EQUALS 100)

|  | 1982 | 1983 | 1984 | 1985 | 1986 | 1987 | 1988 | 1989 |
|---|---|---|---|---|---|---|---|---|
| Forbes 400 Total Net Worth Index | 100 | 128 | 136 | 146 | 170 | 239 | 239 | 293 |
| Consumer Price Index (July) | 100 | 103 | 107 | 111 | 112 | 117 | 122 | 128 |

Source: U.S. Commerce Department, *Forbes* magazine, October 24, 1988, p. 347, and update. In dollars, the total net worth of the Forbes 400 went from 92 billion to about 270 billion.

owners on average could stay only a bit ahead. Retirees did better, managing modest inflation-adjusted advances. Corporate executives and investors were the prime 1980s beneficiaries. Their gains roared ahead of the consumer price index like a sonic boom.

Between 1981 and 1988, as Table 11 shows, the net worth of the Forbes 400 richest Americans roughly tripled. So did their average net worth, and so did the minimum assets needed to qualify for the list. No other data sum up so clearly how the country's wealthiest families flourished under Reagan.

But the sectors changed. As deflation gathered force in 1982 jobs and fortunes were lost in energy, mining, agriculture and portions of basic manufacturing industry. Between January 1981 and July 1987 employment in oil, gas and mining shriveled from 624,000 persons to 430,000. A lot of oil millionaires— the sort Hollywood has always liked to parade in flashy three-hundred-dollar cowboy boots—lost their companies as well as their canary-yellow Cadillacs. Republican party contributions from Texan and Oklahoman independent oilmen, which had been a revolutionary political force in 1980, fell off sharply. People whose money was tied to Mahoning Valley steel, Minnesota farm-equipment dealerships or Oregon timber mills stopped buying condominiums in Scottsdale and Sarasota.

Until 1987, when a boom in exports stimulated by a devalued dollar fueled a resurgence of basic U.S. manufacturing, the

TABLE 12

JOBS: THE SHIFT DURING THE REAGAN YEARS

| Industry | Jan. 1981 | July 1987 |
|---|---|---|
| Total payroll | 90,127,000 | 102,115,000 |
| Oil, gas and mining | 624,000 | 430,000 |
| Construction | 4,302,000 | 5,009,000 |
| All manufacturing | 20,178,000 | 19,098,000 |
| Lumber | 689,000 | 743,000 |
| Furniture | 460,000 | 519,000 |
| Steel | 510,000 | 275,000 |
| Machinery | 2,483,000 | 2,037,000 |
| Electrical and electronic | 2,083,000 | 2,087,000 |
| Autos | 793,000 | 805,000 |
| Apparel | 1,239,000 | 1,127,000 |
| Textiles | 831,000 | 736,000 |
| Leather | 222,000 | 153,000 |
| Miscellaneous manufacturing | 407,000 | 370,000 |
| All services | Not available | 76,853,000 |
| Transportation | 2,935,000 | 3,126,000 |
| Communications | 2,213,000 | 2,218,000 |
| Wholesale trade | 5,321,000 | 5,790,000 |
| Retail trade | 15,075,000 | 18,278,000 |
| Food and drink | 4,698,000 | 5,986,000 |
| Finance, insurance and real estate | 5,255,000 | 6,614,000 |
| Business services | 3,194,000 | 5,101,000 |
| Health | 5,436,000 | 6,884,000 |

Source: Bureau of Labor Statistics (*New York Times*, August 18, 1987)

1980s' great expansion in both employment and corporate profits—and new fortunes—was concentrated in the service industries, particularly communications, retail trade, food and drink,
finance, insurance and real estate, business services and health.
Part of the explanation was that while energy, mining and basic
manufacturing suffered from collapsing commodity prices and
cheap imports, many service industries profited from these phenomena—as well as from the consumer spending wave unleashed by tax cuts, cheap farm products and the tax breaks for
real estate provided by the 1981 tax cuts. Table 12 shows how

employment was expanding in service vocations even as it was shrinking in old-line manufacturing. The best opportunities to make money followed the same pathways.

Many of the lost manufacturing jobs had been high-paying tickets to middle-class status for two generations of postwar blue-collar workers, a process that limited socioeconomic disparity. In 1968 or 1972 hundreds of unionized plants across the North employed large numbers of $20,000-a-year workers in industries where Fortune 500 company CEOs were making $200,000 or $300,000 a year. As service industries took over, with education and talent counting for more and unions for less, much wider cleavages would be the rule—a bottom stratum of low-paid $4.50- and $6.25-an-hour employees supporting an upper echelon of senior executives and professionals making forty, fifty or sixty times as much.

The great new wealth of the Reagan era had its foundations in this new economy, just as a century earlier many of the Gilded Age's new fortunes were made in steel, oil, railroads and heavy machinery. By late 1987 *Fortune*'s profile of the richest people in the world identified five principal categories of wealth accumulation at the billionaire level—real estate, retailing, computers, food and drink, and communications.* A year later, from a slightly different perspective, *Forbes* listed thirty-three men who "had created fortunes large enough ($225 million or over) to join the Forbes 400 in less time than it takes to age good Scotch." Their classification by industry pretty much followed *Fortune*'s: finance, real estate, entertainment/communications, technology and manufacturing. In fact, the manufacturing category in *Forbes*' listings was a little misleading, because three of its four members—Paul Fireman of Reebok, Philip Knight of Nike and Polo's Ralph Lauren—more accurately made their money out of footwear and clothing fashions, a consumerist category. These are the sectors, most of them favored by 1980s public policy, in which *Forbes* and *Fortune*

---

* Parenthetically, two other sectors that notably expanded their share of GNP during the Reagan years—health care and the military—produced few of the era's new large fortunes but, like other service industries, bolstered the decade's concentration of income among middle- and upper-bracket professionals and along the coastal states where health, biotechnology, high-technology, aerospace, research and military facilities were concentrated.

charted the fast money and/or billionaire fortunes of the Reagan era.

The only substantial *Fortune* category of U.S. billionaires *not* listed in the table on page 171—individuals and families with riches derived from oil—makes a different but important point. Oil was declining as a source of new wealth, and most of the individuals and families originally enriched by oil—the Bass brothers ($4.0 billion), Charles and David Koch ($3.0 billion), the Hunts ($2.6 billion in various branches), David and Laurence Rockefeller ($1.5 billion), Gordon Getty, Philip Anschutz and Marvin Davis—were listed by *Fortune* as easing into other endeavors, principally investments and real estate.

Finance alone built few billion-dollar fortunes in the 1980s relative to real estate, communications or computers, but it is almost impossible to overstate Wall Street's role during the decade, partly because disinflation and other federal policies favored financial assets (stocks, bonds, et cetera) over nonfinancial assets and partly because a fair percentage of the new or enlarged fortunes relied on leveraging—playing the spread between the rate at which asset prices increased (or could be pushed up) and the after-tax cost of borrowing money to buy those assets. Innovative financial techniques were essential. And that, in turn, meant that although few financial practitioners were becoming billionaires in the 1980s, the sector *was* producing record incomes for a record number of investment bankers and money managers—enough, by 1987–88, to provide caricatures of greed for books and movies alike.

Populism has always thrived on finance—on the heyday caricature of Wall Street and its overpaid, manipulative paper profiteers. The anti-elite themes of Andrew Jackson, William Jennings Bryan and Franklin D. Roosevelt spewed more resentment at Philadelphia's Bank of the United States and later at Wall Street than at the transgressions of lumber barons, railroad kings or oilmen. Industry and transportation can anger the public with poor wages, unfair working conditions or excessive charges, but the zeniths of U.S. economic trauma and income inequality have involved currency, interest rates, banks, expansive debt, securities manipulation and speculation. In the political reactions following the two prior heydays, financiers and corporate manipulators—such as Jay Gould in the 1880s and

Samuel Insull in the 1920s—were the great targets of reformers and congressional investigative committees alike.

By the late 1980s the financial sector was once again in position to play a similar role. Tables 13 and 14 show that as of 1988 the major new fortunes in finance were being made not by the pedigreed Yale clubmen manning partners' desks at Brown Brothers Harriman or Dillon Read, but by buccaneers—corporate raiders and leveraged buyout specialists, latter-day Goulds and Insulls. And once again the rewards had increased spectacularly. Back in 1981 the financial community's biggest earners had made five to ten million dollars a year. By 1986, however, the top dozen incomes ranged between $35 million and $125 million, in 1987 between $25 million and $100 million and in 1988, between $50 million and $200 million a year. If anything, these figures were probably understated—like the estimate that Michael Milken made $60 million in 1987 when his compensation actually totaled $550 million. Equally significant, the cutoff point for the financial community's "top 100" in 1987 was $4 million of compensation. And this in the year when the stock market had crashed! In order to keep the 1987 list "from becoming a Goldman Sachs yearbook," *Financial World* had to set up a special, *separate* listing for the estimated forty-eight Goldman partners making at least $4 million that year.[18] To make the 1987 or 1988 lists long enough to gather in everyone in the financial community drawing at least $1 million in compensation, experts indicated, would have required several thousand listings.

Paper entrepreneurialism—mergers, acquisitions and junk bonds—was the key to the swollen 1986–88 earnings list. A few people were making huge sums for owning or managing major mutual funds, but most of Wall Street's big money came from restructuring and repackaging corporate America. Selling stock to retail clients, investment management firms or mutual funds paid well; repackaging, remortgaging or dismantling a Fortune 500 company paid magnificently.

The public policy changes of the Reagan era, from antitrust to deregulation, helped make all this possible. Just before the 1988 election, James O'Leary, retired chief economist of the New York–based United States Trust Company, complained about how the merger-buyout craze had been unleashed: "In

TABLE 13

*1987 Billionairedom*

| Name/Company | Estimated Net Worth |
|---|---|
| **Real Estate** | |
| Alfred Taubman | $2.5 Bil |
| Jay & Robert Pritzker | 1.5 |
| Harry Helmsley | 1.3 |
| The Marriott Family | 1.3 |
| Donald Bren | 1.2 |
| Samuel LeFrak | 1.0 |
| **Communications** | |
| Samuel & Donald Newhouse | 7.5 |
| John Kluge | 3.1 |
| Anne Cox Chambers & Barbara Cox Anthony | 2.5 |
| Rupert Murdoch | 2.2 |
| William & Randolph Hearst | 1.5 |
| Katharine & Donald Graham | 1.1 |
| Walter Annenberg | 1.1 |
| **Computers** | |
| David Packard | 3.0 |
| Ross Perot | 2.5 |
| William Hewlett | 2.0 |
| William Gates | 1.2 |
| **Retailing** | |
| Sam Walton | 8.7 |
| Leslie Wexner | 2.4 |
| Milton Petrie | 1.1 |
| Donald Fisher | 1.0 |

TABLE 13 (*Cont.*)

*1987 Billionairedom*

| Name/Company | Estimated Net Worth |
|---|---|
| **Food and Drink** | |
| The Mars Family | 5.0 |
| Edgar & Charles Bronfman | 3.6 |
| The MacMillan Family | 2.9 |
| John Dorrance | 1.5 |
| August Busch | 1.3 |
| John Lupton | 1.3 |
| William & Joseph Coors | 1.2 |
| Michel Fribourg | 1.2 |
| Ernest & Julio Gallo | 1.0 |
| John Simplot | 1.0 |

recent years, we have gone hog wild on deregulation. The antitrust laws aren't being enforced anymore, opening this thing up to abuse."[19] And a few days earlier, Martin Lipton, the New York lawyer who reportedly received history's largest legal fee for advising on a corporate merger, nevertheless complained that "we and our children will pay a gigantic price for allowing abusive takeover tactics and boot-strap, junk-bond takeovers. . . . As with tulip bulbs, South Sea bubbles, pyramid investment trusts, Florida land, REITs, L.D.C. loans, Texas banks and all the other financial market frenzies of the past, the denouement will be a crash."[20]

But the money to be made brought even skeptics aboard the gravy train, working to put more and more companies "into play." Between 1980 and early 1988, the cumulative value of mergers, acquisitions, takeovers and leveraged buyouts, friendly and hostile, exceeded two thirds of a trillion dollars,* which

---

* One brokerage industry analyst, Perrin Long, suggested that only merger fees and LBO profits kept the securities industry profitable during the first nine months of 1988.

## TABLE 14
### FINANCIAL WORLD "WALL STREET 100 INDEX"
### (TOP 12 EARNERS EACH YEAR)
### IN MILLIONS OF DOLLARS

| *Calendar Year 1986* | | *Calendar Year 1987* | |
|---|---|---|---|
| Michel David-Weill, Lazard Frères | $125 | Paul Tudor Jones, Tudor Investment Corp. | $80–100 |
| George Soros, Soros Fund Mgt. | $90–100 | George Soros, Soros Fund Mgt. | $75 |
| Richard Dennis, C&D Commod. | $80 | George Roberts, KKR | $70 |
| Michael Milken, Drexel* | up to $80 | Henry Kravis, KKR | $70 |
| J. M. Davis, D. H. Blair | $60–65 | Michael Milken, Drexel* | $60 |
| Jerome Kohlberg, KKR | $50 | Michel David-Weill, Lazard Frères | $54 |
| Henry Kravis, KKR | $50 | Jerome Kohlberg, KKR | $35 |
| George Roberts, KKR | $50 | John Weinberg, Goldman Sachs | $32 |
| Ray Chambers, Wesray | $45–50 | Donald Carter, Carter Organization | $32 |
| William Simon, Wesray | $45–50 | Theodore Forstmann, Forstmann Little | $30 |
| M. Steinhardt, Steinhardt Partners | $40 | Ray Chambers, Wesray | $28 |
| E. Johnson III, FMR Corp. | $35 | Reginald Lewis, TLC Group | $25 |

### *Calendar Year 1988*

| | |
|---|---|
| Michael Milken, Drexel | $180–199 |
| Gordon Cain, Sterling Group | $120 |
| Henry Kravis, KKR | $110 |
| George Roberts, KKR | $110 |
| Robert Bass | $100 |
| Paul Bilzerian, Singer Co. | $80 |
| Irwin Jacobs, Minstar Inc. | $75–100 |
| Michel David-Weill, Lazard Freres | $65 |
| Peter Peterson, Blackstone Group | $50–60 |
| Richard Rainwater | $50–60 |
| Joseph Schuchert, Kelso & Co. | $50–60 |
| S. Schwartzman, Blackstone Group | $50–60 |

* Now known to have been substantially underestimated.
Source: Financial World Magazine

not only supported escalating stock prices but provided an abundance of commissions, fees and profits.[21] With normal investment banker fees ranging between one half of 1 percent and 1.5 percent of the transaction price, 1980–88 activity generated at least $5 billion in fees, mostly during the second Reagan administration. Back in 1984 investment banker fees had come to only $159 million. By 1988, however, the total fees on reported deals had risen to $1.3 billion.[22]

For 1988 (through November 8), LBOs alone provided Morgan Stanley with $62 million, Goldman Sachs with $45 million, First Boston with $35 million, Kohlberg Kravis Roberts with $28 million, and Kelso with $25 million.[23] Just after Election Day *The New York Times* speculated that Henry Kravis's RJR Nabisco deal could see potential fees "run as high as $500 million."[24] It actually produced $700 million in fees.[25]

Beyond the investment community, few benefited from these mergers and LBOs. Small shareholders being bought out often did well. But the evidence seems compelling that the greatest benefit went to the middlemen—to the advisers, promoters, packagers and refinancers—and that the deal mania was driven less by its merits than by its staggering profits. Similar tendencies had developed during the 1920s, but without the international implications so daunting in the 1980s.

In 1987–88, several of New York's prominent investment banking firms and boutiques—including Goldman Sachs, Wasserstein Perella and the Blackstone Group—sold partial ownership to Tokyo investors laden with U.S. dollar holdings. In 1989 one New York magazine identified the leading principals of Wasserstein Perella and the Blackstone Group as *kagemusha*, "shadow warriors," who represented the interests of Japan.*

---

* Accusations that U.S. capitalists were "selling out America" through alliances with foreign financiers were hardly new to the 1980s. In his early-nineteenth-century attacks on the Bank of the United States, Andrew Jackson had criticized its partial ownership by foreigners. Similarly, late-nineteenth-century populists castigated the alliance between Wall Street capitalists and British financiers. Populist presidential candidate James Weaver decried Wall Street in 1892 as "the Western extension of Threadneedle and Lombard Streets," saying Great Britain was regaining dominion over her long-lost colonies. William Jennings Bryan condemned the transatlantic reach of Britain's gold standard in his famous speech to the 1896 Democratic National Convention. By the late 1980s some U.S. economists, notably David Hale, were speculating that Japan might be developing the same economic bogeyman's

Great wealth and hints of economic disloyalty were beginning to overlap.

Accountants, proxy solicitation firms and lawyers, in particular, also profited, a further confirmation of the preeminence of restructuring and assets manipulation. Attorneys' gains, while not as great as those of the financial community, were impressive. In 1981 the average personal income for lawyers was $60,000 to $70,000; in the American Bar Association *Journal*'s annual survey in 1984 it was $83,643, and by 1989 it had risen to $117,800. At merger-specialist firms like Wachtell, Lipton, Rosen & Katz and Skadden, Arps, Slate, Meagher & Flom, the profits per partner for 1987 reached $1.4 million and $885,000, respectively.[26] Even the starting salary in big New York firms for new young attorneys fresh out of law school had climbed from $35,000 in 1981 to $67,000 six years later. Tables 15A and 15B profile the 1988 earnings of America's best-paid lawyers—top trial lawyers and entertainment attorneys did even better than merger specialists—and illustrate the 1987 partnership earnings of the ten most profitable law firms in New York City.

Similar changes occurred in Washington, D.C., Boston, Philadelphia, Atlanta, Chicago and Los Angeles. During the 1980s the total number of lawyers—counting both partners and associates—in upper-caste New York City law firms, admittedly a subjective calculus, more or less doubled from ten to twenty thousand. Even a smaller city like Boston saw the number of top-firm lawyers double from some fifteen hundred to three thousand. All in all, and also including three to five prominent firms in cities like Seattle or Cincinnati, plus one or two equivalents each in cities like Portland, Maine and Mobile, Alabama, the major law firms in the United States probably counted some fifty to sixty thousand attorneys by 1988. Of those over forty years old, half to two thirds were probably millionaires. In July 1988 *American Lawyer* reported that the average income for the 1,318 partners at the fifteen most profitable law firms in the United States was $739,000.[27] Presumably almost all were mil-

---

role in U.S. politics that Britain had played a century earlier. Implications of economic disloyalty have always been troublesome for globally minded capitalists.

## TABLE 15A

### THE BEST-PAID LAWYERS IN AMERICA, 1988

| Top Ten Trial Lawyers | Estimated 1988 income |
|---|---|
| Joseph D. Jamail | $450 million |
| Herbert Hafif | $ 40 million |
| Gerald Michaud | $ 18 million |
| Walter Umphrey | $ 14.5 million |
| Max Toberoff | $ 12 million |
| Ronald Krist | $ 9 million |
| John O. Quinn | $ 8 million |
| Richard W. Mithoff | $ 7.4 million |
| Ernest Cannon | $ 7 million |
| Stanley S. Schwartz | $ 6.2 million |

| Top Ten Corporate Lawyers | Estimated 1988 income |
|---|---|
| Joseph Flom† | $ 5 million |
| Raoul L. Felder* | $ 3.8 million |
| Harry Brittenham* | $ 3 million |
| Allen Grubman* | $ 3 million |
| Martin Lipton† | $ 3 million |
| Kenneth Ziffren* | $ 3 million |
| John Eastman* | $ 3 million |
| John Branca* | $ 2.5 million |
| Arthur Fleischer† | $ 2.5 million |
| Samuel Butler† | $ 2.4 million |

† mergers and acquisitions; * entertainment and celebrities.
Source: *Forbes*, October 16, 1989

lionaires. The magazine's overall assessment of the state of upper-echelon American lawyerdom in 1988 went as follows:

> For most of the law's heavy hitters, business has been so good that law is fast becoming not just a source of wealth for the few but one of the country's largest sources of high incomes.
>
> Consider this: According to *Forbes*, the average salary and bonus compensation in 1987 for the 800 chief executives of the country's largest corporations was $762,253. That's 800 chief executives with an average income of $762,253. But at the 15 firms in the AM LAW 100 with the highest profits per partner,

TABLE 15B

THE TEN MOST PROFITABLE NEW YORK CITY LAW FIRMS,
1987

| Firm<br>(1987 Rank) | Number of Partners<br>1987 | Profits Per Partner<br>1987 |
|---|---|---|
| Wachtell, Lipton,<br>    Rosen & Katz | 43 | $1,405,000 |
| Cravath, Swaine & Moore | 64 | 1,220,000 |
| Cahill, Gordon & Reindel | 52 | 1,200,000 |
| Skadden, Arps, Slate,<br>    Meagher & Flom | 177 | 1,100,000 |
| Davis, Polk & Wardwell | 92 | 915,000 |
| Sullivan & Cromwell | 89 | 1,080,000 |
| Simpson, Thacher & Bartlett | 84 | 645,000 |
| Willkie, Farr & Gallagher | 80 | 640,000 |
| Cleary, Gottlieb, Steen &<br>    Hamilton | 92 | 580,000 |
| Weil, Gotshal & Manges | 90 | 555,000 |

there were 1,318 partners with average incomes of $739,000.

Another measure of the law business as big business: When we started this survey four years ago, there were five firms with gross revenues of more than $100 million. In 1987 there were 28.[28]

Smooth, prosperous lawyers have not been far behind financiers as a target of populist ire, an animosity as old as Shakespeare, who had one of his fifteenth-century figures suggest, "Let's kill all the lawyers." The legal community, too, had enjoyed a notable boom in previous U.S. financial heydays.

The greatest benefits went to the participating capitalists, whether financiers, corporate executives, investors or business owners. The last, of course, furnished most of the names on the list of richest Americans in 1988, just as in 1888. Multibillion-dollar companies where privately held ownership still resided in individuals—from Mars and Cargill to Deering-Milliken and Koch Industries—provided the best illustrations. Their principal owners were billionaires. And many a decamillionaire's assets lay in nothing more than a small manufacturing company or a dozen fast-food franchises.* A new phenomenon, as Table 16 shows, was the 1981–88 explosion in top CEO compensation packages and the leap of many of *these* individuals into deca-millionaire and capitalist status.

Rewards like these began blurring the economic divisions between top managers of major corporations and entrepreneur-ial, capitalist founders or owners. Chief executives were becom-ing more like owners, as their compensation—in theory, at least—reflected corporate success. Yet the correlations were er-ratic. Heads of money-losing companies were adding only a little less income than the stewards of high-achieving firms.

In April 1988 *Business Week* released a startling statistic: during 1987, a year with just 4 percent inflation, the average CEO compensation at 339 of the nation's largest publicly held corporations rose by 48 percent to $1.8 million.[29] It rose 14 percent more in 1988—to $2.02 million. At *Forbes*, that mag-azine's survey of the chief executive officers of the "Forbes 800" top companies turned up an average total compensation of $1.28 million in 1987, a 28 percent jump from the year before.[30] And *Electronic Business* magazine reported that the one hundred highest-paid executives in high-tech companies earned an average of $785,000 in 1987, and seventeen received more than $1 million.[31] Table 17 shows the 1983–88 rise in CEO salaries using the data from the annual *Business Week* survey.

Where stock options were involved, vice presidents and others below the CEO level occasionally outgained their chairmen. However, surveys based only on salary and bonus confirmed a widening gap between CEOs and other executives during the 1980s. According to one sampling of 1987 pay levels in thirty major companies, the median total *cash* compensation for chief executives was $1,087,500. For the company's second-ranking executive it dropped to $645,000; for the third, fourth and fifth in the hierarchy, to $520,500, $460,500 and $433,800, re-spectively. The results added up to "a widening of the differ-ential" between the man at the top and the next-ranking

* Marketing expert Thomas Stanley estimated in early 1989 that most of the nation's 1.5 million millionaires were small-business owners: "You are ten times more likely to become a millionaire if you own a small business."

TABLE 16

THE TWENTY-FIVE HIGHEST-PAID U.S. EXECUTIVES, 1981–88
(INCLUDING 1988 SALARY, BONUS AND LONG-TERM COMPENSATION)

| *1981* | | *1988* | |
|---|---|---|---|
| *Name/Position/Firm* | *Total Compensation (millions)* | *Name/Position/Firm* | *Total Compensation (millions)* |
| R. Genin/Exec. VP/Schlumberger | $5.7 | M. Eisner/Chmn/Walt Disney | $40.1 |
| F. Hickey/CEO/Gen. Instrument | 5.3 | F. Wells/Pres/Walt Disney | 32.1 |
| J. Kluge/CEO/Metromedia | 4.2 | E. Horrigan/VChmn/RJR Nabisco | 21.7 |
| J. Riboud/CEO/Schlumberger | 3.0 | F. Johnson/CEO/RJR Nabisco | 21.1 |
| H. Gray/CEO/United Technologies | 3.0 | M. Davis/Chmn/Gulf & Western | 16.3 |
| R. Adam/CEO/NL Industries | 2.9 | R. Gelb/Chmn/Bristol-Meyers | 14.1 |
| R. Cizik/CEO/Cooper Industries | 2.8 | W. Stiritz/Chmn/Ralston Purina | 12.9 |
| D. Tendler/CEO/Philbro | 2.7 | B. Kerr/Chmn/Pennzoil | 11.5 |
| A. Busch III/Chmn/Anheuser-Busch | 2.6 | J. Liedtke/Chmn/Pennzoil | 11.5 |
| F. Hartley/Chmn/Union Oil | 2.3 | P. Fireman/Chmn/Reebok | 11.4 |
| S. McLean/Exec. VP/NL Industries | 2.3 | J. Robinson/Chmn/Amer. Express | 10.9 |
| H. Beretz/Pres./Philbro | 2.2 | K. Olsen/Pres/Digital Equip. | 10.0 |
| R. Anderson/Chmn/Rockwell Int'l | 2.2 | D. Petersen/Chmn/Ford Motor | 9.9 |
| D. Lewis/Chmn/Gen. Dynamics | 2.1 | J. Sculley/Chmn/Apple Computer | 9.5 |
| D. Schuman/Chmn/Bausch & Lomb | 1.9 | D. Buntrock/Chmn/Waste Mgt. | 8.4 |
| J. Lesch/CEO/Hughes Tools | 1.8 | P. Rooney/Pres/Waste Mgt. | 7.5 |
| N. Fluor/CEO/Fluor | 1.7 | P. Vagelos/Chmn/Merck | 6.9 |
| L. Crown/Exec. VP/Gen. Dynamics | 1.7 | J. Bryan/Chmn/Sara Lee | 6.8 |
| L. Jesselson/Exec. VP/Philbro | 1.7 | A. Grove/CEO/Intel | 6.4 |
| R. Grohman/CEO/Levi Strauss | 1.7 | S. Wolf/Chmn/UAL | 6.4 |
| W. Agee/CEO/Bendix | 1.7 | J. Lyons/VChmn/Merck | 6.3 |
| R. Gelb/Chmn/Bristol-Myers | 1.5 | J. Williams/Chmn/Warner-Lambert | 6.1 |
| H. Rothschild/Exec. VP/Philbro | 1.5 | L. Gerstner/Pres/Amer. Express | 6.0 |
| C. Witting/VChmn/Cooper Ind. | 1.5 | J. Stookey/Chmn/Quantum Chem. | 5.9 |
| R. Warner/Chmn/Mobil | 1.5 | S. Cook/CEO/Tribune | 5.9 |

Source: *Business Week*, May 10, 1982, May 1, 1989

executives.[32] Not surprisingly, there was also a sharp contrast between top-officer salary increases—up 56.8 percent from 1983 to 1987—and the lesser 32.6 percent increment going to the average merit-recipient white-collar employee.[33] Meanwhile the disparity between CEOs and workers was accelerating even more. In 1979 CEOs made twenty-nine times the income of the

TABLE 17

RISING AVERAGE TOTAL CORPORATE CEO COMPENSATION
(IN THOUSANDS OF DOLLARS)

|              | 1983 | 1984  | 1985  | 1986  | 1987  | 1988  |
|--------------|------|-------|-------|-------|-------|-------|
| Business Week | 900 | 1,100 | 1,200 | 1,250 | 1,800 | 2,025 |

Source: Published Business Week data and information furnished by Business Week regarding yearly percentage increases

average manufacturing worker. By 1985 the multiple was forty. By 1988, *Business Week* said the total compensation of the average CEO in its annual survey had risen to ninety-three times the earnings of the average factory worker, prompting the magazine to editorialize that "executive pay is growing out of all proportion to increases in what many other people make—from the worker on the plant floor to the teacher in the classroom."[34] Chart 6 profiles the extraordinary, unprecedented divergence that occurred during the Reagan years.

Furthermore, there was a negligible correlation between increases in CEO compensation and shareholder gains. One professor dismissed pay-for-performance relationships as "almost non-existent in a lot of companies."[35] The same was true of golden parachutes. For the top one tenth of 1 percent of Americans, national economic restructuring involved negligible risk and enormous gains. Participation in paper entrepreneurialism—even as a loser—was beginning to be its own reward.

These raw compensation numbers understated the full benefit to top-executive bank accounts, for the top tax rates had fallen, as mentioned before, from 70 percent to 28 percent, a boon to the corporate elite, but useless to most workers whose combined income tax and Social Security tax burdens remained much the same.

Highly rewarded participants in one particularly burgeoning American business, entertainment—movies, records and the like became second only to aircraft as a U.S. export in the late 1980s—included not only executives but performers and promoters.[36] Tabulations for the 1986–88 period showed that their compensation was on a par with that of the financial community. Twenty entertainment moguls made the Forbes 400 in

CHART 6

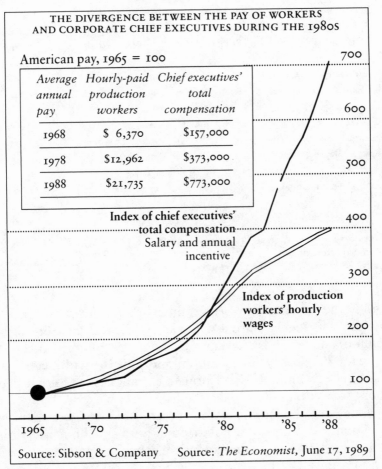

**THE DIVERGENCE BETWEEN THE PAY OF WORKERS AND CORPORATE CHIEF EXECUTIVES DURING THE 1980S**

American pay, 1965 = 100

| Average annual pay | Hourly-paid production workers | Chief executives' total compensation |
|---|---|---|
| 1968 | $ 6,370 | $157,000 |
| 1978 | $12,962 | $373,000 |
| 1988 | $21,735 | $773,000 |

Index of chief executives' total compensation
Salary and annual incentive

Index of production workers' hourly wages

700
600
500
400
300
200
100

1965    '70    '75    '80    '85    '88

Source: Sibson & Company      Source: *The Economist,* June 17, 1989

## TABLE 18

### THE TEN LARGEST CORPORATE GOLDEN PARACHUTES, 1988

|  | Company | Reason for Payment | Total package* ($ thousands) |
|---|---|---|---|
| F. Ross Johnson, CEO | RJR Nabisco | Leveraged buyout | $53,800 |
| E. A. Horrigan, Vice-Chmn. | RJR Nabisco | Leveraged buyout | 45,700 |
| Gerald Tsai Jr., Chmn. | Primerica | Commercial Credit takeover | 46,800 |
| Edward P. Evans, Chmn. | Macmillan | Maxwell takeover | 31,900 |
| Kenneth A. Yarnell, Pres. | Primerica | Commercial Credit takeover | 18,400 |
| John D. Martin, Exec. VP | RJR Nabisco | Leveraged buyout | 18,200 |
| Sanford C. Sigoloff, Chmn. | Wickes | Leveraged buyout | 15,900 |
| Whitney Stevens, Chmn. | J. P. Stevens | West Point-Pepperell takeover | 15,700 |
| Philip L. Smith, Chmn. | Pillsbury | Grand Metropolitan takeover | 11,000 |
| Wilhelm A. Mallory, Sr. VP | Wickes | Leveraged buyout | 7,500 |

* Includes final salary, bonus, long-term compensation, certain retirement benefits and estimated future annuity payments as well as parachute.
Source: *Business Week*, May 1, 1989.

1988, and tabulations of entertainment's top forty earners for the years 1988–89 started with singer Michael Jackson ($125 million) and producer Steven Spielberg ($105 million), took note of actor Bill Cosby ($95 million) and finished with actor Mel Gibson ($20 million).[37] Performers earning less than that over those two years didn't make the list.

As the decade closed, the distortion of American wealth raised questions not just about polarization but also about trivialization. Less and less of the nation's wealth was going to people who produced manufactures or commodities. Services were ascendant—from fast food to legal advice, investment vehicles, data bases and videocassettes. New heyday wealth has always been scorned for representing unfamiliar or unfashionable vocations or sectors—the "beer barons" of Victorian England are an example. Similar disdain applied to late-1980s fortunes made in everything from candy bars to pet food, cosmetics, cable television and electronic games. The mounting concentration of

wealth in the service industries, however, raised a larger problem. It was one thing for new technologies to reduce demand
for farmers, steelworkers and typists, enabling society to concentrate more resources on health, money management and leisure. But the distortion lay in the disproportionate rewards to
society's economic, legal and cultural manipulators—from lawyers and investment advisers to advertising executives, mer-
chandisers, consumer finance specialists, fashion designers,
communicators, media magnates and entertainment promoters.
Unfortunately, heyday biases in these directions are as American
as apple pie. As disposable income concentrates even more
strongly than usual in the hands of the upper 10 to 20 percent
of Americans, vocations dealing in short-term objectives and
satisfactions profit. Humdrum activities and long-term objectives suffer.

A related boom occurred in nonfinancial assets—art and
homes, in particular—linked to the taste and demand of investors, entrepreneurs, corporate managers, lawyers, doctors and
other service-sector elites. Inasmuch as the value of housing in
the United States represented most Americans' principal asset
and added up to several times the value of all the stocks on the
New York Stock Exchange, the effect of the 1980s on residential
housing values significantly amplified regional and sectoral
wealth trends.* Paralleling circumstances in Britain and Japan,
the biggest gains came in areas in or near the nation's financial
centers. As Appendix I shows, between 1981 and 1989 home
values soared 50 to 125 percent on a metropolitan area–wide
or statewide basis in Boston, Connecticut, New York City,
Washington, D.C., Philadelphia, Los Angeles, San Francisco,
San Diego and Hawaii, with the largest increases in the better
residential neighborhoods. In sharp contrast, inflation-adjusted
housing prices actually fell for the 1981–89 period in many
places, from Tulsa and Baton Rouge to Denver and Omaha,
where local economic troubles mirrored agriculture, energy or
declining manufacturing sectors. Although home prices started

* According to the Census Bureau, in 1984 home ownership was reported by
two thirds of all households and accounted for 41 percent of net worth. For
the nearly 80 percent of the population with a net worth below one hundred
thousand dollars, a lopsided 77 percent of that net worth was represented by
equity in homes and cars.

sagging in 1989 in parts of the Northeast and California, the decade's revaluations in the U.S. housing market had quietly redistributed hundreds of billions of dollars (at least on paper)—and done so with even more bias than income shifts.

In the process, some Americans lost not just housing value or opportunity but also the roof over their heads. By 1989 tent cities and shantytowns were taking shape, from New York City to San Francisco, and homeless people were organizing temporary tent cities in front of the Illinois and California state capitols. Across the nation, requests for emergency shelter were rising steadily, in small regional centers and big cities alike. In May 1989 Congressman Henry Gonzalez, chairman of the House Committee on Banking, Finance and Urban Affairs charged that by the Reagan administration's reduction of low- and moderate-income housing programs in the face of rising prices "we have made Americans nomads in their own land. Talk about refugees—we have families roaming this land, some of them living in cars and under bridges.* We're headed for the way of . . . Brussels, West Berlin, London and Paris, where 12 to 15½ years ago they were having rent squatters, they were having forcible evictions and violence."[38]

For America's richest two or three hundred thousand families, by contrast, art and antiques roughly tripled during the Reagan era, witness the increase in value from 1981 to 1989 in a cross section of art categories from the Sotheby's Index (see Appendix J). While homelessness mounted at the lower end of the economic spectrum, the art and furnishings of a representative eleven-room cooperative apartment on New York's Park Avenue could well have risen from a $675,000 value in 1981 to $1.5 million in 1989 simply by the workings of supply and demand. Similar, if lesser, explosions in art prices had taken place in the 1920s and Gilded Age booms. When the top one half of 1 percent of Americans are rolling in money, the residential luxuries

---

* Nomadism and homelessness have been recurrent characteristics of U.S. financial heydays and their aftermath. The circumstance of the late 1920s and (especially) 1930–36 are well known. But similar trends were unmistakable in the 1880s and 1890s, especially in the wake of the 1893 depression: in December of that year Governor Lorenzo Lewelling of Kansas issued by executive proclamation the so-called Tramp Circular drawing parallels to Elizabethan England and prerevolutionary France.

they crave—from Picassos and eighteenth-century English furniture to Manhattan town houses and Malibu beach homes—soar in markets virtually auxiliary to those in finance.

By 1989 the realignment of American wealth was beginning to evoke criticism, albeit less than in Britain and Japan. Following the revelation of Michael Milken's $550 million earnings for 1987, a conservative Southern survey, the Long Marketing North Carolina Poll, found a 53 percent local majority favoring a cap on the incomes of professional athletes, corporate executives, movie stars, stockbrokers and the like. Survey taker W. H. Long observed that "clearly, in America today and certainly in North Carolina today, a slowly growing majority detest excess in the earnings market."[39] Yet by any reasonable yardstick, American populist resentment was still far less than in the early 1890s or the early 1930s. Lester Thurow was not alone when he said in 1989 that "it looks like America (again) has an oligarchy," but the implications he raised awaited further events.[40] Americans do not react against wealth per se. As we have seen, however, some upper-bracket wealth accumulation was a result of favoritism in Washington policies ranging from tax cuts to tight money, permissive financial deregulation and abnormally high real interest rates. Only if that favoritism could later be said to have hurt other Americans and jeopardized the *larger* economy—important charges during prior heydays—would the scene be set for a classic populist reaction against an abusive, self-serving economic elite.

## COASTAL WINNERS, INTERIOR LOSERS: THE NEW GEOGRAPHY OF 1980S WEALTH

The political map of American popular economic frustration— and, at extremes, *revolt*—has an old geography, coasts against hinterland, and it took shape again in the 1980s.

The gap between the wealthy states and metropolitan areas and the poorer areas, mostly rural, low-income urban or small-town, grew sharply in the 1980s. To be sure, some upper-bracket neighborhoods lost ground along with their local farm or energy economies—in Houston and Tulsa, for example. But in general, American affluence indisputably shifted its geography toward the upscale residential concentrations of business owners, corporate executives, skilled service-industry professionals (not least, money managers, lawyers, doctors and communicators) and well-off retirees.

By 1988, as the U.S. Commerce Department released its 1987 regional per capita income data, the political implications were considerable. Disparities between the most prosperous sections of the country—New England, the Middle Atlantic States and the Far West—and the poorer areas (the Great Lakes, Plains, Southwest, Rocky Mountains and Southeast) had widened again after having narrowed during the sixties and seventies. Not only did this confirm much of the "bicoastal economy" thesis that the Democrats had profitably spotlighted in 1986 (yet largely put aside in 1988), but it also reconfirmed the bias and sectional vulnerability of Republican financial heyday economics.*

The precedents were all too clear. A similar division had accompanied the agricultural depression that devastated the South, Midwest and Plains from the early 1870s to the mid-1890s, while deflation worked nearly the same havoc in the Rocky Mountain mining states, just as it would a century later. Meanwhile, much of California, most of the Northeast and a fair part of the expanding Great Lakes section enjoyed Gilded Age prosperity. Once again during the 1920s, economist Wesley C. Mitchell noted that in terms of national income only three sections of the country showed a major gain from 1921 to 1928—the Middle Atlantic States, the east-north-central states (Great Lakes) and the Pacific. The South, Farm Belt and Mountain states all suffered from the post–World War I deflation in agriculture and most extractive industries.[41] As we shall see, political insurgency has *always* followed suit—the only question has been one of degree.

Chart 7 illustrates how the classic pattern of regional income gaps reemerged under the heyday economic policies of the 1980s. Maps tell the story best. The five maps on pages

* An important caveat should be stated here. By early 1988, the relative decline of the interior was ending, to some extent because of improving conditions in the heartland, particularly the Great Lakes, but also because of softening circumstances in the financial, service and high-tech centers in the New York–Boston corridor. By late 1989 clear patterns of weakness were becoming apparent in the same Northeastern coastal states that had led the Reagan-era boom, and lesser concerns were apparent in California.

CHART 7

**Regional
Differences Widen**

Per capita personal income as percent
of U.S. average

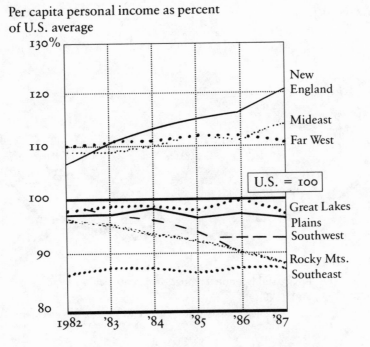

**New England:** Connecticut, Maine, Vermont, New Hampshire,
Rhode Island, Massachusetts. **Mideast:** District of Columbia,
Delaware, Maryland, New Jersey, New York, Pennsylvania.
**Great Lakes:** Illinois, Michigan, Ohio, Indiana, Wisconsin. **Plains:**
Minnesota, North Dakota, South Dakota, Iowa, Kansas, Missouri,
Nebraska. **Southeast:** North Carolina, South Carolina, Alabama,
Arkansas, Florida, Georgia, Kentucky, Louisiana, Mississippi,
Tennessee, Virginia, West Virginia. **Southwest:** Arizona, New
Mexico, Oklahoma, Texas. **Rocky Mountain:** Idaho, Colorado,
Montana, Utah, Wyoming. **Far West:** California, Nevada, Oregon,
Washington.

NOTE: Excludes Alaska and Hawaii.
Source: Department of Commerce
Source: *Wall Street Journal*, October 6, 1988

## MAP 1

**The Bicoastal Boom**   Annual rates of economic growth from first
quarter 1981 through the fourth quarter 1985

BICOASTAL

**4.0** ☐ COASTAL STATES IN BICOASTAL ECONOMY REPORT
**1.4** ☐ ALL OTHERS

ALASKA
HAWAII
*NOT SHOWN*

Sources: The Bi-Coastal Economy report, 1987 Statistical Abstract

**SHARE OF POPULATION** BY PERCENT

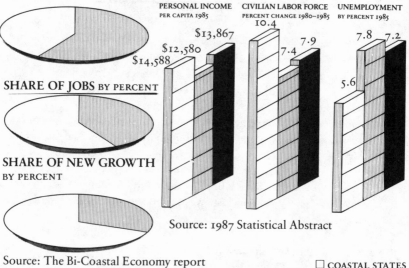

**SHARE OF JOBS** BY PERCENT

**SHARE OF NEW GROWTH**
BY PERCENT

Source: The Bi-Coastal Economy report

PERSONAL INCOME
PER CAPITA 1985
$13,867
$12,580
$14,588

CIVILIAN LABOR FORCE
PERCENT CHANGE 1980–1985
10.4
7.4      7.9

UNEMPLOYMENT
BY PERCENT 1985
7.8    7.2
5.6

Source: 1987 Statistical Abstract

☐ COASTAL STATES
▥ ALL OTHERS
■ U.S. AVERAGE

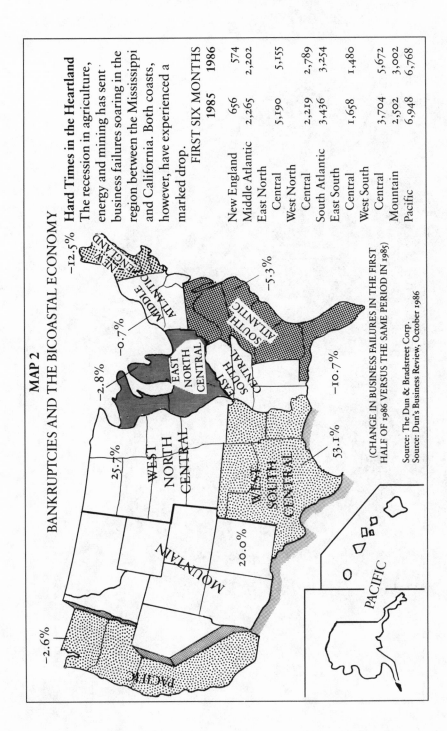

MAP 2

BANKRUPTCIES AND THE BICOASTAL ECONOMY

**Hard Times in the Heartland**
The recession in agriculture, energy and mining has sent business failures soaring in the region between the Mississippi and California. Both coasts, however, have experienced a marked drop.

| | FIRST SIX MONTHS | |
|---|---|---|
| | 1985 | 1986 |
| New England | 656 | 574 |
| Middle Atlantic | 2,265 | 2,202 |
| East North Central | 5,190 | 5,155 |
| West North Central | 2,219 | 2,789 |
| South Atlantic | 3,436 | 3,254 |
| East South Central | 1,658 | 1,480 |
| West South Central | 3,704 | 5,672 |
| Mountain | 2,502 | 3,002 |
| Pacific | 6,948 | 6,768 |

−12.5%
−5.3%
−0.7%
−2.8%
25.7%
53.1%
−10.7%
20.0%
−2.6%

NEW ENGLAND
MIDDLE ATLANTIC
SOUTH ATLANTIC
EAST NORTH CENTRAL
EAST SOUTH CENTRAL
WEST NORTH CENTRAL
WEST SOUTH CENTRAL
MOUNTAIN
PACIFIC

(CHANGE IN BUSINESS FAILURES IN THE FIRST HALF OF 1986 VERSUS THE SAME PERIOD IN 1985)

Source: The Dun & Bradstreet Corp.
Source: Dun's Business Review, October 1986

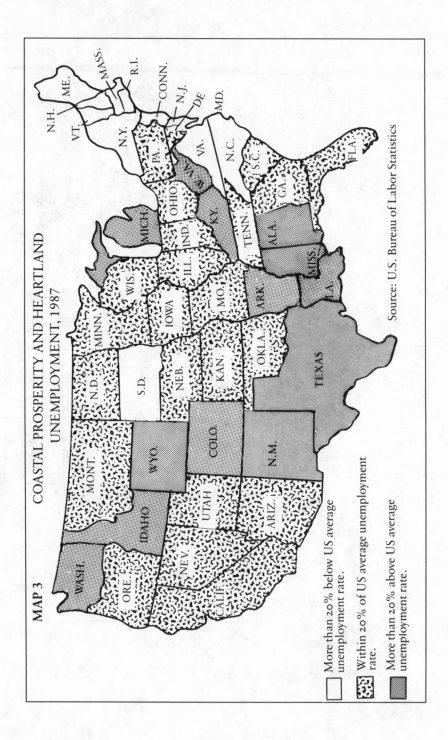

MAP 3        COASTAL PROSPERITY AND HEARTLAND
                    UNEMPLOYMENT, 1987

☐  More than 20% below US average
   unemployment rate.

▨  Within 20% of US average unemployment
   rate.

▓  More than 20% above US average
   unemployment rate.

Source: U.S. Bureau of Labor Statistics

188–90 and 195–96 illustrate the "bicoastal economy" thesis advanced in 1985–86, as well as the extent to which it was further supported but also modified by 1988–89 data.

The prosperity during the Reagan era of the eastern seaboard and the Pacific coast, principally California, was easy enough to explain. Both coasts had the nation's greatest concentration of service industries, from finance and insurance to entertainment, but also profited from rising defense outlays and the stepped-up volume of U.S. imports attendant on the trade deficit. As ports like Boston, Norfolk, Charleston, Savannah, Long Beach, Tacoma and Seattle boomed during the 1980s, jobs and business opportunities grew. California, Florida, Georgia and North Carolina even managed to expand their manufacturing employment in 1982–86, when factory jobs in the old Rust Belt were hemorrhaging. Eastern seaboard prosperity was so striking that one economist puzzled over the "Atlantic coast mystery."[42] Besides the service industry boom, the Northeast enjoyed a greater increase in two-earner households, as well as a growing disproportion of federal spending.

In 1988 Bernard Weinstein, a Texas specialist in Sunbelt economics, contended that since the late 1970s a redistribution of federal spending had favored the portions of the country that were already richest—New England and the Middle Atlantic—versus the low-income South Atlantic and Southwest. Of the ten wealthiest states based on 1978 per capita income—mostly in the North—five ranked in the top ten in 1987 per capita federal outlays. Of the ten poorest, by contrast—eight in the Sunbelt—only one could even make the top twenty states in 1987 per capita federal outlays. Federal spending, in short, was reinforcing existing 1980s wealth concentration. For example, in fiscal year 1987, federal procurement in the South amounted to only $609 per capita compared with $795 for the United States as a whole and a striking $1,334 for New England.[43]

Federal outlays were shifting their geographic directions for specific reasons, too. Expanded federal interest payments involved recycling more money to the country's richest (creditor) locales. And increasingly sophisticated military weaponry involved shifting larger amounts of defense outlays to high-technology and research centers, also predominantly coastal.

As we have seen, weakness in the heartland and the South

also reflected the strong dollar, which hurt exports and attracted a devastating volume of imports. The combined damage to the interior states was enough to reverse the prior half century's pattern of declining regional income gaps. Census Bureau officials acknowledged a falloff in the industrial, agricultural and mining regions while services, defense and high-tech industries prospered.[44] Back in 1979 just one region substantially trailed the national per capita income average—the Southeast, traditionally America's poorest section. By 1986, though, three regions—the Southeast, Rocky Mountains and Southwest—had per capita incomes 10 percent or more below the national average. And the Rust Belt, hurt by manufacturing woes, fell below the national income average for the first time on record. Negative reactions in the heartland and the South were an important reason why the Republicans lost control of the U.S. Senate in 1986.

Table 12 on page 167 has already documented the 1981–87 national decline in manufacturing jobs. Rust Belt centers saw an even greater loss—11 percent in Ohio, 18 percent in Illinois.[45] A few large companies like Peoria-based Caterpillar laid off percentages of their work force reminiscent of the Great Depression.

In the Farm Belt, meanwhile, the 1981–87 collapse in commodity and land prices was worse than in the 1920s. Table 19 shows what happened to land prices in the major agricultural states in both periods. *Huge amounts of wealth vanished in the farm states even as much larger amounts were being created in the financial markets.* The saving difference, however, would come in the Reagan administration's mid-1980s decision to support farm incomes through (1) reflation (money-supply expansion and currency devaluation) and (2) unprecedented federal outlays on farm programs. The latter rose from a level representing slightly over a quarter of farmers' net cash income in 1981 to a level representing almost 60 percent at the peak of the crisis in 1986. Without these public expenditures, the farm economy might have gone into the abyss. *With* these subsidies, the value of farmland in states like Illinois, Iowa and Minnesota bottomed out in early 1987.

Farmers' losses, however, were enormous. In Minnesota, for example, the per-acre price of average land fell from $1,947 in

## TABLE 19

### THE DECLINING VALUE OF FARMLAND, 1920–29, 1981–89

*Average Value per Acre of Farm Real Estate (in Dollars)*

| | 1920 | 1921 | 1922 | 1923 | 1924 | 1925 | 1926 | 1927 | 1928 | 1929 |
|---|---|---|---|---|---|---|---|---|---|---|
| Michigan | 75 | 76 | 75 | 75 | 73 | 71 | 70 | 69 | 69 | 69 |
| Wisconsin | 99 | 100 | 94 | 92 | 90 | 87 | 84 | 82 | 81 | 80 |
| Minnesota | 109 | 108 | 95 | 89 | 85 | 80 | 78 | 73 | 71 | 71 |
| Ohio | 113 | 96 | 91 | 92 | 92 | 88 | 86 | 82 | 80 | 81 |
| Indiana | 126 | 117 | 95 | 93 | 89 | 85 | 81 | 74 | 73 | 73 |
| Illinois | 188 | 181 | 149 | 146 | 137 | 137 | 130 | 118 | 114 | 113 |
| Missouri | 88 | 83 | 71 | 69 | 63 | 61 | 57 | 55 | 54 | 54 |
| North Dakota | 41 | 40 | 38 | 35 | 31 | 30 | 28 | 27 | 26 | 26 |
| South Dakota | 71 | 69 | 58 | 50 | 46 | 45 | 42 | 38 | 37 | 36 |
| Nebraska | 88 | 82 | 71 | 68 | 63 | 60 | 60 | 58 | 57 | 57 |
| Kansas | 62 | 62 | 55 | 54 | 51 | 50 | 49 | 49 | 49 | 49 |

Source: U.S. Agriculture Department

*Average per Acre Price of Average Land (in Dollars)*

| | 1981 | 1982 | 1983 | 1984 | 1985 | 1986 | 1987 | 1988 | 1989 |
|---|---|---|---|---|---|---|---|---|---|
| Illinois | 2768 | 2531 | 2020 | 2036 | 1702 | 1337 | 1198 | 1285 | 1456 |
| Indiana | 2443 | 2105 | 1629 | 1799 | 1460 | 1092 | 934 | 1043 | 1191 |
| Iowa | 2486 | 2406 | 1945 | 1955 | 1321 | 950 | 825 | 1009 | 1203 |
| Michigan | 1480 | 1509 | 1399 | 1285 | 1148 | 1010 | 1062 | 765 | 905 |
| Minnesota | 1947 | 1922 | 1566 | 1513 | 1116 | 669 | 628 | 727 | 928 |
| Missouri | 1212 | 1180 | 1014 | 1016 | 871 | 669 | 690 | 638 | 755 |
| N. Dakota | 785 | 819 | 810 | 784 | 748 | 645 | 479 | 504 | 510 |
| Ohio | 2203 | 2061 | 1500 | 1496 | 1280 | 1003 | 1006 | 1109 | 1202 |
| S. Dakota | 700 | 679 | 493 | 469 | 453 | 274 | 285 | 312 | 408 |
| Wisconsin | 1602 | 1612 | 1322 | 1410 | 1127 | 817 | 758 | 687 | 812 |

Prices as of January 1
Source: LandOwner Newsletter
    219 Parkade, Cedar Falls, IA 50613

1981 to $628 in 1987. Inasmuch as Minnesotans had thirty million acres in cultivation or fallow, that represented a $20–40 billion loss of paper wealth to state farmers.[46] Losses of a similar magnitude occurred in Illinois and Iowa. In the thinly populated Dakotas, farmland lost $10 billion to $15 billion in value, a much sharper per capita decline. Estimates by the Conference Board suggested that the total value of farmers' land in the United States declined from $712 billion in 1980 to $392 billion in 1986. By 1988, however, prices were starting to re-flate—as Table 19 also shows.

But by 1988 fewer farmers could benefit from this recovery, as many had left their farms, voluntarily or through foreclosure. The U.S. farm population dropped to under 5 million in 1987, down from over 6 million in 1980 and almost 9 million in 1975, as prosperous, larger farmers replaced poor, smaller ones. However, by 1987, speculators and other absentee investors accounted for about 31 percent of farm transactions, up from 23 percent in 1983. As landholdings concentrated, thousands of farmhouses were torn down, thousands of miles of fence ripped out. In autumn 1987 Don Paarlberg, a former senior official in the Eisenhower, Nixon and Ford agriculture departments, feared a social revolution as he saw outside capital—from doctors, lawyers, businessmen and wealthy investors—flooding in to buy up agricultural holdings as farmland prices stabilized. "We are drifting toward a structure of agriculture which approaches what we twice (after the Revolution and in the Civil War) previously rejected—a wealthy, hereditary landowning class, with new entrants almost ruled out unless they are well-to-do."[47]

For 1988, income data showed a Middle West recovery, but it was most pronounced in the industrial Great Lakes area, where the devalued dollar had revived manufacturing. Map 4 draws the lines on the basis of state-by-state changes from June 1987 to July 1988 in personal income, and Map 5 illustrates the parallel changes in home values. Though the Rust Belt was beginning to rejoin the "bicoastal economy," the small-town Great Plains remained devastated.

In the meantime, the rise of the service industries was also redrawing the American economic map in historically familiar ways. Most of the benefits came *within* metropolitan areas,

MAP 4

COASTAL INCOME GAINS, HEARTLAND INCOME STAGNATION, 1988
State Personal Income    In percent change from June, 1987, to June, 1988

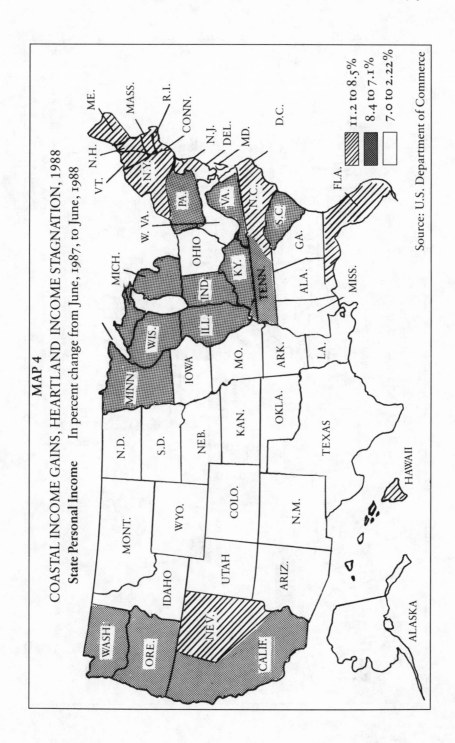

Source: U.S. Department of Commerce

11.2 to 8.5%
8.4 to 7.1%
7.0 to 2.22%

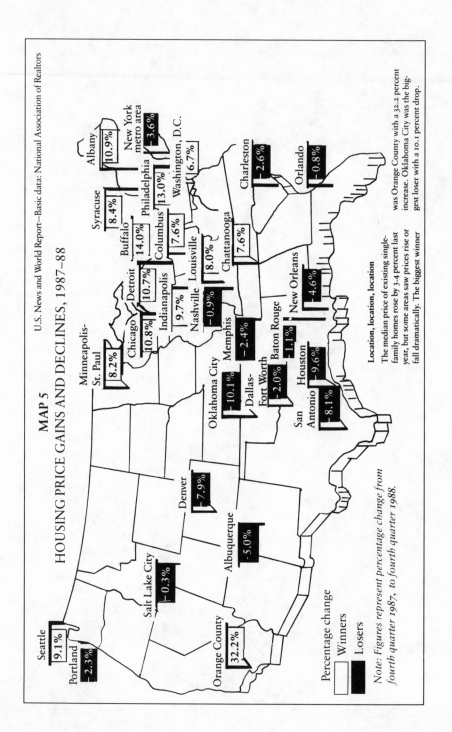

MAP 5

HOUSING PRICE GAINS AND DECLINES, 1987–88

U.S. News and World Report—Basic data: National Association of Realtors

Seattle 9.1%
Portland -2.3%
Salt Lake City -0.3%
Denver 7.9%
Albuquerque -5.0%
Orange County 32.2%

Minneapolis-St. Paul 8.2%
Chicago 10.8%
Detroit 10.7%
Indianapolis 9.7%
Buffalo 14.0%
Syracuse 8.4%
Albany 10.9%
New York metro area 3.6%
Philadelphia 13.0%
Washington, D.C. 6.7%
Columbus 7.6%
Louisville 8.0%
Nashville -0.9%
Chattanooga 7.6%
Charleston -2.6%
Orlando -0.8%
New Orleans -4.6%
Memphis -2.4%
Baton Rouge -1.1%
Oklahoma City -10.1%
Dallas-Fort Worth -2.0%
Houston -9.6%
San Antonio -8.1%

Percentage change
☐ Winners
■ Losers

*Note: Figures represent percentage change from fourth quarter 1987, to fourth quarter 1988.*

**Location, location, location**
The median price of existing single-family homes rose by 3.4 percent last year, but some areas saw prices rise or fall dramatically. The biggest winner was Orange County with a 32.2 percent increase. Oklahoma City was the biggest loser with a 10.1 percent drop.

albeit these were expanding, sometimes considerably. The Conference Board reported the service-industry trend turning five cities—Boston, New York, Chicago, Atlanta and Los Angeles—into "unofficial regional capitals," and development followed several common lines.[48] Downtown core areas boomed, accompanied in New York, Boston and Chicago by historic preservation and gentrification. A century earlier, architects in New York City likewise enjoyed an orgy of commissions for brownstones, town houses and—literally—miles of Fifth Avenue mansions. During the 1980s, too, housing builders and developers went where the money was. By the end of the decade, more and more New Yorkers found themselves acknowledging a harsh reality: the city was dividing between the rich and the poor—and losing its middle class.

But if the decade's residential impetus favored the top third of American incomes, suburbanization was still the predominant movement. Young professionals might be drifting back to city downtowns, but within the metropolitan areas, jobs and families were moving to the suburbs. In some cases, whole companies were picking up, leaving Manhattan or Chicago for the peripheries of Atlanta, Dallas, Southern California or exurban New Jersey. The new suburbs created by these 1980s movements became staunch cheering sections for the policies that nurtured them, and one sidebar to the elections of 1984 and 1988 was the huge margins turned in by a little-known group of counties for both Reagan and Bush.[49] Some of America's richest townships, according to the 1985 Census, were new upscale municipalities like Hunter's Creek, Texas, and Rancho Santa Fe, California.[50] Nevertheless, the larger polarization was procoastal, because the overwhelming weight of the suburban concentration was there. Of the twenty-one U.S. counties listed in Table 20 for having the highest 1985 per capita income, fourteen were suburban—and of these, seven were in the heavily white-collar Washington, D.C. suburbs and six were in the environs of New York City. The gap between suburbia and the rest of the United States was widening.

There *were* exceptions to the metropolitan and predominantly coastal nature of wealth concentrations. The 1980 Census, coming amid inflation, had mapped rural or small-town wealth pockets in agricultural and extractive regions like Idaho potato

## TABLE 20

### U.S. COUNTIES WITH THE HIGHEST PER CAPITA INCOME, 1985

| County | Amount | County | Amount |
|---|---|---|---|
| Loving, Texas | $34,173 | New York, New York | $17,319 |
| Falls Church, Virginia | 20,699 | Pitkin, Colorado | 17,304 |
| Arlington, Virginia | 20,094 | Somerset, New Jersey | 17,248 |
| Alexandria, Virginia | 19,783 | Juneau, Alaska | 17,071 |
| Montgomery, Maryland | 19,589 | Morris, New Jersey | 17,004 |
| Fairfax, Virginia | 18,731 | Nantucket, Massachusetts | 16,943 |
| Marin, California | 18,668 | Los Alamos, New Mexico | 16,871 |
| Bristol Bay, Alaska | 18,618 | Bergen, New Jersey | 16,850 |
| Fairfield, Connecticut | 17,708 | Fairfax City, Virginia | 16,812 |
| Westchester, New York | 17,649 | Nassau, New York | 16,326 |
| | | Howard, Maryland | 16,222 |

Source: Bureau of the Census

country, coastal Alaska or the Texas Oil Patch.* Those were
ebbing by the late 1980s, though, to be supplanted by new
nonmetropolitan centers of per capita prosperity that had less
to do with natural resources and more to do with the *new* "three
Rs" of affluent demographics—retirement, research and recreation.

By 1985 three of the twenty-one richest counties were a product of these forces—Pitkin and Nantucket (both recreation) and
Los Alamos (research). Two other kindred counties made the
top fifty—Palm Beach and Collier, both Florida retirement and
recreation areas. In 1987 one economist suggested that Americans' fifth major migration wave was to "penturbs"—small
towns and cities able to combine economic opportunity and
quality living, most notably college and university towns, research parks, historic renewal areas, old seaports, retirement
centers, and recreational and resort communities.[51]

---

* Loving County, Texas, with just a few hundred people, still reflected this
phenomenon in 1985.

But if the glittering side of the equation was that a two-worker professional couple could cross the United States without ever being more than fifty miles from a penturban outpost boasting nouvelle cuisine and a BMW dealer, there was a darker aspect. Even fewer parts of America were more than fifty miles from a demographic backwater of the 1980s—some major unemployment pocket, shut-down mine, declining central city, wiped-out small town or other monument to a no-longer-relevant crop or product. Home to the poorest third of Americans, many of these areas had stagnated during the 1980s, creating a tragic geographic parallel to the widening socioeconomic contrasts between billionaires and the homeless. Small-town America was also being polarized, and the balance was on the negative side of the ledger.

Demographic as well as economic Darwinism followed from the market orientation of the 1980s and its bias toward those already successful. Population concentrations dependent on the affluent flourished, while those holding the downwardly mobile or participants in less favored sectors withered. The governing Washington politicians of prior conservative heydays never interfered with these trends, painful as they might be, and neither did those of the Reagan era. The pendulum of political economics had to swing first.

Yet the imbalance was intensifying. As Upper American townships and neighborhoods boomed during the Reagan years the poorer regions and metropolitan areas of the United States lost relative ground. Growth data for 1984–86—three years of mid-1980s recovery—showed that two thirds of the 106 most prosperous metropolitan areas, mostly located in the Northeast, California or Florida, enlarged their edge with faster-than-average income growth; of the poorest 105 areas, two thirds grew at below-average rates.[52] Regions, neighborhoods and people without capital, skills or education were losing their lifelines.

Impoverished small cities definitely became more noticeable during the 1980s. Forgotten municipalities like East St. Louis, Illinois, Benton Harbor, Michigan, and Camden, New Jersey, all largely black, sank below stereotypical big-city slums like the South Bronx, eliciting attention as America's new version of apartheid.[53] As of the 1980 Census, a number of major U.S. cities—Newark, Atlanta, Miami, Baltimore and Cleveland—had counted at least 20 percent of their population living below the poverty line. The problem worsened by mid-decade, because as big cities lost more middle-class white population, the relative percentages both of blacks and of people below the poverty line increased. The gap between the big-city slums and the rest of metropolitan America was getting bigger.

Beyond the cities, education and economic class were more important than race. Hard times in small-town and rural areas fell largely on *white* Americans. In addition to the problems of agriculture, closed-down mines and small manufacturing plants also focused fear of an irreversible rural decline—at least outside the penturbs. Just before the 1988 Republican National Convention, *The Wall Street Journal* began a front-page series by stating that the United States "is in the midst of a coast-to-coast, border-to-border collapse of much of its rural economy," affecting roughly a quarter of the nation's population.[54]

Involving much more than agriculture, this collapse of large chunks of nonmetropolitan America reached from fishing and cannery towns like Eastport, Maine, all the way to rural California's mining and timber counties, over a dozen of which had double-digit unemployment rates in 1988. The coasts had rural and small-town backwaters, too—just fewer of them. Weak commodities prices were an explanation, but so were the new global wage differentials of the 1980s. Cheap, willing, rural nonunion American labor was no longer cheap enough. "Poverty in America wears many faces," said Congressman George Miller of California, and the rural poverty rate—17 percent in 1987—was "growing twice as fast as urban poverty."[55]

This plight wasn't easy to see from busy airports, interstate highways and suburban shopping centers, but fifty years after John Steinbeck wrote *The Grapes of Wrath* about Depression-era migrants, the *Los Angeles Times* observed that modern-day Joad families were again bundling into cars and leaving behind farm foreclosures in Illinois, oil-field layoffs in Oklahoma, closed mines in Minnesota. " 'What we're experiencing now in Oregon is something that last happened in the Dust Bowl Days,' said Bob More, whose twenty-four-bed shelter in North Bend, Oregon, overflowed in 1988 with 994 homeless people. 'We're seeing folks from the Farm Belt, from the oil patch. In February, most of our people came from the Midwest.' "[56] Bill Faith, head

of the Ohio Coalition for the Homeless, said, "Rural homelessness is growing faster than we can keep track of it. People
are living in railroad cars and tarpaper shacks. Shelters in tiny
towns we've never heard of are operating at or above capacity
and are turning people away."[57]

Even economists and sociologists along the Atlantic and Pacific coasts worried about local "dual" economies—"the two
Oregons," "the two Pennsylvanias" or "the two Carolinas."
While southeast Pennsylvania, for example, was booming
around a service-industry base, the Appalachian western part
of the state was digging out from the devastation of steel and
related heavy industries. And in North Carolina, metropolitan
areas with prosperous banking, insurance and research enterprises sat amid small towns traumatized by lost textile mills,
apparel plants or shoe factories.

The heyday type of economic maldistribution has a slow political fuse. In the late nineteenth century and the 1920s increased regional inequality took a while to produce more than
agrarian grumbling and heartland splinter parties. Careful observers could have mapped the areas of economic pain and
deflation—principally commodity-producing regions—by the
votes that were cast for Grangers, Greenbackers and Populists
in 1872–92 and then for Robert La Follette's Progressive presidential campaign in 1924. However, it was only after the economic crises of 1893 and 1929 that the economic insurgency
of the country's have-not regions reached critical mass in the
1896 and 1932 elections.

By the end of the 1980s, the circumstantial parallels of the
Reagan era were only half developed. A political revolt in the
Farm Belt had helped cost the Republicans the Senate in 1986—
North and South Dakota, hurt by disinflation, elected only Democrats to the U.S. House and Senate that year, an unprecedented
outcome—and two years later the Republicans suffered their
greatest 1984–88 presidential vote-share declines in the farm,
oil and mining states, though they managed to win most of
them. By contrast, except for New England, where Massachusetts governor Dukakis was a favorite son, Bush basically held
Reagan's East Coast support, especially in the booming New
York–Washington corridor, and Bush also kept his losses in
California small enough to carry that state. Where he lost the

most ground was in the nation's troubled interior—in the states where "Republican prosperity" commercials were rarely played.

## MORE LOSERS: GENDER, AGE AND RACE IN AMERICAN WEALTH PATTERNS

The 1980s were also tough on people whose weakness was a matter of education, family status, sex, age or race, though the strong, the well-educated, the well-married and the well-off *within* these groups made gains above the national average.

Overall, a disproportionate number of women, young people, blacks and Hispanics were among the decade's casualties. Even as record numbers of female corporate directors, black millionaires and twenty-six-year-old investment bankers and rock stars were entrenching themselves in Upper America, a much larger and growing underclass of high school dropouts, unwed mothers, female heads of households, unemployable young black males and homeless persons of all races and ages was beginning to provoke worried questions about the nation's future. The realignment of economic opportunity—the rich and well-educated grasped it, while the poor and uneducated could not—devastated the lives of many low-income Americans by removing the jobs and circumstances needed for homes and family cohesion.

Nominal statistics could be misleading. Women gained on men by increasing their share of new jobs and narrowing the male-female salary gap. In 1979 the median weekly earnings for women working full-time came to just 62.5 percent of the median weekly earnings for men. By 1983 that had climbed to 66 percent, and by 1987 to 70 percent.[58] And by 1988 the unemployment rate for women had actually dropped below that for men. But one economist underscored how much of the female gain was merely comparative: "Men's salaries selectively have gone down. Blue-collar men have been enormously affected and unions have made major pay concessions. And there have been deep cuts in the white-collar workforce (of male managers)."[59]

Furthermore, the extra costs of day care, marital stress, reduced shopping opportunity and lost leisure weren't counted as

offsets, nor were the even harsher facts: unwed women's preg-
nancies, young husbands who couldn't find adequate work, broken homes and divorce courts. Single-parent families, mostly
with a female head, grew from 13 percent of the total in 1970
to 22 percent in 1980 and then to 27 percent in 1987. So while
the inflation-adjusted median family income of married couples
was going up by almost 9 percent from 1980 to 1986, that of
female-headed families rose by only 2 percent.[60]

Lauri Bassi, a young Washington economist, documented another perverse link: women's share of *poverty* was rising simultaneously with women's share of *employment* (and despite
increasing female wages) because divorce was forcing previously
nonworking females into inadequate jobs of the minimum-wage
type. Failure of fathers to pay child support worsened the pressure.[61] Family breakups that sent women to work did more than
accelerate the 1980s per capita income increase; they also
mooted much of its ostensible benefit.

Yet women in professional jobs and upper-income circumstances were achieving striking gains. While males with a high
school education or less lost ground in the 1980s, the only
females working full-time to lose constant-dollar earning power
from 1980 to 1986 were high school dropouts, many of whom
became single mothers. Female college graduates actually out-
paced males of equivalent education in income gains, so that
women's economic circumstances polarized even more than
men's during the Reagan years. The bottom 25 to 35 percent
of women (working and nonworking), however, represented an
important portion of the decade's major losers. Overall, a lot
more women than men voted against George Bush for a plausible reason: a disproportion of females were becoming a have-
not constituency.

The realignment of income to the old away from the young,
starting before the Reagan era, grew during the 1980s into one
of the century's major upheavals. Senator Daniel Patrick Moynihan worried in 1987 that "we've become the first society in
history in which the poorest group in the population is the
children."[62]

In 1959 the elderly constituted a disproportionate number of
the poor. Some 35 percent of those over sixty-five years of age
had incomes below the federally determined poverty line, com-

TABLE 21

CHANGES IN FEMALE AND MALE EARNINGS 1973–86

## HOW EARNINGS CHANGED OVER TWO DECADES

Changes in individual earnings for men and women who work full time. adjusted for inflation

| | Age 25–34 | | Age 35–44 | | Age 45–54 | |
|---|---|---|---|---|---|---|
| MEN | 1973–79 | 1979–86 | 1973–79 | 1979–86 | 1973–79 | 1979–86 |
| 1–3 years high school | −7% | −14% | −11% | −7% | −2% | −3% |
| 4 years high school | −6 | −10 | −3 | −4 | −3 | −1 |
| 1–3 years college | −4 | −3 | −8 | +1 | −9 | +4 |
| 4 years college | −9 | +9 | −6 | +1 | −5 | +6 |
| 4 + years college | −6 | +12 | −7 | +4 | −7 | +10 |
| WOMEN | | | | | | |
| 1–3 years high school | 0% | 0% | +3% | −4% | +1% | −1% |
| 4 years high school | +2 | +1 | 0 | +9 | 0 | +6 |
| 1–3 years college | −1 | +5 | +1 | +12 | 0 | +10 |
| 4 years college | −3 | +16 | −8 | +23 | −7 | +16 |
| 4 + years college | −5 | +18 | −6 | +13 | +13 | +8 |

Source: Frank Levy, University of Maryland, based on calculations from Census Bureau data. Does not conform exactly to presidential terms but gives the most revealing indication of underlying trends in the 1970s and the 1980s.

Source: *Los Angeles Times*, October 29, 1988

pared with 22.4 percent for the population as a whole and 26.9 percent for children under 18.[63] Through the 1960s, however, *both* poverty rates fell—that for young people dropped to 14 percent in 1968, that for the elderly to 25 percent. This simultaneous progress ended during the 1970s and 1980s. Among the elderly, poverty kept dropping, down to just 12.2 percent in 1987. By contrast, the percentage of children in poverty bottomed at 14 percent, climbed to 16 percent during the seventies, and then edged over 20 percent during the Reagan years. Former Congressional Budget Office director Rudolf Penner acknowledged in 1987 that "the children have suffered a great deal as we have given more and more benefits to the elderly."[64] Chart 8 illustrates the change.

The same undertow hurting "children"—the Census definition specified "related children under 18"—also affected other younger Americans. A 1988 study of sixteen- to twenty-four-year-olds, both youths and young family heads, published in 1988 by the William T. Grant Foundation, found their inflation-adjusted purchasing power 27 percent lower and the percentage of young people living below the poverty level in 1986 almost double that of 1967.[65]

Another study found that inflation-adjusted income for families with children, headed by an adult under the age of thirty, collapsed by roughly one fourth between 1973 and 1986. Many young families were in depression-level circumstances; others had been broken up, still others kept from marriage. The proportion of twenty- to twenty-four-year-old males—of *all* races—married and living with their spouses dropped from 39.1 percent in 1974 to 21.3 percent in 1986.[66]

In 1984, according to ABC News polls, young voters cast 57 percent of their ballots for Reagan. By 1988, despite the lack of any real effort by the Democrats to target and explain the relative economic decline of young Americans during the 1980s, turnout among eighteen- to twenty-four-year-old voters declined and the GOP share of their vote for president dropped to 52 percent. Even so, election-year and postelection polls found young voters much more Republican than the country as a whole, an irony in light of Reagan-era income trends. As Table 29 suggests, on *economic* grounds the eighteen- to twenty-four-year-old electorate was a vulnerable Republican constituency.

But for the elderly, circumstances improved. During the early 1980s, as inflation-adjusted wages fell, retirees' pensions, especially Social Security, held steady or rose. Part of the explanation was that older voters were using political power to get more money.

In 1982, by one calculation, the federal government spent ten times as much per capita on the elderly as on children.[67] In 1962–73, a different era, older people between the ages of sixty-five and seventy-nine had drawn down on their resources after retirement, consuming wealth built up during their working days. Meanwhile young families between eighteen and thirty

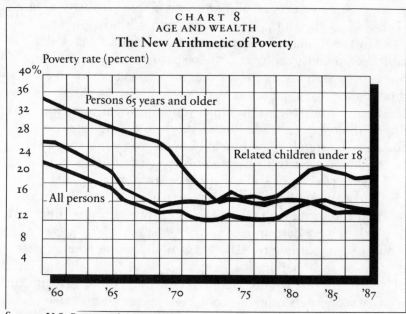

CHART 8
AGE AND WEALTH
**The New Arithmetic of Poverty**

Poverty rate (percent)

Persons 65 years and older

Related children under 18

All persons

Source: U.S. Bureau of the Census

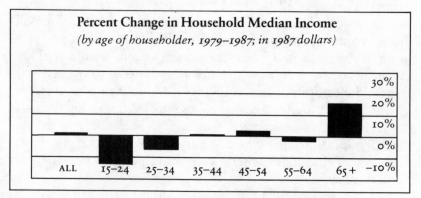

**Percent Change in Household Median Income**
*(by age of householder, 1979–1987; in 1987 dollars)*

Source: U.S. Census data, American Demographics, March 1989

were able to accumulate. But between 1973 and 1983 this traditional pattern reversed, with the average household wealth of the sixty-five- to sixty-nine-year-old age group in constant 1985 dollars increasing from $169,366 to $321,562 while average wealth for twenty-five- to thirty-four-year-old households *shrank* from $59,624 to $49,046.[68]

By 1988 the gap had widened as older Americans' stocks, bonds and real estate gained value and as Social Security payments to the aged climbed. Younger wage earners, by contrast, found their FICA taxes higher. The basic Social Security fiscal equation itself was profoundly redistributive on a generational basis.

Overall, federal spending was tilting. Although persons sixty-five and over constituted 12.1 percent of the population in 1986, benefits for the aged accounted for fully 27.2 percent of federal outlays. According to the Office of Management and Budget, federal funds received by older people rose from $44 billion in 1971 to $217 billion in 1984 and roughly $400 billion in 1988. Besides Social Security and Medicare, that also included housing assistance and food stamps. Most states reduced property taxes for people over sixty-five, thereby increasing levies for everyone else. Younger Americans sensed or knew that in some cases their parents were living better as retirees than they had as members of the work force.

Racial minorities were also net losers. In 1987 the income of the typical black family—at $18,098—equaled just 56.1 percent of the typical white family's income, the lowest comparative percentage since the 1960s.[69] The gap had widened most in the Midwest, where blacks lost high-paying jobs in trade-shrunken heavy industries. But the simultaneous advance of black professional and two-earner families obliged the Center on Budget and Policy Priorities to acknowledge an unprecedented polarization: "The income gap between lower- and upper-income black families is now wider than at any other point on record. Income inequality is now significantly greater among black families than among whites."[70] The unskilled and uneducated underclass was coming undone, but sociologists could legitimately point to "the first secure generation of middle-class blacks."[71] They constituted only a thin demographic layer, however, so overall economic discontents barred Republican inroads among blacks in the 1988 presidential election—and among Hispanics, too. The 70 to 82 percent of the Hispanic vote Michael Dukakis won in Texas, California and New Mexico was only ten points below his percentage among blacks. While Hispanics liked the Republican positions on a number of cultural issues, economic resentments drew them to the Democrats. Between 1978 and 1987 federal statistics showed the poverty rate among Hispanics increasing from 21.6 percent to 28.2 percent.

For women, young people and minorities the effect of economic polarization during the 1980s was largely negative. The nation as a whole also suffered as unemployable young people drove up the crime rate and expanded the drug trade. Broken families and unwed teenage mothers promised further welfare generations and expense. And none of it augured well for the future skills level and competitiveness of the U.S. work force. Yet popular concern for these developments was restrained by the memory of the expensive failure of liberal programs ten to twenty-five years earlier. Many had destabilized the very groups and cultures they were supposed to help. Equality had been an unworkable objective. Those recollections almost certainly helped prolong the Darwinian alternatives of the 1980s.

Even so, American history is a cavalcade not only of individualism and freedom of opportunity but of egalitarianism and cyclical populism. Excessive stratification—unprecedented concentrations of wealth on one side and diminishing prospects for another 30- to 40 percent of the population—has eventually incited political upheaval. The timing varies, and so do the dynamics, yet past a certain point the "unfairness" of heyday economics typically offends the electorate, and the countertrends generated attract elements well beyond liberalism or even populism. Important conservative and traditionalist sectors of the community also react negatively to dollar-chasing and to the practices of the new elites rising on Darwinian values.

This is especially true when private greed is seen as a threat to the national interest. Theodore Roosevelt, who exemplified patrician distaste for parvenu wealth at the end of the nineteenth century, was sufficiently worried that the capitalist organizers of the trusts might "enslave" the country that he discussed with historian Brooks Adams the possibility of leading "some great outburst of the emotional classes" to crush the oligarchs.[72] Traditionalists voiced similar fears during the 1920s, and in the 1980s, too, adherents of "cultural conservatism" tried to stake out a position separate from and sometimes even critical of the prevailing Darwinian conservatism of deregulation, Laffer Curves, marketplace theory and unrestrained global capitalism. The emergence of heyday capitalism in the United States has been a seamless web of many ideas, but so has the correction of its abuses.

By 1989 that correction was still to come. Despite the unprecedented flamboyance of America's great fortunes, the growing national concern about homelessness and the increasing rhetoric about imbalances in public policy, no more than a vague framework existed for the sort of insurgent psychologies and politics that had helped to end prior heydays. Few orators or demagogues had begun blaming the rich or self-serving elites for national problems, including America's loss of relative international wealth, and the economy was in its seventh straight year of recovery. Sociologist Christopher Jencks summed up the watchfulness among critical academicians: "When you talk to people, you get an awful lot of this kind of generalized anger. From a political point of view, I think the potential for a lot of very difficult and dangerous things is there, but it hasn't been happening yet."[73] As the rich grew richer, all that could be said was that more and more Americans were beginning to notice.

*Chapter*

*7*

*George Bush*
*and the Threshold of the 1990s*

If your daughter's in cotillion
And your son's enrolled at Choate
And your wife is worth a million
I'm sure to get your vote

GRIDIRON CLUB PARODY OF
GEORGE BUSH, MARCH 1988

That the Great Divide between rich and poor in America has
widened is perhaps the most troubling legacy of the 1980s.

*BUSINESS WEEK*, SEPTEMBER 1989

Our biggest fear is that the Democrats surface with a leader
who is able to capitalize on the theme of economic populism.

GOP POLLSTER VINCENT BREGLIO, 1989

By the time of Bush's inauguration in January 1989 the triumph
of Upper America was both complete and precarious—precarious because its success was becoming so obvious. Widespread
resentment over extreme wealth was inevitable, though still
unfocused.

As 1989 unfolded, so did a new wave of conspicuous consumption. By April many stock market indexes had regained
their October 1987 pre-crash levels. Spring sales at Sotheby's
and Christie's set records, including $4 million for Andy War-
hol's painting of Marilyn Monroe. The world's most expensive
automobile, a 1931 Bugatti Royale, had sold at auction in 1987
for $9.8 million; in spring 1989 the price rose again. From Bel-
Air to Beverly Hills, entertainers, movie executives and foreign

investors rolling in money gave Southern California a new real estate term: "tear-downs"—the replacement of old homes with $5–30 million kitsch palaces including tanning parlors, motorized chandeliers, petting zoos and heliports.[1] In late summer lavish multimillion-dollar birthday parties for financier Saul Steinberg and publisher Malcolm Forbes—his was complete with charging Moroccan cavalrymen—added to a sense of excess.*

Financial players were becoming as reckless as they had been in 1929. Soon after Reagan left office, undercover FBI agents moved into Chicago's commodity trading pits, where rigging had become rampant. Massive indictments followed by summer. Insolvent, recklessly managed savings and loan associations, centered in Texas and the Southwest, promised to cost the American taxpayer $200 billion before the end of the 1990s. In New York, where Drexel Burnham, the nation's fifth-largest securities firm, had agreed to pay an enormous fine as part of a settlement of criminal securities fraud charges, federal prosecutors also indicted its prize employee, Michael Milken, the originator of junk bonds, themselves increasingly in disrepute and default. When government figures showed that Milken had actually earned a stunning $550 million in 1987, even billionaire David Rockefeller suggested that "such an extraordinary income inevitably raises questions as to whether there isn't something unbalanced in the way our financial system is working."[2]

George Bush had earlier told a newspaper interviewer that he didn't like "this fast-buck stuff," and on Inauguration Day he would repeat his concern:

> In our hearts, we know what matters. We cannot only hope to leave our children a bigger car, a bigger bank account . . . and what do we want the men and women who work with us to say when we're no longer there? That we were more driven to succeed than anyone around us?

But just what change Bush could or would represent was not entirely clear. In 1988 he had briefly tried out a populist image—

---

* Steinberg himself understood the precarious symbolism; he commented that if the circumstances of his party were stock, "I'd short it."

eating pork rinds, campaigning with country music star Loretta Lynn, speaking to a succession of police and sheriffs' rallies. And when he first got to the White House, he laid out a horse-shoe pitch. Yet the America Bush truly represented was that of old multigenerational wealth—of trust funds, third-generation summer cottages on Fisher's Island and grandfathers with Dillon Read or Brown Brothers Harriman—which accepted the economic policy of the Reagan era despite its distaste for its arriviste values.

That was clear in the people Bush selected for his cabinet. The secretaries of state, treasury and commerce—James Baker III, Nicholas Brady and Robert Mosbacher—were old Bush friends, graduates of the best private schools, second- or third-generation multimillionaires with a collective net worth of about $250 million. As treasury secretary in 1987–88, Baker had insisted on Latin American debt-repayment policies benefiting Chemical Bank, in which he had several million dollars' worth of stock. He claimed sentimental reasons for holding his stock, which came to him in a merger between Chemical and the Texas Commerce Bank, founded by his grandfather. The ethical embarrassments of Bush's upper-class associates were a far cry from those of Ronald Reagan's hustling middle-class friends and aides, but the political evolution was simple enough: in two decades of presidential control, the Republicans had evolved from "cloth coat" Middle Americanism under Richard Nixon to aggressive new-money capitalism under Ronald Reagan and finally to the old-money, Episcopal establishment under George Herbert Walker Bush.

In economic policy the transformation was not particularly notable. Back in March 1988 Bush had deplored arriviste values, but had also reaffirmed his underlying free market preference: "Let individuals have as much leeway and flexibility as possible . . . as free a market as possible." Bush added that people's motivations were probably beyond government reach, making it not appropriate to seek "a legislative way to channel a person's energies into something that could be more productive."[3] As president, he restated his strong opposition to new taxes and to any tinkering with the income-tax-rate reduction passed during the Reagan years. Indeed, one of Bush's own principal priorities

of 1989 was yet another preference for those well off—a reduction of the capital gains rate from 28 percent (where a 1986
compromise had pegged it to match the new top income tax
rate) down to 15 percent. At first, even some Republicans responded skeptically. Senator Bob Packwood of Oregon, a principal architect of the 1986 tax law as chairman of the Senate
Finance Committee, called the proposal "a step away from the
perceived fairness of the new tax system by the $18,000-a-year
sawmill worker" who might believe the rich were getting out
of paying their share.[4] Nor did Bush favor spending more than
nominal new sums on health and education, which provoked
Congressman William Gray of Philadelphia, an ordained minister and former Democratic chairman of the House Budget
Committee, to criticize the new president on April 22 by quoting
Scripture: "Where a person's treasure is," said Gray, "there
you'll find his heart."[5] As the year unfolded, Bush's unwillingness to support new funds for domestic programs, even ones he
endorsed, faced growing criticism—at least inside the Washington Beltway.

But there were signs of a changing national attitude. *The New
Republic* published the decade's first substantial case for bringing down the federal deficit through a steep tax on upper-bracket
luxury consumption.[6] A 1987 poll by the University of Chicago's
National Opinion Research Center had found that 59 percent
of Americans believed the wealthy weren't taxed enough, and
in 1989 slightly more than 50 percent of those polled by the
Center said the government should reconsider raising taxes for
wealthy individuals, or making direct payments to the poor, to
reduce the income gap between the haves and have-nots. Just
11 percent opposed the idea. The Center's Tom Smith actually
observed that "the soaking-the-rich approach [to raising government revenues] has been quite popular among Americans
since the 1930s."[7] In a similar vein, a national survey taken by
Gallup in February for the Times-Mirror corporation found 82
percent of respondents in favor of raising income taxes for those
with incomes over eighty thousand dollars. The public's simultaneous lopsided agreement—by 58 percent to 30 percent—that
the gap between rich and poor was widening prompted Andrew
Kohut, the Gallup president, to say he was shocked by the

numbers.[8] Few Americans called the rich-poor gap a top national priority; their growing perception of its existence was what was significant.

In March the House Ways and Means Committee released a report showing that the percentage of U.S. family income in the hands of the top 1 percent climbed from 8.1 percent in 1977 to 9.0 percent in 1980 and 11.6 percent in 1985.[9] A 12 percent share was predicted for 1990. A few weeks earlier *The Washington Post* had noted the provocative findings of a new Census Bureau study: "In the private economy left to itself, before either taxes or transfer payments [the government word for benefits], the richest fifth of all people had 52.4 percent of all income in 1986, the poorest fifth only 1 percent and the next-poorest fifth only 7.6 percent."[10] *The New York Times* reported evidence that in contrast to most economic recovery periods, the 1983–88 upturn had *increased* the income inequality already apparent in 1981–82 recession circumstances.[11] *Business Week*, in turn, protested against the unprecedentedly large gap between the 1988 compensation of corporate chief executives and the pay of workers.

Popular culture was also beginning to confirm a new mood. Viewership had been slipping since 1984, but by 1989 there was no doubt that *Dallas, Dynasty* and *Falcon Crest* and the other prime-time television nouveau riche epics of the Reagan years had lost much of their earlier audience. In May *The Wall Street Journal* reported "the message is clear: Rich is out." Meredith Berlin, editor in chief of *Soap Opera Digest*, echoed the verdict: "We're all sick and tired of watching shows about rich people as the economy presses on a lot of others."[12] Morton Downey, Jr., the controversial television talk-show personality, started lacing his fading appeal with attacks on the rich, and a band of radio talk-show hosts—in the news for helping defeat a pay raise for Congress and stir up a consumer boycott of Exxon—invited consumer activist Ralph Nader to keynote the organizational meeting of a new network of populists. In a sense, broadcast audiences were voting with their dials on the very theme Michael Dukakis had cast aside the previous summer and that George Bush had sought to minimize by criticizing avarice and promising a "kinder, gentler America."

Speculation that a stronger Democratic presidential nominee

could have defeated Bush hung over the opening months of his presidency. His 53 percent was the weakest Republican presidential victory in a two-way race since 1908; and he was the GOP's first twentieth-century newly elected chief executive to see his party simultaneously lose ground in the Senate, House, state governorships and state legislatures. A switch of 535,000 votes in eleven states, analysts noted, could have elected even Dukakis. Bush had lost three Pacific states and barely carried pivotal California. Commodity deflation had also hurt the Republicans in the oil and farm states, with Iowa and Wisconsin turning Democratic and the Democratic presidential vote jumping by seven to eleven points between 1984 and 1988 in Texas, Oklahoma and Louisiana. In the Midwest Dukakis carried four dozen counties that had not voted for a Democratic president since 1964.

Meanwhile, affirmative government was making a philosophic comeback, and with it growing demands for new revenues and new regulations reminiscent of similar transitions as the Progressive Era replaced the Gilded Age and the New Deal replaced the Roaring Twenties. The tidal shift had begun in 1986, when the Republicans lost the Senate, thereafter undertaking reevaluations that led in 1988 to Bush's call for a "kinder, gentler America."

The new president quickly replaced the Coolidge portrait in the White House with Theodore Roosevelt's, reflecting his belief in TR's turn-of-the-century commitment to conservation, patrician reform and somewhat greater regulatory involvement, themes Bush thought he could reenact in the 1990s. His proposals in the area of the environment and campaign finance were in this vein. HUD Secretary Jack Kemp's proposals for "urban homesteading" and sale of public housing units to their occupants also suggested a new GOP outlook.

But what Reaganomics had set loose was the *larger* essence of heyday Republicanism: a central belief in "economic man," barely restrained markets and the sort of incentive economics that several generations of critics have dismissed as "trickledown." At critical turning points in U.S. history, the Republicans have played a useful role by reestablishing these priorities against excessive inflation, bureaucracy or welfare. But this same Republican values system becomes increasingly selfish, speculative and counterproductive as GOP cyclical dominance becomes entrenched.

During the late nineteenth century and again in the 1920s the combination of decreased government regulation, tax reduction, disinflation, rising inequality of wealth, financial speculation, booming markets and expansive debt helped to inflate an economic bubble. After the collapse of 1929 Republicans paid a large political price. In the mid-1890s, however, Republicans had been luckier. They escaped the economic consequences of the Gilded Age by narrowly losing the 1892 presidential election to Cleveland, a Democrat almost as conservative as themselves, just before the panic and depression of 1893, leaving Democrats with the consequences, including the loss of over a hundred House seats in the 1894 midterm elections. In 1896 the Democrats lost the presidency, enabling the Republicans to regain the White House with the political price already paid by disarrayed Democrats.

But at the end of the 1980s it was not a Democrat but George Bush who followed Reagan as the Dow-Jones Industrial Average went on to regain the highs made before the 1987 crash. Other speculative records were being set not only in art auctions and rare coin purchases but also in leveraged buyouts and takeovers in one industry after another.

By autumn the Bush administration was also displaying renewed heyday biases. Heavy White House pressure for reduction of capital gains taxation stirred the new Democratic House Speaker, Thomas Foley, to predict a resurgence of the tax shelter industry. Senator Ernest Hollings of South Carolina, chairman of the Senate Commerce Committee, lamented the risky precedents in partially funding the savings and loan industry bailout with off-budget bonds. Next, he said, "You'll have drug bonds, nuclear-waste clean-up bonds, go-to-Mars bonds."[13] Nevertheless, the president's nominee as chairman of the Securities and Exchange Commission, Richard Breeden, favored more deregulation of the financial markets and opposed curbs on leveraged buyouts and corporate takeover activity. Meanwhile, Bush's continued opposition to tax increases reflected Republican support for business and financial activity at the cost of new money for education, the aging, the U.S. transportation infrastructure, housing, drug control and the rising number of children in poverty. In domestic economics, despite new rhetoric, the essential policies of the Reagan years continued.

Globally, the Bush administration did seem firmer toward U.S. trading partners, whereas during the Reagan regime, as one commentator said, "the Japanese could have bought the Lincoln Memorial and moved it to Tokyo without anyone complaining."[14] Yet even internationally the philosophic changes of the 1980s persisted. During the Reagan years conservatives had become the newest version of "one-worlders," and marketplace principles drove the new internationalism as tables of investment bankers at London's Le Gavroche, New York's Regency or Geneva's Perle du Lac replaced Marxist international peace conferences or United Nations meetings. Here, too, the commitment to market economics, the free flow of capital and the uninhibited accumulation of wealth were deeply held principles of Republican faith, *not* lightly heeded policies that could be changed in response to cautionary signals.

Thus the new Bush administration also found itself caught in the financial and debt impetus of the Reagan years, declining to take serious action against deficits, leveraged buyouts or the merger wave. Yet, as in prior Republican bubbles, enterprise had increasingly degenerated into speculation and worse, promoting a serious misallocation of national income and resources. Past zeniths had supported John Maynard Keynes's famous description that "speculators may do no harm as bubbles on a steady stream of enterprise. But the position is serious when enterprise becomes a bubble on a whirlpool of speculation."[15]

The persistence of a heyday milieu in 1989 framed the debate of the 1990s. Besides promoting speculation, past realignments of wealth to the rich—shifts of 3 to 5 percent of national income from the grass roots to the top 1 percent of the population— have hurt the bottom half of Americans by effects ranging from rural and small-town decay to urban crime, weakened families and lost economic opportunity for the unskilled. Indeed, previous American polarizations of wealth—combining easy money at the top with loss of hope and faith at the bottom— were also accompanied by the same conspicuous consumption and short-term "now" values that conservative spokesmen found themselves deploring in the last months of the 1980s.

The imbalance of the late 1980s, unfortunately, went be-

yond the confines of America's domestic economy by also affecting the United States' place in the world. Policies of sharp
tax-bracket reductions, unprecedented federal deficits and borrowing at high real interest rates, along with deregulation, permissive finance, massive borrowing overseas and consequent
sales of U.S. assets and companies, accelerated America's relative
economic decline beyond what would have occurred in a less
avaricious environment. Had national decision-makers been
willing to bear revenue burdens similar to those of the Eisenhower era—a hardly punitive 14 to 15 percent of GNP collected
in non–Social Security taxes instead of the inadequate 12 percent
taken under Reagan—the "selling of America" might not have
been necessary. Washington's excessive commitment to private
wealth worked against the national interest.

By 1989, among the major Western powers, the conservative
tide was beginning to show signs of reversal. From Tokyo to
London, voters increasingly opposed a political culture of money
accumulation, rising economic polarization and the imposition
of regressive taxes to pay for upper-bracket reductions. In Britain, with its regressive poll tax and unpopular proposals to
reform the national health service and privatize water and elec-
tricity, the Conservative party lost to Labour by 40 percent to
35 percent—after a strong middle-class swing—in June's elections for the European Parliament. Prime Minister Margaret
Thatcher's job ratings sank enough to start Conservatives worrying about the next British elections. Canada's Liberal opposition moved far ahead of the Conservatives in summer polls as
the public reacted against the government's proposed 9 percent
national consumption tax, and Japan's Socialists stunned the
world by winning July elections for the upper house of Parliament by opposing the Liberal Democrats' 3 percent consumption tax and saying the revenues would be better raised by taxing
stock market and real estate profits.[16]

Japanese economist Hiroshi Takeuchi noted that in the 1950s
and 1960s the nation's most prominent businessmen were industrialists whose efforts benefited the nation as a whole. The
success stories of the late 1980s involved almost obscene
amounts of money made in real estate and stock speculation.
"Our values, our belief in hard work and industry, are falling

apart," said Takeuchi. "Those who work the hardest get the least. That undermines everything."[17]

Few Americans were going that far as the decade drew to a close. But more and more were finding it difficult to accept $30 million golden parachutes and Michael Milken's $550 million annual income as they also read reports that 21 percent of children lived in poverty and that the nation was mortgaging its future by borrowing abroad to keep taxes down. Not surprisingly, as tent cities began to spring up around the country, 83 percent of Americans told the Gallup poll that they saw poverty increasing—and a plurality blamed "circumstances beyond [the poor person's] control." The U.S. Labor Department reported twenty thousand child-labor-law violations in 1988, up from thirteen thousand in 1986, and New York governor Mario Cuomo proposed state legislation to deal with a 500 percent rise in New York City establishments illegally employing children.[18] In speeches increasingly evocative of the New Deal, Cuomo also contended that middle-class voters were "beginning to figure out that the rich are doing better than ever, while they are stalled at best."[19]

This was the central political question as the old decade gave way. Many progressives took it for granted that middle-class Americans soon would reject an era of "benign neglect" that had given us working families without homes, the mentally ill without shelter, schools that don't teach and highways and bridges that collapse.[20] And public opinion data were beginning to support these assumptions. In October Richard Wirthlin, former pollster for the Reagan White House, reported a surprising surge—voters now ranked the triple category of "poverty, hunger and homelessness" as the nation's second most important problem, after drugs.[21]

Yet in the past, middle-class America had needed more than liberal rhetoric to reject an alliance with the rich to pursue shared political interests with the poor. In 1929 the Great Depression provided that stimulus even though a majority of middle-class voters appeared to stick with Herbert Hoover in the election of 1932. Around the turn of the century, in contrast, substantial elements of middle- and upper-middle-class America had responded to a different impetus—the "new nationalism" expressed by Theodore Roosevelt and theologized by Herbert Croly in his book *The Promise of American Life*.

In words that would apply again almost a century later, Croly blamed an excess of individualism—encouraging business to seek its rewards regardless of the social cost—for "a morally and socially undesirable distribution of wealth" that threatened the "social bond" upon which American democracy rested.[22] The remedy, he said, was a "new nationalism"—a renewal of national spirit through democratically controlled (as opposed to oligarchic) government activism. Higher taxes, additional economic regulation, a greater commitment to easing inequality and belief in the usefulness of the central government all had a role to play, as did a redefinition of purpose going beyond moneymaking and the marketplace. Roosevelt, who had led his Rough Riders in a famous charge up San Juan Hill during the Spanish-American War, added a strong dash of conventional patriotism, and the result was one of America's more significant reform periods, which some 1989 progressives found themselves invoking as a possible precedent for the 1990s.[23]

The case for confronting the 1990s through a new economic patriotism was not unreasonable. Americans, concerned about homelessness and other signs of mounting poverty, became aware of a generalized slackness in the national spirit. In August 1989 an ABC News survey found 60 percent of those questioned describing the state of the U.S. economy as "not so good" or "poor," and, more pointedly, a Business Week poll found 64 percent of Americans predicting that within ten years the U.S. economy would be dominated by foreign companies. By October, Americans were fearful enough of the changing global balance of economic power that a Gallup survey found over 60 percent opposed to foreign investment in the United States and to the arrangement by U.S. companies of partnerships and ownership transfers with foreign corporations. December saw survey data showing that large majorities of Americans believed that Japan had already displaced the United States as the world's leading economic power. The public sensed that somehow the wealth of future generations was slipping away.

One could reasonably assume that the 1990s would be a time in which to correct the excesses of the 1980s, for the dangers posed by excessive individualism, greed and insufficient concern for America as a community went beyond the issue of fairness and, by threatening the ability of the United States to maintain its economic position in the world, created an unusual meeting ground for national self-interest and reform. As the 1980s ended, other events were also suggesting new political directions. The extraordinary upheavals in Eastern Europe, spurring democracy and decreasing the Russian military threat, also reduced the political importance of the longtime Republican reputation for a strong defense against Soviet aggression. By increasingly lopsided majorities, voters saw coping with the commercial and financial threat of Japan as the new challenge for the United States. With the Republican national coalition rooted mainly in the distant psychologies of the 1960s and 1970s, a second new issue also put Republican appeal in jeopardy: the electorate's adverse reaction to the U.S. Supreme Court's *Webster* decision, which affected women's abortion rights. The pro–abortion rights trend apparent in the 1989 state elections raised doubts whether the Republicans could maintain their highly effective alliance of economic and religious conservatives. Thus historical patterns suggesting that a new U.S. political cycle might begin in the 1990s took on a new plausibility.

As for the framework of the U.S. economy, by 1989 concentration of wealth, mounting debt and financial recklessness were reminiscent enough of the Gilded Age and the 1920s to sharpen questions about similar eventual consequences, inasmuch as both prior heydays had been followed by speculative implosions, populist turbulence, increased regulatory reform and some downward redistribution of wealth. Pressures were also growing to reduce the central role of money in U.S. politics and culture. What would develop along these lines remained to be seen. But normally optimistic Americans spoke of the future with foreboding, and the decade ended as it had begun: amid a rising imperative for a new political and economic outlook, and with the imminent prospect of a very different chapter in the annals of the wealth and power of the United States.

# Notes

## Chapter 1
### THE BEST OF TIMES, THE WORST OF TIMES

1. Thomas J. Stanley, *Marketing to the Affluent* (Homewood, Ill.: Dow Jones-Irwin, 1988).
2. "Upbeat Race to the White House," *Detroit News*, February 21, 1988.
3. *ABC News/Money Magazine Consumer Comfort Index*, April 28, 1988.
4. "Brace for More Japanese Takeovers," *Fortune*, March 14, 1988.
5. William Raspberry, "The Underclass as Tocqueville Saw It," *Chicago Tribune*, June 18, 1986, op-ed page.
6. "The 400 Richest People in America," *Forbes*, October 26, 1987, p. 106.
7. "Party Palace," *New York* magazine, January 9, 1989, p. 24.
8. "The Bull Market's Biggest Winners," *Fortune*, August 8, 1983, pp. 36–43.
9. Congressional Budget Office, *The Changing Distribution of Federal Taxes: 1975–90*, October 1987, Table 8, p. 48.
10. "Low Wages and Social Discontent," *Christian Science Monitor*, April 14, 1989.
11. *Declining American Incomes and Living Standards*, Economic Policy Institute, 1987, p. 10.

12. *Measuring the Effects of Benefits and Taxes on Poverty: 1986*, Census Bureau, 1988, p. 5.

13. "Gap Grows Between Rich, Poor," *Columbus Dispatch*, July 16, 1988.

14. *The State of Working America*, Economic Policy Institute, p. 1.

15. "America's Income Gap," *Business Week*, April 17, 1989, p. 78.

16. Frank Levy, *Dollars and Dreams: The Changing American Income Distribution* (New York: Russell Sage Foundation, 1987), p. 193.

17. "Average White Male No Longer Leads the March to Prosperity," *Los Angeles Times*, October 20, 1985, Business Section, p. 1.

18. "Future Pressures on Living Standards," *Wall Street Journal*, August 3, 1987, p. 1.

19. "Some Swing Group Voters Miss Out on Prosperity," *Washington Post*, September 22, 1988.

20. "The Next Priority," *Inc.*, May 1989, p. 28.

21. "In the Workplace," *Chicago Tribune*, January 26, 1987, Business Section, p. 4.

22. Lester Thurow, "Pound GOP on Jobs Issue," *Atlanta Constitution*, July 17, 1988.

23. "Pay Isn't Keeping Pace with the Economy," *Philadelphia Inquirer*, July 27, 1988.

24. "45 Percent of New Yorkers Are Outside Labor Force," *New York Times*, August 3, 1988, p. 1.

25. *ABC News/Money Magazine Consumer Comfort Index*, April 28, 1988.

26. "Poll Finds Less Work, More Play in America," *Chicago Tribune*, March 17, 1988.

27. "A Shifting Job Market Is Squeezing the Working Poor," *Business Week*, March 21, 1988, p. 16.

28. "The Winter of Workers' Discontent," *Business Week*, February 1, 1988, p. 18.

29. "Caught in the Middle," *Business Week*, September 12, 1988, p. 80.

30. "Many Find Gold Years Tarnished," *Los Angeles Times*, June 18, 1988, p. 1.

31. "Retirement Prospects Grow Bleaker as Job Scene Changes," *Wall Street Journal*, August 26, 1987, p. 1.

32. "Even with Good Pay, Many Americans Are Unable to Buy a Home," *Wall Street Journal*, February 5, 1988.

33. Ibid.

34. *Time*, November 3, 1986.

35.  "Wooing the Wealthy Reader," *New York Times*, October 14, 1987, p. D1.

36.  Jim Hightower, "You've Got to Spread It Around," *Mother Jones*, May 1988, p. 56.

37.  Walter Dean Burnham, *The Current Crisis in American Politics* (New York: Oxford University Press, 1982).

38.  "Worldwide Inequality: Gap Between the Rich and Poor Is Widening," *Los Angeles Times*, October 21, 1984, p. 1.

39.  Ibid.

40.  David Hale, "Picking Up Reagan's Tab," *Foreign Policy*, Spring 1989, p. 152.

41.  "Thatcher Less Popular," *Sunday Telegraph*, October 9, 1988.

42.  "Rich Man, Poor Man in Japan," *New York Times*, December 26, 1988.

43.  USA Today/CNN poll, *USA Today*, January 25, 1988, p. 1.

44.  "Steady Progress Disrupted by Turbulence in Economy," *Wall Street Journal*, March 11, 1987.

45.  "Americans Uneasy About the Nation's Future," *New York Times*, February 21, 1988, p. 1.

46.  Several 1988 election-year polls produced findings in this vein, notably majorities saying that the Japanese economic threat to the U.S. national security exceeded the Soviet military threat.

47.  "Ticket Likely to Help Boost Other in Party," *Washington Post*, July 4, 1988.

48.  See, for example, "The Dukakis Seeds of Defeat" in the *Boston Globe* of November 21, 1988, as well as "Slowness to Return Blows Reflects Dukakis' Faith in His Competence" in the November 6, 1988, *Washington Post*.

49.  "The Electronic Election," *Boston Globe*, November 13, 1988, p. B12.

50.  "To Broaden Political Base, Bush Must Keep Running," *Christian Science Monitor*, November 14, 1988.

51.  "It's Your Choice," *Boston Globe*, November 2, 1988.

*Chapter 2*
WEALTH, POPULISM AND THE GENIUS OF
AMERICAN POLITICS

1.  Lawrence Goodwyn, *The Populist Movement* (New York: Oxford University Press, 1978), p. xxix.

2.  Eric Foner, "Politics and Ideology in the Age of the Civil War" (New York: Oxford University Press, 1980), p. 49.

3. Tom Wolfe, "Radical Chic," *New York*, July 15, 1970, p. 41.

4. Ibid., p. 56.

5. Ibid.

6. James Q. Wilson, *The Amateur Democrat*, (Chicago: University of Chicago Press, 1966).

7. Thomas D. Edsall, *The New Politics of Inequality* (New York, W. W. Norton, 1984), p. 56.

8. *Congressional Record*, December 3, 1969, p. H1169-5.

9. "New Allies for LBJ," *Wall Street Journal*, April 19, 1967.

10. "What, No Pool in the Foyer?" *Time*, September 21, 1987, pp. 50–52.

11. "High Life Afloat: Superduper Yachts," *Time*, September 7, 1987, pp. 72–74.

12. Lewis Lapham, *Money and Class in America* (New York: Weidenfeld & Nicolson, 1988), p. 188.

13. Daniel P. Moynihan, "The Family and the Nation—1986," *America*, March 22, 1986.

14. "The Dream Busters," *Washington Times*, April 13, 1987, Commentary section, p. 1.

15. Michael Novak, "The Politics of Envy," *Washington Times*, November 7, 1986.

16. Ibid.

17. *Rebuild America*, March/April 1988, p. 1.

18. Richard Hofstadter, *American Political Traditions* (New York: Vintage Books, 1948), p. 220.

19. David Burner, *The Politics of Provincialism* (New York: Alfred A. Knopf, 1968), p. 156.

20. Ibid., p. 166.

21. Ibid., p. 167.

22. Arthur M. Schlesinger, Jr., *The Cycles of American History* (Boston: Houghton Mifflin, 1986), p. 241.

23. Ibid.

24. "Jackson Campaign Strength," *Wall Street Journal*, March 15, 1988, p. 16.

25. "The Eighties Are Over," *Newsweek*, January 4, 1988.

26. "Income Share Debate Waged Anew," *Los Angeles Times*, May 5, 1987.

27. Support for takeover restrictions was 63–64 percent.

28. "Political Round-Up," *Washington Times*, March 24, 1988.

29. "The End of the American Dream," *Industry Week*, April 4, 1988.

30. "Weary Bush Seeks to Hammer Home His Message," *Financial Times*, November 8, 1988.

## Chapter 3
### WEALTH AND POVERTY

1. Richard Hofstadter, *Social Darwinism in American Thought* (Boston: Beacon Press), 1955, p. 58.
2. Ibid., p. 201.
3. Matthew Josephson, *The Robber Barons* (New York: Harcourt Brace, 1962), p. 315.
4. Albert Jay Nock, *Memoirs of a Superfluous Man*, quoted in Lewis Lapham, *Money and Class in America* (New York: Weidenfeld & Nichols, 1987), p. 39.
5. Robert Akerman, "Suddenly There's a Lot of Thought About Parallels Between 1929 and Now," *Atlanta Constitution*, January 18, 1987, op-ed page.
6. Bruce Barton, "The Man That Nobody Knows," quoted in Stuart Bruckey, *The Wealth of the Nation* (New York: Harper & Row, 1988), p. 147.
7. Sinclair Lewis, *Babbitt* (New York: Harbrace Books, 1949), p. 143.
8. George Gilder, *Wealth and Poverty* (New York: Basic Books, 1981).
9. Ibid., with the respective citations appearing on pp. 245, 40, 204, 245 and 188.
10. Jude Wanniski, *The Way the World Works* (New York: Basic Books, 1978).
11. Alvin Rabushka, *From Adam Smith to the Wealth of America* (New Brunswick, N.J.: Transaction Books, 1985).
12. "Law and Economics: A New Order in the Court?" *Business Week*, November 16, 1987, p. 93.
13. Ibid.
14. "Reagan's Economics: Throwback to Coolidge," Knight-Ridder News Service, *Hartford Courant*, April 26, 1981.
15. Josephson, op. cit., p. 315.
16. "Advice for the GOP," *Wall Street Journal*, January 15, 1987.
17. Josephson, op. cit., p. 178.
18. Warren Sloat, *1929* (New York: Macmillan, 1979) p. 92.
19. Joshua S. Goldstein, *Long Cycles* (New Haven: Yale University Press, 1988), Appendix B.
20. "Supply-Side Tax Tonic Has Been a Fantasy," *Los Angeles Times*, December 21, 1987.
21. Benjamin Friedman, *Day of Reckoning* (New York: Random House, 1988), pp. 198–201.

22. "The Spirit of Independence," *Inc.*, July 1988, p. 47.
23. "Today's Corporate Leaders Achieve Folk Hero Status," *Columbus Dispatch*, October 24, 1986.
24. Robert Reich, "The Executive's New Clothes," *New Republic*, May 13, 1985, pp. 26–27.
25. Vincent P. Carosso, *The Morgans: Private International Bankers, 1854–1913* (Cambridge: Harvard University Press, 1987), and Maury Klein, *The Life and Legend of Jay Gould* (Baltimore: Johns Hopkins University Press, 1987).
26. William D. Burt, "A New View of a Legendary Robber Baron," *Reason*, April 1987, p. 50.
27. Several *Harvard Business Review* articles on this subject appeared during 1986 and 1987.
28. Will and Ariel Durant, *The Lessons of History*, quoted in "Income Share Debate Waged Anew," *Los Angeles Times*, May 5, 1987.

## Chapter 4
### WEALTH AND FAVORITISM

1. "You've Got to Spread it Around," *Mother Jones*, May 1988, p. 32.
2. *Survey of Consumer Finances 1983*, Federal Reserve Bulletin, September/December 1984.
3. *Reducing the Deficits*, Economic Policy Institute Briefing Paper no. 812, Washington, 1988, p. 8.
4. George J. Mitchell, "Regressive Tax Reform," Letter to the Editor, *Wall Street Journal*, December 29, 1987.
5. Richard Vedder and Christopher Frenze, "Latest Data Attest Cuts in Top Rate Play Robin Hood," *Wall Street Journal*, April 28, 1987.
6. "Poor Pay Disproportionate Share of Sales Taxes," Associated Press, *Tulsa World*, March 27, 1988.
7. "State Tax Burden Less for Wealthy, Study Says," Associated Press, *Kansas City Star*, April 10, 1988.
8. Charles Murray, *Losing Ground* (New York: Basic Books, 1984).
9. "Reagan Years: As Some Suffer, Others Prosper," *Los Angeles Times*, February 3, 1985.
10. See David Stockman, *The Triumph of Politics* (New York: Harper & Row, 1986).
11. Friedman, op. cit., p. 252.

12. William Greider, *Secrets of the Temple* (New York: Simon & Schuster, 1987), p. 401.

13. George F. Will, "What Dukakis Should Be Saying," *Washington Post*, September 15, 1988.

14. Lawrence M. Friedman, *A History of American Law* (New York: Simon & Schuster, 1973), p. 447.

15. E. Pendleton Herring, "Politics, Personalities and the Federal Trade Commission," *American Political Science Review*, vol. 28 (1934), p. 1021.

16. Ellis Hawley, "Three Facets of Hoover Associationalism," in *Regulation in Perspective* (Cambridge: Harvard Business School Press, 1981), p. 95.

17. Martha V. Gottron, ed., *Regulation: Process and Politics* (Washington: Congressional Quarterly, 1982), p. 89.

18. "Rolling Back Regulation," *Time*, July 6, 1987, p. 51.

19. Michael Kinsley, "Reregulation Revisited," *Washington Post*, February 27, 1986.

20. "Rolling Back Regulation," p. 51.

21. "Deregulation Is Hot Seminar Topic," *Richmond Times-Dispatch*, April 20, 1986, p. E-4.

22. "Rolling Back Regulation," p. 52.

23. Greider, op. cit., p. 170.

24. Ibid., pp. 456–57.

25. Thomas K. McCraw, *Regulation in Perspective* (Cambridge: Harvard University Press, 1981), p. 76.

26. "Rodino Sees Demise of Antitrust Enforcement," *Newark Star-Ledger*, March 6, 1988.

27. "Wave of Mergers, Takeovers Is Part of Reagan Legacy," *Washington Post*, October 30, 1988.

28. "Takeovers: Today's Pools," *Philadelphia Inquirer*, November 23, 1986.

29. "Deregulation a Rough Jolt for Workers," *Boston Globe*, March 9, 1986, p. A1.

30. "Deregulation Gone Haywire," *Atlanta Journal and Constitution*, November 27, 1983.

31. "Five Years Later," *Columbus Dispatch*, December 11, 1988.

32. "Deregulation Gone Haywire."

33. "With Deregulation, Big Get Bigger," *Philadelphia Inquirer*, December 19, 1987, p. 9-A.

34. "Off Our Backs," *Des Moines Register*, April 24, 1988.

35. "Deregulation Is Adding to Transportation Woes," *Cleveland Plain Dealer*, November 16, 1986.

36. "Off our Backs."

37. "Federal Deregulation Runs into a Backlash, Even from Business," *Wall Street Journal*, December 15, 1983, p. 1.
38. Ibid.
39. Charles A. Beard, *The Economic Basis of Politics and Related Writings* (New York: Vintage Books, 1957), p. 170.
40. George McKenna, *American Populism*, (New York: G. P. Putnam's Sons, 1974), pp. 75, 79.
41. Lawrence Goodwyn, *The Populist Movement* (New York: Oxford University Press, 1978), p. 12.
42. Fred Shannon, *American Farmers Movements* (New York: Anvil Books, 1957), p. 50.
43. McKenna, *American Populism*, pp. 89–90.
44. McKenna, op. cit., pp. 137–38.
45. Greider, op. cit., p. 294.
46. Herbert Hoover, *The Memoirs of Herbert Hoover* (New York: Macmillan & Company, 1952), vol. 3, p. 30.
47. Greider, op. cit., p. 692.
48. Ibid., p. 78.
49. Ibid., p. 542.
50. Friedman, op. cit., p. 172.
51. Greider, op. cit., p. 563.
52. Ibid.
53. Ibid., p. 519.
54. Ibid., pp. 461, 591.
55. "Debts—Public and Private," *New York Times*, January 29, 1933.
56. "Consumer Debt: A Lode That Lures Wall Street," *Wall Street Journal*, December 31, 1988.
57. "Takeovers: Today's Pools," *Philadelphia Inquirer*, November 23, 1986.

*Chapter 5*
AMERICA'S SHRINKING SHARE OF GLOBAL WEALTH

1. "Best Is 'Almost Free' for Billionaire Buyer," *Boston Globe*, April 18, 1988.
2. "Japan Is Said to Be Richest," *New York Times*, August 22, 1989.
3. "Low Dollar Means U.S. Has Become Bargain Basement," *Wall Street Journal*, November 30, 1988.
4. "A Wealth of Billionaires," *Forbes*, July 24, 1989, pp. 117–210.

5. "Sale of Firestone to Japanese Not a Threat," *Los Angeles Times*, March 19, 1988, Part IV, p. 1.

6. "An Appraisal: Foreign Takeovers of U.S. Firms to Surge," *Wall Street Journal*, January 11, 1988.

7. Richard A. Gephardt, *Remarks to American Chamber of Commerce International Forum*, February 28, 1989.

8. Lester Thurow, "When the Lending Stops," *New Perspectives Quarterly*, Fall 1987, p. 14.

9. "For Sale: America," *Time*, September 14, 1987.

10. "Yen for a Good Buy," *Boston Globe*, April 18, 1988.

11. "How Japan Is Winning Dixie," *U.S. News and World Report*, May 9, 1988, pp. 43–59.

12. "The Selling of America (Cont'd)," *Fortune*, May 23, 1988, p. 64.

13. "Truth About Foreign Investment," *Dallas News*, October 17, 1988.

14. Jonathan Yates, "Why Make It Easy for Foreign Investors?" *Philadelphia Inquirer*, March 20, 1989.

15. "Sell Hawaii, Lease California," *New West*, October 1988, p. 12.

16. "Japanese Move in by Another Degree," *Chicago Tribune*, January 22, 1989.

17. Friedman, op. cit., p. 226.

18. "U.S. Once Again Weighs Price of Foreign Ownership," *Christian Science Monitor*, November 21, 1988.

19. *Competitiveness Index*, Council on Competitiveness, Washington, D.C., June 1989.

20. Lester Thurow, "The Great Wall," *Alexander & Alexander World*, First Quarter 1989.

21. "Foreign Investors," *Industry Week*, February 1, 1988, p. 30.

22. Warren Brookes, "Beating Up on Big Business," *Washington Times*, March 30, 1988, p. F1.

23. "Star-Spangled Sale," *Dallas News*, March 27, 1988, p. H1.

24. "Investment Income Deficit Seen for U.S.," *Chicago Tribune*, March 15, 1989.

25. "U.S. Trade Falls Short in Service," *Philadelphia Inquirer*, Sept. 13, 1989.

26. U.S. Commerce Department estimate, 1987.

27. "Foreign Investment: A Boom or Binge for United States," *Minneapolis Star-Tribune*, November 15, 1987.

28. Quoted in Martin and Susan Tolchin, *Buying into America: How Foreign Money Is Changing the Face of our Nation* (New York: Times Books, 1988), p. 194.

29. "Japan Is Number One in Per Capita Output," *Philadelphia Inquirer*, March 19, 1988.
30. "Japan Most Creditworthy Nation," *Investors' Daily*, April 4, 1988.
31. *The Economist*, January 14, 1989.
32. "U.S. Markets Lose World Stock Dominance," *Investors' Daily*, July 21, 1987.
33. "Tokyo Stock Market Outperforms U.S.," *New Orleans Times-Picayune*, July 24, 1988.
34. David D. Hale, *Monthly Economic Forecast*, Kemper Financial Services, January 1989.
35. "When Tokyo Picks Up the Tab," *Wall Street Journal*, September 18, 1987, p. 5D.
36. Masahiro Sakamoto, "Pax Americana's Twin Deficits," *New Perspectives Quarterly*, Fall 1987, p. 8.
37. "Japan Is Number One in Per Capita Output," *Philadelphia Inquirer*, March 19, 1988.
38. "Japan Said to Have Passed U.S. in Aid to Third World," *Washington Post*, May 10, 1988.
39. "Japan Asserts American-Style Clout in Toronto," *New York Times*, June 20, 1988.
40. "U.S. Banks Fall from Top 10 List," *Columbus Dispatch*, July 31, 1988.
41. "U.S. Companies Court Japanese Moneymen for Venture Capital," *Christian Science Monitor*, April 29, 1988.
42. "U.S. Market Share Drops in Electronics," *New York Times*, January 5, 1989.
43. Ibid.
44. "Foreign Licenses at Record High," *New York Times*, March 18, 1989.
45. "Germany Beats World's Chemical Sales," *Wall Street Journal*, May 3, 1988.
46. "West Germany's New Military Giant," *Financial Times*, July 13, 1988.
47. "Pentagon Eases Stand Against Foreign Stakes in U.S. Defense Firms," *Wall Street Journal*, April 28, 1988, p. 1.
48. "Japan Arms Firms Poised for Export Assault," *Chicago Tribune*, October 23, 1988.
49. Joan Feldman, "The Dilemma of 'Open Skies,' " *New York Times Magazine*, April 2, 1989.
50. "Foreigners Harvest U.S. Agribusiness," *Des Moines Register*, October 11, 1987.

51. "Firestone Wasn't Pushed Out of Tires, It Jumped," *Los Angeles Times*, March 19, 1988, Business Section, p. 1.
52. "The Selling of America," *Los Angeles Times*, January 24, 1988, p. IV-3.
53. "MergerMania," *Miami Herald*, March 27, 1988.
54. "America, a Wholly-owned Subsidiary of...", *New York Times*, March 30, 1988, op-ed page.
55. "For Sale: America," *Time*, September 14, 1987.
56. "Heritage to the Highest Bidder," *Washington Post*, April 9, 1989.
57. "Foreign Investors: Allies or Aggressors," op. cit., p. 27.
58. "Is Texas Losing Its Independence?" *Forbes*, December 14, 1987, p. 184.
59. "U.S. Is Losing the Trade Contest," *St. Petersburg Times*, December 11, 1988.
60. "Foreigners Buy Up USA," *USA Today*, July 28, 1988.
61. More recent data were not available from the Canadian embassy in Washington as of April 1989.
62. "Foreign Investment Reached New Highs in 1987," *Investors' Daily*, March 29, 1988.
63. Friedman, op. cit., p. 74.
64. "U.S. Arms Exports Show a Sharp Decline," *Christian Science Monitor*, March 22, 1988.
65. "For Sale: America," *Time*, September 14, 1987, p. 53.
66. Ibid.
67. "As Foreigners Grab Up U.S. Real Estate," *Baltimore Sun*, Jan. 1, 1989.
68. "Japanese Clout in U.S. Business," Baltimore Sun, Jan. 15, 1989.
69. "Japanese Feeding Corporate Buyout Binge," *Atlanta Journal and Constitution*, December 25, 1988.
70. "Japanese Clout in U.S. Business," op. cit.
71. "Californians Catch a Ride on Japan's Skyrocketing Economy," *Washington Post*, April 23, 1989.
72. "Gephardt Populist Theme Powers New Surge," *Los Angeles Times*, January 24, 1988.
73. R. W. Apple, "Signs of England's Decline Are Too Obvious to Ignore," New York Times Service, October 27, 1985.
74. "In Britain, Battle Is on for Compassion Vote," *New York Times*, May 25, 1987.
75. "Incomes of Poor Down by 15% Under Tories," *Financial Times*, June 8, 1987.
76. "Thatcher's Jungle, Kinnock's Zoo," *Financial Times*, June 8, 1987.

77. "Thatcher Launches Drive in Areas With Heavy Joblessness," *Washington Times*, June 15, 1987.
78. "Thatcher's Poll Tax," *Philadelphia Inquirer*, April 24, 1988.
79. "Thatcher's Tax Cutter," *Economist*, March 19, 1988, p. 9.
80. "Thatcher's Poll Tax."
81. "Tax Revolt Boosts Scottish Nationals," *Christian Science Monitor*, March 1, 1989.
82. "Britain's Real Estate Boom," *Investors' Daily*, May 13, 1988.
83. Ibid.
84. "Iron Lady Battles Opponents on High Moral Ground," *Washington Times*, May 30, 1988.
85. "Britain's Economic Lion Is Strong and Roaring," *Christian Science Monitor*, May 17, 1988.
86. "In Japan, a Feeling of Imbalance," *Boston Globe*, December 26, 1988.
87. "If They're So Rich, Why Do They Feel So Poor," *Philadelphia Inquirer*, June 19, 1988.
88. "Rich Man, Poor Man in Japan," *New York Times*, December 26, 1988.
89. "In Japan, a Feeling of Imbalance."
90. "Japan Infected, Too, by Pursuit of Money," *Chicago Tribune*, March 29, 1989.

## Chapter 6
### THE NEW PLUTOGRAPHY OF 1980S AMERICA

1. "They're Like Us Except They're Rich," *USA Today*, May 22, 1987, p. 1.
2. "How Rich Is Rich," *Millionaire*, August 1988, p. 79.
3. Ibid., p. 83.
4. Gustavus Myers, *History of the Great American Fortunes* (New York: Random House, Modern Library, n.d.), p. 273.
5. Ibid., p. 146.
6. Ibid., p. 147.
7. "How the Nouveaux Riches Got That Way," *Forbes*, October 24, 1988, p. 108.
8. Myers, op. cit., p. 273.
9. Ibid., p. 344.
10. "The Tribune 4,047," *Forbes*, October 24, 1988, p. 91.
11. Ibid., p. 90.
12. "The Legacy of Dollar Mark Hanna," *Forbes*, October 24, 1988, p. 70.

13. Josephson, op. cit., p. 339.
14. Stuart Chase, *Prosperity: Fact or Myth* (New York: Charles Boni Paper Books, 1929), p. 122.
15. "Why Mike Milken Stands to Qualify for the Guinness Book," *Wall Street Journal*, March 31, 1989.
16. R. R. Doane, *The Movement of American Wealth* (New York: Harper Bros., 1939).
17. Scott Burns, "Disaffected Workers Seek New Hope," *Dallas News*, August 21, 1988, p. H1.
18. "What Stock Crash?" *Wall Street Journal*, June 6, 1988.
19. "On the Heavy-Debt Road to Big Buy-outs," *Christian Science Monitor*, November 7, 1988.
20. "Dire Prophecy on Takeovers," *New York Times*, November 4, 1988.
21. "Wall Street—Not Main—Benefits from Buyouts," *Los Angeles Times*, May 1, 1988.
22. "Corporate Takeover Activity Record $311 Billion in 1988," *Washington Post*, January 31, 1989.
23. "A Growing Backlash Against Greed," *New York Times*, Nov. 13, 1988.
24. Ibid.
25. "RJR Nabisco Buyout Nets Bankers $700 Million in Fees," *Dallas News*, December 9, 1988.
26. "Law Firm Income Surging," *New York Times*, July 5, 1988, p. D10.
27. Ibid., p. D1.
28. "The AM LAW 100," *American Lawyer*, July/August 1988, p. 6.
29. "Top Execs' Pay Jumps 48% to $1.8 Million," *USA Today*, April 22, 1988, p. 1.
30. "Top 800 CEOs Average $1.28 Million," *Washington Times*, May 17, 1988.
31. "High Tech Executives' Pay Soars," *Investors' Daily*, November 8, 1988.
32. "The Top Man Gets Richer," *Industry Week*, June 6, 1988, p. 51.
33. Ibid., p. 52.
34. "Bring CEO Pay Down to Earth," *Business Week*, May 1, 1989, p. 146.
35. "The Top Man Gets Richer."
36. "Are Chief Executives Overpaid?" *Wall Street Journal*, April 21, 1988.
37. "The Magic Kingdom," *Forbes*, October 2, 1989, pp. 139–41.

38. "Lawmaker Warns of Social Nomads," *Chicago Tribune*, May 9, 1989.
39. *Long Marketing poll*, Greensboro, North Carolina, release May 1, 1989.
40. Lester C. Thurow, "Choosing an Economic Path," *Boston Globe*, April 4, 1989.
41. Stuart Chase, op. cit., p. 35.
42. Courtenay Slater, "Atlantic Coast Mystery," *American Demographics*, March 1988.
43. Harold T. Gross and Bernard L. Weinstein, "Frost Belt vs. Sun Belt in Aid Grants," *Wall Street Journal*, August 23, 1988.
44. "Income Up in Coastal States," *Columbus Dispatch*, August 21, 1987.
45. Economic Analysis Section, U.S. Commerce Department.
46. "Erosion in Value of State Farmland," *Minneapolis Star-Tribune*, August 9, 1987.
47. "Farm Crisis Survivors Are Reaping Rewards," *Chicago Tribune*, March 27, 1988, p. 1.
48. Conference Board press release, New York, July 8, 1987.
49. Some good examples of new satellite and suburban counties (identified by their nearby cities) that have begun to be important and lopsided sources of votes for the GOP presidential candidates would be: Shelby, Alabama (Birmingham); Seminole and Martin, Florida (Orlando and Palm Beach); Cobb and Gwinnett, Georgia (Atlanta); Williamson, Tennessee (Nashville); Lexington, South Carolina (Columbia); Rankin, Mississippi (Jackson); Collin and Denton, Texas (Dallas); Chesterfield, Henrico and Virginia Beach (Richmond, Norfolk). All gave Bush 70 percent more of their vote in 1988; Reagan's percentages in 1984 were even higher.
50. "Kenilworth, Illinois, called Wealthiest U.S. Suburb," *Boston Globe*, March 31, 1987.
51. The economist was Seattle-based Jack Lessinger. See "Predicted: Penturbs Where Life Is Simpler," *USA Today*, May 26, 1987.
52. "Income Gap Between U.S. Cities is Growing," *Investors' Daily*, May 5, 1988.
53. "Urban Wastelands," *Wall Street Journal*, June 22, 1988.
54. "Smalltown America Battles a Deep Gloom as its Economy Sinks," *Wall Street Journal*, August 4, 1988.
55. Ibid.
56. "Homelessness Beyond the Big Cities," *Los Angeles Times*, March 28, 1989.

57. "As Farms Falter, Rural Homelessness Grows," *New York Times*, May 2, 1989.

58. "Women Narrowing the Salary Gap With Men," *Los Angeles Times*, February 2, 1988.

59. "Women Outpacing Men in Employment Gains," *Chicago Tribune*, December 19, 1988.

60. "People Patterns," *Wall Street Journal*, September 7, 1988.

61. "Men Helped Feminize Poverty," *Wall Street Journal*, February 17, 1988.

62. Moynihan, op. cit. kids.

63. "Consuming Our Children," *Forbes*, November 14, 1988.

64. "Nation's Elderly Are Mobilized for the Election Year," *Philadelphia Inquirer*, March 26, 1988.

65. "Needed: Pathways Out of Poverty," *Christian Science Monitor*, November 18, 1988.

66. Ibid.

67. "Consuming Our Children," p. 230.

68. Ibid., p. 224.

69. Greenstein, "Study Finds an Increasing Number of Young Families in Poverty," *Boston Globe*, November 18, 1988.

70. Ibid.

71. Ibid.

72. Richard Hofstadter, *American Political Traditions* (New York: Vintage Books, 1948), p. 220.

73. "Growing Gap Shown Between Rich, Poor," *Boston Globe*, May 15, 1989.

*Chapter 7*
GEORGE BUSH AND THE THRESHOLD OF THE 1990S

1. "Million-Dollar Birthday Cakes," *Time*, May 1, 1989.

2. "Wages Even Wall Street Can't Stomach," *New York Times*, April 3, 1989.

3. "Bush Pledges Minimal Controls," *Los Angeles Times*, March 27, 1988.

4. "Bush Defends Capital Gains Tax-Cut Plan," *USA Today*, March 15, 1989.

5. "Gray: Bush Shortchanges Nation's Poor," *Philadelphia Inquirer*, April 23, 1989.

6. James S. Henry and Marshall Pomer, "The 1 Percent Solution," *New Republic*, February 6, 1989.

7. "What Role Can the Wealthy Play," *Jackson Clarion-Ledger*, October 15, 1989.

8. "Public's Views Could Aid Democrats," *Washington Post*, March 9, 1989.

9. Background Material on Data and Programs Within the Jurisdiction of the Ways and Means Committee, March 15, 1989.

10. "The Poor Are Still Poor," *Washington Post*, December 30, 1988.

11. Leonard Silk, "Rich and Poor: The Gap Widens," *New York Times*, May 12, 1989.

12. "Fans of TV Soaps Sour on Glitz," *Wall Street Journal*, May 8, 1989.

13. "S&L Deal: Both These Plans Are Turkeys," *Chicago Sun-Times*, August 6, 1989.

14. Richard Reeves, "Send Clear Signals to Japan," *Philadelphia Inquirer*, March 23, 1989.

15. John Maynard Keynes, quoted in the *Left Business Observer*, July 27, 1989, p. 8.

16. "Japan in the Mood for Change," *Economist*, July 15, 1989, p. 32.

17. "Japan: Angst Washes Over One Nation," *Los Angeles Times*, July 30, 1989.

18. "Child Workers at Risk," *Christian Science Monitor*, October 31, 1989.

19. Interview with Mario Cuomo, *New Perspectives Quarterly*, Fall 1989.

20. Robert Kuttner, "A New Era of Ideological Detente," *Boston Globe*, October 27, 1989.

21. The Wirthlin Group National Quorum Memorandum, October 1989.

22. John B. Judis, "Herbert Croly's Promise," *New Republic*, November 6, 1989.

23. See, in particular, the argument in John B. Judis, op. cit.

# *Appendix A*

Approximate Numbers of Millionaires, Decamillionaires,
Centimillionaires and Billionaires in the United States, 1848–1990

| | Millionaires (1) | Decamillionaires (2) | Centimillionaires (3) | Billionaires (4) |
|---|---|---|---|---|
| 1848 | 50 | 1 | | |
| 1875 | 1,000 | 50 | 1 | |
| 1892 | 4,047 | 200 | 6 | |
| 1910 | 5,000 | | | |
| 1918 | 10,000 | | | 1 |
| 1927 | 15,000 | | | 2 |
| 1929 | 20,000 | | | 2 |
| 1944 | 13,000 | | | — |
| 1953 | 27,000 | 800 | | — |
| 1957 | | | 44 | 1 |
| 1961/1962 | 80,000 | 2,500 | | 1 |
| 1965 | 90,000 | | | |
| 1968/1969 | 121,000 | | 153 | 2 |
| 1972–1973 | 180,000 | | | 4 |
| 1976 | 250,000 | | | 2 |
| 1978 | 450,000 | | | 1 |
| 1979 | 519,000 | | | |
| 1980 | 574,000 | | | ? |
| 1981 | 638,000 | | | ? |
| 1982 | | 38,885 | 400 | 13 |
| 1983 | | | 500 | 15 |
| 1984 | | | 600 | 12 |
| 1985 | 832,000 | | 700 | 13 |
| 1986 | | | 900 | 26 |
| 1987 | 1,239,000 | 81,816 | 1,200 | 49 |
| 1988 | 1,500,000 | 100,000 | 1,200 | 51 |

(1) The statistics and estimates for millionaires are drawn from
multiple sources.

(2) The decamillionaire data for 1982–88 comes from Thomas

J. Stealey, *Marketing to the Affluent* (Homewood, Ill.: Dow Jones-Irwin, 1988). The prior numbers are estimates, save for 1848, when there was only 1 decamillionaire—John Jacob Astor.

(3) The data for 1953 and thereafter are derived or estimated from the various tabulations of Forbes and Fortune magazines.

(4) The billionaire tallies come from the Forbes and Fortune surveys of the richest Americans during the 1980s.

## NOTE FOR TABLE 9A, ON PAGE 161

*FORTUNE's listing of winners in the stock market is made up of individuals whose personal wealth in corporate shares increased by more than $100 million between August 12, 1982, and July 1, 1983. Only common stocks publicly traded in the U.S. were counted. Options, warrants, and convertible securities were omitted as having somewhat hypothetical value until the rights they convey are exercised. Family foundations were excluded, but trusts that benefit the investors were included. Most of the gains listed are paper profits, but bull market profits realized by sales before July 1 were taken into account. Stocks bought during the bull market were valued from the date of purchase. One company on the list, TeleVideo Systems, went public during the period. Only the gains achieved above the offering price of $18 per share were attributed to TeleVideo's founder, K. Philip Hwang. Mark Taper won't get to collect his full $304-million share of First Charter Financial because he had agreed before July 1 to sell it to Financial Corp. of America for $27 million less. Shares held in the names of spouses and dependent children were considered part of the investors' fortune, but the holdings of grown children, brothers and sisters, and more distant relatives were treated independently. Computer Directions Advisors Inc. of Silver Spring, Maryland, and Corporate Data Exchange of New York City helped FORTUNE develop the data.*

# *Appendix B*

ESTIMATED PERCENTAGES OF TOTAL WEALTH HELD BY
THE TOP ONE HALF OF 1 PERCENT OF U.S. HOUSEHOLDS

SOURCE: Joint Economic Committee

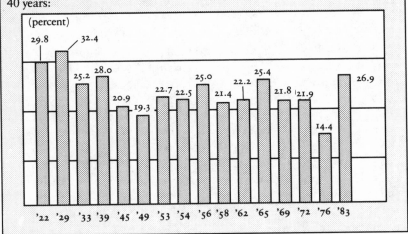

The share of wealth held by the "super-rich"—the wealthiest 0.5 percent
of U.S. households—has risen sharply in the last decade after falling for
40 years:

(percent)

The figures for 1922 through 1983 were compiled by the Joint Economic Committee
of Congress based on data furnished by the Federal Reserve Board.

# Appendix C

## FAMILY INCOME DATA, 1970–87
### (all figures in 1987 dollars)

| | Median Family Income | After-Tax Median Family Income | Median Household Income | Median After-tax Household Income | Per Capita Income |
|---|---|---|---|---|---|
| 1970 | 28,880 | NA | 25,564 | NA | 9,299 |
| 1973 | 30,820 | NA | 26,884 | NA | 10,591 |
| 1975 | 28,970 | NA | 24,918 | NA | 10,174 |
| 1977 | 30,025 | 25,518 | 25,454 | NA | 10,850 |
| 1980 | 28,996 | 23,763 | 24,427 | 20,061 | 10,740 |
| 1981 | 27,977 | 22,266 | 23,835 | 19,398 | 10,592 |
| 1982 | 27,591 | 22,610 | 23,750 | 19,433 | 10,573 |
| 1983 | 28,147 | 22,954 | 23,976 | 19,739 | 10,892 |
| 1984 | 29,923 | 23,374 | 24,526 | 20,260 | 11,301 |
| 1985 | 29,302 | 23,005 | 24,952 | 20,483 | 11,635 |
| 1986 | 30,534 | 23,220(est) | 25,807 | 21,097 | 12,096 |
| 1987 | 30,853 | 23,508(est) | 25,986 | 21,410 | 12,287 |

*Source:* The median family income, median household income, median after-tax household income and per capita income figures come from the U.S. Census Bureau publication *Money Income of Households, Families and Persons in the United States: 1987.* The after-tax median family income figures come from *Tax Foundation's Tax Features,* July/August 1987, p. 1, and is based on median family income for all families with one earner employed full time year-round.

# Appendix D

## THE REPUBLICANS AND THE RICH: POPULAR PERCEPTIONS IN THE OPINION POLLS, 1981–88

**PART I—THE REAGAN ADMINISTRATION**
**NBC NEWS NATIONAL POLL, JANUARY 1982:** Do you think that upper-income, middle-income and lower-income Americans have been helped or hurt by Reagan economic policies?

|  | Helped | No Difference | Hurt | Not Sure |
|---|---|---|---|---|
| Upper-income | 67% | 7% | 13% | 13% |
| Middle-income | 24 | 14 | 53 | 9 |
| Lower-income | 10 | 8 | 75 | 7 |

**Time/Yankelovich Clancy Shulman National Poll, September 1988:** As a result of President Reagan's policies, are the following groups better off or worse off economically?

|  | Better | Neither | Worse | Not Sure |
|---|---|---|---|---|
| Wealthy Americans | 75% | 7% | 9% | 9% |
| Middle-class Americans | 41 | 8 | 47 | 4 |
| Low-income Americans | 26 | 7 | 60 | 7 |

**Conference Board/National Family Opinion National Poll, Autumn 1988:** Compared to eight years ago, how do you feel the circumstances of each of the following groups are today?

|  | Better | Same | Worse |
|---|---|---|---|
| High-income Families | 82% | 15% | 3% |
| Middle Class | 20 | 40 | 39 |
| Poor People | 11 | 23 | 67 |

PART II—GEORGE BUSH

**Time/Yankelovich Clancy Shulman National Poll, October 1988:**
Suppose George Bush were elected as our next president, do you think Bush will:

|                              | Yes  | No   | Not Sure |
|------------------------------|------|------|----------|
| Be good for the middle class? | 46%  | 46%  | 8%       |
| Favor the wealthy?           | 62   | 31   | 7        |

# Appendix E

## CYCLES OF AMERICAN PRESIDENTIAL POLITICS SINCE 1800

All six U.S. presidential cycles to date have begun with two decades of lopsided success by the newly ascendant party, and no similar domination has occurred at any other time.

| Cycle | Initial Period of One-Party Dominance | Minority Interruption |
|---|---|---|
| Jeffersonian Era Democratic-Republican Party 1800–28 | Jefferson 1800–1808 Madison 1808–16 Monroe 1816–24 (24 years) | Quincy Adams (National Republican) 1824–28 |
| Jacksonian Era Democratic Era 1828–60 | Jackson 1828–36 Van Buren 1836–40 Polk 1844–48 (16 of 20 years) | Harrison-Tyler (Whig) 1840–44 Taylor-Fillmore (Whig) 1848–52 |
| Civil War Republican Era 1860–96 | Lincoln-Johnson 1860–68 Grant 1868–76 Hayes 1876–80 Garfield-Arthur 1880–84 (24 years) | Cleveland 1884–88 1892–96 (No presidential candidate of either party won a majority of the popular vote between 1876 and 1892) |

| Cycle | Initial Period of One-Party Dominance | Minority Interruption |
|---|---|---|
| Industrial Republican Era 1896–1932 | McKinley-Roosevelt 1896–1908 Taft 1908–12 (16 years) | Wilson (Democrat) 1912–20 |
| New Deal Democratic Era 1932–68 | Roosevelt-Truman 1932–52 (20 years) | Eisenhower (Republican) 1952–60 |
| Civil Disturbance Republican Era 1968–?? | Nixon-Ford 1968–76 Reagan 1980–88 Bush 1988–?? (20 of 24 years) | Carter (Democrat) 1976–80 |

All of these six eras began with watershed elections in which (1) the previous incumbent party was defeated and (2) a new alignment of party presidential voting—resting on a new coalition—was established, which kept its essential shape for at least twenty years. Interestingly, all three Republican hegemonies have produced a "capitalist heyday" during the second half of the cycle.

# *Appendix F*

## PUBLIC OPPOSITION TO THE 1986 TAX REFORM

American voters never rallied behind the 1986 tax reform, with its claimed simplification of taxes and its reduction of the top personal income tax rate to 28 percent in exchange for elimination of a number of tax shelters, credits and deductions. Here are the negative verdicts delivered in the major polls:

*Overall Assessment:* Respondents to a late March 1988 ABC News/ Washington Post survey indicated by 55 percent to 31 percent that "reform" has made the system worse, not better.

*Simplification:* According to April 1988 USA Today/CNN polling, 85 percent of a national sample called the new law too complicated and 67 percent described it as more confusing than the previous tax law.

*Fairness:* In the USA Today sampling, 66 percent thought the new tax law was unfair. February 1989 Gallup polls for the Times-Mirror Corporation found a 39 percent plurality calling the new law "less fair" than the old one; only 13 percent thought it was "fairer."

*Taxes Higher, Not Lower:* Early 1988 polls found respondents saying they were paying more taxes. In the ABC News/Post sampling, 58 percent thought they were paying more (in 1987 federal taxes), while only 22 percent thought they were paying less.

*1986 Tax Reform Beneficiaries:* In the USA Today poll, 60 percent thought the 1986 tax act benefited the rich, 78 percent thought it benefited special interests.

*The New York Times* of September 25, 1989, noted that "the public seems never to have accepted the 1986 changes."

# Appendix G

## SHIFTS IN PER CAPITA INCOME IN THE
## WORLD'S RICHEST NATIONS

Gross Domestic Product per Capita Adjusted for Purchasing Power 1980–1986

|                | 1981     | 1982     | 1983     | 1984     | 1985     | 1986     | 1987 |
|----------------|----------|----------|----------|----------|----------|----------|------|
| USA            | $13,077  | $13,424  | $14,282  | $15,705  | $16,548  | $17,324  |      |
| Canada         | 12,306   | 12,516   | 13,205   | 14,427   | 15,366   | 16,105   |      |
| W. Germany     | 9,594    | 10,144   | 10,669   | 11,418   | 12,114   | 12,741   |      |
| France         | 9,526    | 10,331   | 10,694   | 11,203   | 11,701   | 12,218   |      |
| United Kingdom | 8,422    | 9,061    | 9,678    | 10,224   | 10,913   | 11,498   |      |
| Italy          | 8,700    | 9,252    | 9,568    | 10,247   | 10,833   | 11,406   |      |
| Japan          | 8,852    | 9,615    | 10,172   | 11,012   | 11,798   | 12,339   |      |

* Source: Organization for Economic Cooperation and Development

Unadjusted Gross Domestic Product per Capita (based on currency exchange rates *not* adjusted for purchasing power):

## Top 12 Nations, 1985–88*

| 1985 | | 1986 | | 1987 | | 1988 | |
|---|---|---|---|---|---|---|---|
| United Arab Emirates | $19,270 | Switzerland | $17,680 | Switzerland | $21,330 | Switzerland | $27,260 |
| United States | 16,690 | United States | 17,480 | United States | 18,530 | Luxembourg | 22,600 |
| Switzerland | 16,370 | Norway | 15,400 | Norway | 17,190 | Japan | 21,310 |
| Kuwait | 14,480 | United Arab Emirates | 14,680 | United Arab Emirates | 15,830 | Iceland | 20,160 |
| Norway | 14,370 | Canada | 14,120 | Japan | 15,760 | Norway | 20,020 |
| Canada | 13,680 | Kuwait | 13,890 | Sweden | 15,550 | United States | 19,780 |
| Sweden | 11,890 | Sweden | 13,160 | Canada | 15,160 | Sweden | 19,150 |
| Japan | 11,300 | Japan | 12,840 | Denmark | 14,930 | Finland | 18,610 |
| Denmark | 11,200 | Denmark | 12,600 | Kuwait | 14,610 | Germany | 18,530 |
| Germany | 10,940 | Finland | 12,160 | Finland | 14,470 | Denmark | 18,740 |
| Finland | 10,890 | Denmark | 12,160 | Germany | 14,400 | Canada | 16,760 |
| Australia | 10,830 | Germany | 12,080 | France | 12,790 | France | 16,080 |

* Source: World Bank

# *Appendix H*

## THE U.S. MERCHANDISE TRADE DEFICIT
## AND CURRENT ACCOUNT DEFICIT, 1981–88

|      | Merchandise Trade Deficit (U.S. $ Billions) | Current Account Deficit (U.S. $ Billions) |
|------|---------------------------------------------|-------------------------------------------|
| 1981 | − 34.6                                      | + 8.2                                     |
| 1982 | − 38.4                                      | − 7.0                                     |
| 1983 | − 64.2                                      | − 44.3                                    |
| 1984 | − 122.4                                     | − 104.2                                   |
| 1985 | − 133.6                                     | − 112.7                                   |
| 1986 | − 155.5                                     | − 133.2                                   |
| 1987 | − 170.3                                     | − 143.7                                   |
| 1988 | − 137.1                                     | − 126.5                                   |

\* Costs, insurance and freight basis
Source: U.S. Department of Commerce

# Appendix I-1

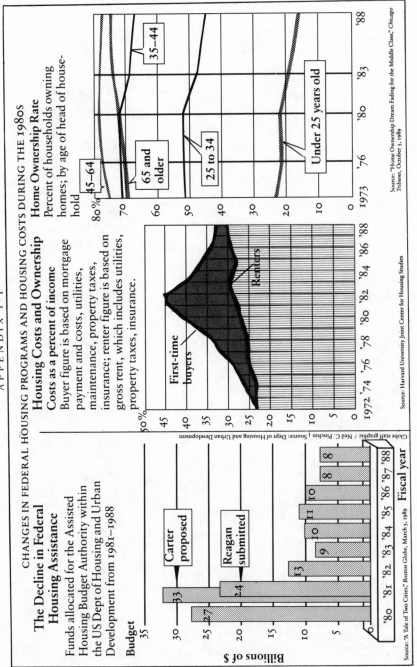

CHANGES IN FEDERAL HOUSING PROGRAMS AND HOUSING COSTS DURING THE 1980s

## The Decline in Federal Housing Assistance

Funds allocated for the Assisted Housing Budget Authority within the US Dept of Housing and Urban Development from 1981–1988

**Budget**

Billions of $

35

30 — 33 — Carter proposed

25 — 27

20 — 2.4 — Reagan submitted

15

10 — 9 — 3

5 — 11 — 10 — 8 — 8

6

'80 '81 '82 '83 '84 '85 '86 '87 '88 **Fiscal year**

Globe staff graphic / Neil C. Pinchin ; Source: Dept of Housing and Urban Development

Source: "A Tale of Two Cities," *Boston Globe*, March 5, 1989

## Housing Costs and Ownership

**Costs as a percent of income**

Buyer figure is based on mortgage payment and costs, utilities, maintenance, property taxes, insurance; renter figure is based on gross rent, which includes utilities, property taxes, insurance.

50%
45
40
35
30
25
20
15
10
5
0

First-time buyers

Renters

1972 '74 '76 '78 '80 '82 '84 '86 '88

Source: Harvard University Joint Center for Housing Studies

## Home Ownership Rate

Percent of households owning homes; by age of head of household

80%
70
60
50
40
30
20
10
0

45–64

65 and older

35–44

25 to 34

Under 25 years old

1973 '76 '80 '83 '88

Source: "Home Ownership Dream Fading for the Middle Class," *Chicago Tribune*, October 3, 1989

# Appendix I-2

## COMPARATIVE CHANGES IN SALES PRICES OF SINGLE-FAMILY HOMES BY METROPOLITAN AREA, 1981–88

| | Median Sales Price, 1981 (000s) | Median Sales Price, 1988 (000s) | Percentage Change |
|---|---|---|---|
| *Areas of Greatest Increase* | | | |
| Albany/Schenectady/Troy, New York | $46.1 | $92.2 | +100% |
| Anaheim/Orange County, California | 131.7 | 211.4 | +61 |
| Baltimore, Maryland | 57.7 | 88.7 | +54 |
| Boston, Massachusetts | 80.2* | 181.2 | +126 |
| Detroit, Michigan | 48.5 | 73.1 | +51 |
| Hartford, Connecticut | 81.4 | 167.6 | +106 |
| Honolulu, Hawaii | 100.0† | 215.1 | +115 |
| Los Angeles, California | 111.4 | 180.1 | +60 |
| New York/Northern New Jersey/Long Island | 73.8 | 184.8 | +150 |
| Philadelphia, Pennsylvania | 59.2 | 102.4 | +73 |
| Providence, Rhode Island | 50.0 | 130.6 | +161 |
| Rochester, New York | 45.9 | 75.7 | +65 |
| San Diego, California | 97.4 | 147.8 | +52 |
| San Francisco, California | 121.6 | 206.4 | +70 |
| Syracuse, New York | 43.2 | 74.6 | +73 |
| Washington, D.C. | 88.3 | 132.5 | +50 |
| *Areas of Least Increase (or Decrease)* | | | |
| Baton Rouge, Louisiana | 69.6 | 64.7 | −7 |
| Denver, Colorado | 76.2† | 81.8 | +7 |
| Des Moines, Iowa | 52.5 | 55.8 | +6 |
| El Paso, Texas | 52.6 | 59.6 | +13 |

| | Median Sales Price, 1981 (000s) | Median Sales Price, 1988 (000s) | Percentage Change |
|---|---|---|---|
| Houston, Texas | 72.7 | 61.8 | −15 |
| Oklahoma City, Oklahoma | 54.1 | 56.2 | +4 |
| Salt Lake City/Ogden, Utah | 62.9 | 67.7 | +7 |
| Tulsa, Oklahoma | 59.2 | 65.0 | +9 |

* Figure used is for *1982*, not 1981.
† Estimated figure.

Note that in the cities showing the smallest increases, all of these gains trailed the 1981−88 inflation rate, so that homeowners suffered a loss in real terms.

Source: National Association of Realtors (February 1989)

# *Appendix J*

## THE 1980–89 WEALTH EFFECT ON THE VALUES OF ART

SOTHEBY'S ART INDEX,*
1980–89
(1975 = 100)

|  | Sep. 1980 | Jan. 1982 | Jan. 1985 | Jan. 1989 | Sep. 1989 |
|---|---|---|---|---|---|
| *Old Master Paintings* | 255 | 201 | 278 | 469 | 660 |
| *Impressionist Art* | 206 | 248 | 356 | 1255 | 1525 |
| *Modern Paintings* | 204 | 249 | 336 | 1138 | 1415 |
| *English Furniture* | 256 | 279 | 382 | 822 | 822 |
| *Aggregate of all art categories* | 253 | 249 | 324 | 740 | 905 |

* Sotheby's Art Index reflects the subjective analyses and opinions of Sotheby's art experts, based on auction sales and other information deemed relevant. Nothing in Sotheby's Art Index is intended or should be relied upon as investment advice or as a prediction or guarantee of future performance or otherwise.

# Index

ABOUT THE AUTHOR

KEVIN PHILLIPS was chief political analyst for the 1968 Republican presidential campaign and later served as assistant to the attorney general. Since 1971 he has been the editor-publisher of *The American Political Report*. Since 1979 he has also edited and published the *Business and Public Affairs Fortnightly*. Phillips is a contributing columnist to the *Los Angeles Times*, a member of the political strategists' panel of *The Wall Street Journal*, and a regular commentator for National Public Radio and CBS Radio Network. He served as a commentator for CBS Television at the 1984 and 1988 Republican and Democratic presidential conventions. He is also a periodic contributor to the Op-ed page of *The New York Times* and the Outlook section of *The Washington Post*.

Phillips's first book, *The Emerging Republican Majority*, was described by Newsweek as "the political bible of the Nixon Era." It predicted the coming conservative era in U.S. national politics.

In 1987 the *National Journal* listed Kevin Phillips as one of 150 people in Washington you would want to have on your side in a fight. In 1988 *U.S. News and World Report*—in their special issue on the "New Establishment"—included Phillips in their forty-member who's who in U.S. politics.